THE EARLY CAREER
OF SAMUEL JOHNSON

THE EARLY CAREER
OF SAMUEL JOHNSON

Thomas Kaminski

New York   Oxford
OXFORD UNIVERSITY PRESS
1987

Oxford University Press

Oxford   New York   Toronto
Dehli   Bombay   Calcutta   Madras   Karachi
Petaling Jaya   Singapore   Hong Kong   Tokyo
Nairobi   Dar es Salaam   Cape Town
Melbourne   Auckland

and associated companies in
Beirut   Berlin   Ibadan   Nicosia

Library of Congress Cataloging-in-Publication Data
Kaminski, Thomas.
The early career of Samuel Johnson.
Includes index.
1. Johnson, Samuel, 1709–1784.
2. Authors, English—18th century—Biography.
I. Title.
PR3533.K36   1987   828'.609 [B]   86-16256
ISBN 0-19-504114-3 (alk. paper)

2 4 6 8 10 9 7 5 3 1
Printed in the United States of America
on acid-free paper

PREFACE

Few lives have undergone as much scrutiny as Samuel Johnson's. Although the young Johnson who edited the *Gentleman's Magazine*, compiled the Harleian catalogue, and walked the streets of London with Richard Savage was in many ways a man unknown to Boswell, many generations of Johnsonians from John Nichols through James Clifford have probed his literary remains, hoping to get a glimpse of him. Yet the researches of these men have often been fruitful without satisfying. Although a great deal of evidence, documentary as well as hearsay, has accumulated over the past two centuries, some has escaped careful analysis because of its apparent insignificance, and some has eluded interpretation in spite of the resourcefulness of the investigators. The present study is an attempt to subject all of the available evidence pertaining to Johnson's early career to rigorous and consistent analysis and to develop contexts that allow scattered facts and cryptic references to be interpreted. In doing this I hope to provide a coherent picture of Johnson's early years as a hack writer.

This study is carefully limited in both time and scope. By Johnson's early career I mean the period from his initial excursion to London in 1737 until his signing of the contract for the *Dictionary* in 1746. I have neglected Johnson's literary attempts that preceded his coming to London, for these were undertaken at irregular periods and do not have about them the air of a commitment to a life of writing. Although it might be argued that the *Dictionary* itself should be included in such a study (it is certainly a production of Johnson's years of obscurity), it has nevertheless been omitted, for a similar handling of the *Dictionary* would in all likelihood make this study half again as long as it is. In addition, the great literary works that Johnson accomplished while engaged on that great scholarly one—*The Rambler* and *The Vanity of Human Wishes*—are perhaps less in need of further dis-

v

cussion than some of the little-known pieces that crowd the
Gentleman's Magazine.

Nor is this work a complete biography of Johnson during these
years. I have tried to restrict myself to matters relevant to his
career as an author. Thus Johnson's trip to the Midlands during
1739 and 1740, which receives considerable discussion in the
standard modern biographies, is only glanced at briefly here.
Nevertheless, in the process of investigating Johnson's earnings,
a topic certainly apposite to his life as a writer, I have been inevitably drawn into such tangential considerations as the extent of
his poverty, the situation of his lodgings, and even the possible
extravagance of his wife. His relations with many of the middling
and low literary figures of the day are considered when their
activities help shed light on Johnson's own undertakings. Richard
Savage has, of course, received special consideration, for no study
of Johnson's early years in London could possibly be complete
without his incorrigible presence.

I have used recent developments in social and political history
to place Johnson in his times and to set his ideas in context. Perhaps the greatest help of all has come not from Johnson studies
themselves but from the expanding field of the history of the
book trade, for no accurate picture of Johnson's life as a hack
writer could be drawn so long as the circumstances in which he
and his contemporaries worked remained obscure. Although our
knowledge of the trade is by no means complete, the discoveries
of the past several decades have brought many aspects of the
literary underworld of the eighteenth century back into the light
of day.

Although Johnson's numerous and various works during this
period have not been ignored by modern scholars, his career as
a whole has never been subjected to a systematic investigation. It
is just such an orderly presentation and assessment that I am
seeking to provide here. I have thus been less zealous to analyze
works individually than to demonstrate how they elucidate Johnson's position as hack writer, magazine editor, or library cataloguer. Many of Johnson's contributions to the *Gentleman's Magazine* receive little consideration, for some have been sufficiently
discussed by other scholars, while others are too trifling to call
for or to bear up under detailed analysis. Only the Parliamentary
debates receive extensive treatment. I have, though, paused fre-

quently in my narrative to examine representative works, especially pieces that point up the exigencies of periodical publication in the eighteenth century or that call attention to the variety of the tasks placed before Johnson. (When I have found it necessary to include any quotations from Johnson's Latin poems, I have commonly subjoined my own translations in parentheses.)

For many of Johnson's works that failed to reach print, such as the aborted translation of the *History of the Council of Trent* or the 1745 edition of Shakespeare, I have tried to develop the contexts in which each was undertaken and to explain the attempt in terms of its significance to the career of an unknown author.

The conclusions that I draw in this study do not always correspond to the traditional view of Johnson's early career, and so I do not expect them to pass without severe scrutiny. It has been my practice throughout to prefer scanty evidence to no evidence: when sparse documentation has conflicted with unsubstantiable tradition, I have trusted the first and drawn my conclusions accordingly. I have no foolish confidence that I have solved all the riddles of Johnson's early career; I hope, rather, to have asked new questions. If the primary effect of this study is to stimulate the search for more evidence and to suggest broader contexts in which to understand Johnson's life as a writer-for-hire, no one shall be happier than I.

I have incurred many debts over the course of this project. Although I cannot here repay them, I wish at least to acknowledge them.

The first debt of any scholar is to his libraries, and I have been particularly fortunate in beginning my researches at the Harvard College Library and concluding them at the Newberry Library in Chicago. I wish to express my special thanks to Richard Brown and Mary Wyly of the Newberry's Office of Research and Education for allowing me the continued use of the collection during a six-month period of 1982 when the library was officially closed for renovation. I can now only marvel at the thoughtfulness and ingenuity of Karen Skubish and the reading-room staff in providing efficient service under most difficult conditions.

The following institutions generously provided photocopies

of manuscript material in their possession: the British Library, the University of Nottingham Library and the Trustees of the Portland Estate, the Boston Public Library, and the Cornell University Library (with special thanks to Donald Eddy for some kind personal attention).

Of the many librarians and archivists who responded to my various queries, I wish to single out Richard Bowden of the Marylebone Library, who not only did me the favor of examining the Marylebone rate books for 1738, but also corrected some of my misconceptions about property ownership in eighteenth-century England.

I wish to thank Loyola University of Chicago for two summer research awards, as well as for access to word-processing equipment that facilitated the preparation of the final draft. I must also here thank Mrs. Patty Szott, who, before the advent of the word processor, typed draft after draft of chapter after chapter, and whose efficiency should make even computers blush.

It is, of course, most pleasant to thank friends. Kenneth Harris and Frank Calvillo read the earliest version of this work and provided helpful comments. George DeVoe exuberantly shared both his research and his insights while pursuing his own work on Samuel Johnson's poetry. John Shea's precise reading saved me from a number of infelicities. James Sack read my chapters on politics with a friendly eye towards helping me avoid obvious historical blunders. A. D. Barker read excerpts from my manuscript and graciously shared with me his superior knowledge of the early years of the *Gentleman's Magazine*. My wife, Noreen Kaminski, kept my prose from becoming excessively mannered and buoyed my spirit when I lacked confidence.

There are three men to whom I owe a special debt of gratitude. When this work was in its early stages, I benefited so greatly from the conversation, the encouragement, and the example of W. J. Bate that I scarcely know how to acknowledge my debt. He may be said to have formed my mind to the task. Donald Greene read the penultimate draft of this work and provided such trenchant criticisms that I can only be thankful that I had the benefit of his learning while the work was still in the process of revision. Finally, O M Brack Jr. read two complete drafts with a keen eye for weak argument, errors of detail, and slovenly expression; yet I have benefited at least as much from his friendship as from his criticisms. I suspect that none of these men will find this work completely above his censure, but each will, I think, see in it improvements for which he rather than the author deserves the credit.

Chicago   T. K.
June 1986

CONTENTS

I   The Road to St. John's Gate   3

II   The World of the *Gentleman's Magazine*   24

III   A Miner in Literature   41

IV   Translating for Booksellers   62

V   Savage, Poverty, and Politics   83

VI   Resisting Fate   107

VII   The Parliamentary Debates   123

VIII   The Editor   144

IX   In Search of Reputation   172

Appendices   198

Abbreviations Used in Notes   205

Notes   207

Index   259

THE EARLY CAREER
OF SAMUEL JOHNSON

CHAPTER I

THE ROAD TO
ST. JOHN'S GATE

So the young author panting for a name,
And fir'd with pleasing hope of endless fame,
Intrusts his happiness to human kind,
More false, more cruel than the seas and wind.
Samuel Johnson, "The Young Author"

On March 2, 1737, Samuel Johnson left Lichfield for London in the company of David Garrick, with an unfinished draft of *Irene* in his pocket. That same day Gilbert Walmesley wrote to his friend the Rev. John Colson that Johnson set out "to try his fate with a tragedy, and to see to get himself employed in some translation, either from the Latin or the French. Johnson is a very good scholar and poet, and I have great hopes will turn out a fine tragedy-writer."[1] Johnson was coming to London to make his name by his literature. He carried along with him the good wishes of his friends and the knowledge of his own abilities, but he could not have anticipated the great struggle that lay before him as he sought success in the literary world of London.

At twenty-seven Johnson was no longer a youth, and the previous ten years had already taught him that much more was to be endured in life than enjoyed. From his year at Oxford he had learned that although his genius might be recognized, he could not expect it to be readily rewarded. His adult life was littered with a succession of failures. He was temperamentally unsuited for carrying on his father's book trade. He had had no success at all in the string of teaching positions that he had sought or held between his duties at Stourbridge School and the failure of his own school at Edial. He had spent months at a time lounging in Lichfield, perhaps studying, perhaps not, and sulking in Birmingham, where melancholy often provoked him to abuse Ed-

mund Hector, the friend with whom he was staying.[2] Various
literary pursuits had come to nothing. In 1733 he had contributed some essays to Thomas Warren's *Birmingham Journal,* but
he was unable to rouse himself to regular composition. Hector
had to extort from Johnson his translation of Father Lobo's *Voyage to Abyssinia* by representing to him the distress his delay caused
the printer's family. Even then Johnson would not leave his bed,
Hector hurriedly taking down his dictated abridgment of the text.
During 1734 he had issued proposals for an edition of Politian's
Latin poems, to which he was to add a history of Latin poetry
from Petrarch to Politian and a life of his author. As one might
suspect, the project aroused little interest in the Midlands; whether
the proposals ever reached London is unknown. The response
was so small that the work was never carried out; indeed, it may
never have been begun.[3]

Later that year Johnson wrote a tactless letter to Edward Cave,
the publisher of the *Gentleman's Magazine,* offering his services as
an author.

> As You appear no less sensible than your Readers of the de-
> fects of your Poetical Article, you will not be displeased, if, in
> order to the improvement of it, I communicate to You the Sen-
> timents of a person, who will undertake on reasonable terms
> sometimes to fill a column.
>
> His opinion is, that the Publick would not give You a bad
> reception, if . . . You admitted not only Poems, Inscriptions, &c
> never printed before, which he will sometimes supply You with;
> but likewise short literary Dissertations in Latin or English, Crit-
> ical Remarks on Authours Ancient or Modern, forgotten Poems
> that deserve Revival, or loose pieces . . . worth preserving. By
> this Method your Literary Article . . . will, he thinks, be better
> recommended to the Publick, than by low Jests, awkward Buf-
> foonery, or the dull Scurrilities of either Party.[4]

Cave could not have been pleased with the implication that the
pieces he printed were either vulgar or jejune and must have
disliked the haughty tone of his correspondent. Unfortunately
for Johnson, Cave was just then preparing to open up a portion
of the magazine to essays and articles submitted by his readers
and as a result would receive for free the variety, though perhaps
not the quality, of pieces that Johnson was offering to sell.

Each of these false starts has a half-hearted quality about it.
Johnson seems to have been easily discouraged from carrying out

what he had proposed; any stumbling block was enough to halt work. But going to London was a decisive step. With the failure of his school at Edial, there may have seemed nothing else for him to do. As a married man he was forced to find a suitable means of support. Even if his pride had not smarted at the idea of living on his wife's money, as it certainly must have, the obvious realization that her "fortune" was not inexhaustible would have been enough to force him to find work.[5] Edial had been an investment, an attempt to turn Tetty's limited assets into a continuous source of income, but it did not become self-sustaining and had to be abandoned. Yet the two years since his marriage had not been totally wasted; if his school was a failure, he had nevertheless made considerable progress on his tragedy. He was coming to London to finish *Irene,* to polish it, and to bring it to the stage. The journey had at least the appearance of a serious commitment to a life of writing.

Many years later, when Johnson was in a large company, he jokingly reminisced at Garrick's expense about their arrival in London, "when I came with two-pence half-penny in *my* pocket, and thou, Davy, with three half-pence in thine."[6] Although Johnson probably exaggerated their poverty to annoy Garrick, neither came well provided. At most Johnson probably carried a few pounds. The less money he had, the greater the probability that he would seek out some work immediately upon his arrival. Such little tricks and incentives were not uncommon with Johnson, always so painfully conscious of his habitual laziness. He may also have had a naive confidence in his ability to find suitable employment in town.

Little is known of Johnson's first stay in London. Boswell informs us that he took lodgings in Exeter Street with Norris the staymaker and that he frequently visited Henry Hervey; but of his other activities little more than conjecture remains. Lucy Porter, Johnson's step-daughter, told Boswell that Walmesley had given him a letter of introduction to Henry Lintot the bookseller and that Lintot gave him work. But this seems unlikely, especially since Boswell recalled Johnson saying Cave was the first publisher for whom he had worked in London.[7]

Before long Johnson was in need of money. According to Hawkins, who cites a witness "now living . . . and of whose ve-

racity the least doubt cannot be entertained," Johnson and Garrick jointly applied to Wilcox the bookseller for a loan of five
pounds.[8] Walmesley's letter to Colson suggests that Johnson had
hoped to sustain himself in London by doing a translation, and
when he left Lichfield he may have already envisioned the translation of Father Paul Sarpi's *History of the Council of Trent* that he
was to undertake for Cave over a year later. He probably offered
this or some other such project to Wilcox, prompting the bookseller's suggestion, as he contemplated Johnson's great size, that
he become a porter.[9] Johnson was ignorant of Grub Street if he
expected a member of the trade to take up such an offer from
an ungainly, unknown, overconfident country scholar. The most
Johnson would have been offered was probably some menial task
at a meager wage.[10] In all likelihood he obtained no work, living
off his part of the loan from Wilcox until he could receive money
from home. If his hope of supporting himself in London had
failed, he could still solace himself with the idea that this left him
considerably more time to work on *Irene*.

Johnson's economy at this time was in strict keeping with his
means. He dined at the Pine Apple in New-street for eight pence
a day "with very good company," his regular fare consisting of
a six-penny cut of meat and a penny's worth of bread. His lodging with a tradesman and his simple meals suggest that he followed some of the precepts of an old Birmingham acquaintance,
an Irish painter who had counseled him that

> thirty pounds a year was enough to enable a man to live [in Lon-
> don] without being contemptible. He allowed ten pounds for
> clothes and linen. He said a man might live in a garret at eigh-
> teen-pence a week; few people would inquire where he lodged;
> and if they did, it was easy to say, "Sir, I am to be found at such
> a place." By spending three-pence in a coffee-house, he might
> be for some hours every day in very good company; he might
> dine for six-pence, breakfast on bread and milk for a penny, and
> do without supper. On *clean-shirt-day* he went abroad, and paid
> visits.[11]

It is important to place this sort of frugality in perspective. Thirty
pounds a year could keep a gentleman above poverty so long as
he lived with care. The actual value of this sum is best understood by comparing it to the income of a common laborer of
Johnson's day. Such a man might earn a mere eighteen pounds

a year, and although his wife and children might eke out this total somewhat, the necessities of an entire family would often be provided on less than the Irish painter's yearly allotment. Their fare, in truth, would not be so hearty as Johnson's, but then, in spite of all the hoopla about the roast beef of old England, it remained true throughout most of the eighteenth century that perhaps half of England's population ate little meat or none at all.[12]

Although Johnson was not living a life of plenty, nor was he in distress. His limited funds—we cannot say income, for he was probably living off capital—were not cause for reproach; nor did they indicate poverty, that is, the want of necessities. He lived as a gentleman of slender means, but he lived among gentlemen. He was obviously proud of his companions at the Pine Apple, "several of [whom] had travelled," and he carried himself among them as a man of education and breeding.[13] Throughout his life, whether comfortably off or sorely distressed, he was always solicitous of the respect due a gentleman. At Oxford he had enrolled as a commoner, and thereby used up in one year the small store of money that might have supported him through several years as a batteller or through the entire course as a servitor. But his pride would not permit such a lowering of his social position.[14] A man was not a gentleman by virtue of his wealth but by his birth, his merit, and his breeding. And though, as he later said, he could hardly tell who his grandfather was, he certainly felt that his own merit, indeed genius, compensated for a lack of ancestors.[15] In every particular his behavior in these early years adumbrates the attitudes on subordination and social position recorded by Boswell.

When Tetty returned to London with him half a year later, his living arrangements would become more regular and more expensive, but for this temporary bachelor's life, meager provisions were sufficient for him to live above contempt.

After several months of taking in London, Johnson retired to Greenwich with the hope of finishing *Irene*. He had become so involved in the life of the city that he ignored his original purpose for coming. His fascination with "the full tide of human existence" made further work on the long-labored play impossible. *Irene* may have for a time seemed distant or irrelevant, but it was the key to his future. At Greenwich he again began work on the play, composing in his head while walking in the Park.[16]

The same pangs of conscience that drove him from London probably also inspired the letter to Edward Cave of July 12, 1737, explaining his project for a translation of Sarpi's *Historia del Concilio Tridentino*, a seventeenth-century piece of ecclesiastical history critical of the Counter Reformation. He suggests that since the French translation by Pierre François Le Courayer was recently well received in England, the time was right for a new English version. He argues that the style of the old seventeenth-century English translation is "capable of great Improvements," and he offers to provide a specimen of his own work, should Cave approve the project.[17] A more ambitious translator, submitting several pages of elegant prose with his letter, might have done more to convince Cave, but in all probability Johnson had not yet opened the work he so confidently offered to adorn with his style.

Johnson's offer arose from the current celebrity of Sarpi's book. Le Courayer, a disaffected French Catholic priest exiled from his native country because of his latitudinarian views, was residing in England under the protection of Lord Percival and Archbishop William Wake. He had become a member of Queen Caroline's private circle, and it was at her request that he undertook his own translation. Le Courayer's French version had been published at London only the year before, and Johnson was offering to make Sarpi's Italian text and Le Courayer's French notes accessible to English readers. There were many factors, though, to discourage the undertaking. It was a very large work. The original Italian edition is a closely printed folio of eight hundred pages. At the time of Johnson's letter, Cave was struggling with his first major independent publication after the *Gentleman's Magazine*, Du Halde's *Description of the Empire of China and Chinese Tartary*. After seventeen months of delays, this work had only just begun going to press in February 1737. Cave's problems with this production may have made him wary of publishing another large tome.

In addition, Le Courayer's translation would itself be a competitor with this new English version. The influence of his royal patroness had helped Le Courayer garner nearly five hundred subscribers, many from the English aristocracy and the upper echelons of the Church. Johnson could argue that his translation would make the work available to the English audience, but Cave may have felt that the only audience that could be counted on to purchase such an expensive and specialized work had already purchased Le Courayer's. Finally, Johnson's translation, complete with notes and commentary, would be more a work of scholarship than one of general interest, and scholarship was not the concern of the booksellers. Scholarship for the most part was the product of patronage, which could take the form of a government sinecure, a university post, or a position in the Church. Some such benefice was necessary for the leisure of study. But the booksellers were men of business, not patrons of learning. There were innumerable hacks floating around London who could turn French or Italian into readable English. If a translation had a potential market, a version quickly done by one of these, preempting any rivals, was the bookseller's desire. Since a translator was paid for his work by the sheet, it was to his advantage not to dwell on correctness of style but to turn out text as quickly as possible. From his proposal Johnson appears intent on rivaling Le Courayer. There is little wonder that Cave demurred. He had no care to provide the nation with an elegant new edition of a hundred-year-old piece of Church history—at least not without some certainty of gain. Johnson had sought a patron but found only a bookseller. A year later, after Johnson had proved himself as an author by writing *London,* Cave would reconsider this proposal.[18]

Cave's rejection of the Sarpi project probably had little effect on Johnson, for he appears to have concentrated his hopes on his play. His primary intention all along, we may assume, had been to become a tragic poet. Other doors had been closed to him by his lack of a university degree: he could not enter the law or any other profession; his school had little credibility; and even his qualifications as a translator may have been questioned. But the university did not qualify a man to be a poet, genius did. Pope had no degree and needed none. Just as he had tried to distinguish himself at Oxford by translating Pope's *Messiah* into elegant Latin hexameters, Johnson now hoped to rise suddenly in London by a single great exertion of his genius. This time he would not imitate Pope or any other writer, ancient or modern; he would instead attempt the most difficult of the genres—tragic poetry. Unlike Pope, who had followed a poetical *cursus honorum,* starting with pastorals and proving his genius through a number of poems formed on solid classical principles, Johnson, with his characteristic impatience, sought to leap to the top of the literary world with one great bound. It was with *Irene* that he first intended to "drive the world about a little."

But rather than overpowering London he was captivated by it, and he returned to Lichfield in the summer of 1737 as he had left it months before, with *Irene* unfinished in his pocket.[19] No particular prospects of work would be needed to lure him back to London, for his very lack of application that spring may have left him sanguine in his hopes for success. Not having finished *Irene,* he had not yet experienced the great blow of having it rejected. He was invigorated by the city and confident of his talent. If others had foundered, he would prevail. And even when he was assailed with doubts, this much was certainly true: in Lichfield he had no prospects, in London there was at least hope.

According to Boswell, Johnson remained in Lichfield for only three months, long enough to finish his play and take care of whatever business remained. Then, once again filled with great expectations, he brought Tetty to London and established himself as a permanent resident of that city.

Johnson returned to London with Tetty towards the end of 1737 and took up lodgings in Woodstock Street near Hanover Square. In the early eighteenth century, London was rapidly spreading westward. Hanover, Cavendish, and Grosvenor Squares had been built during the 1720s and 1730s, attracting many of the fashionable inhabitants of the old city who wished to escape its squalor. Much of the land surrounding these elegant new squares had been leased to speculators who tried to cash in on the movement westward. The housing there was often thrown up quickly; the streets were unpaved. Yet the area was looked on as a haven from the mob that inhabited the city, and it attracted many middle-class residents.[20]

Few readers accustomed to the tales of Johnson's dire poverty during his early years in London would expect to find him and Tetty in such surroundings. Tetty's pretensions to quality, which were not totally unfounded, and her detestation of the city may have led them to seek a "genteel" quarter of London. Though perhaps an odd couple, they were certainly a respectable one. In all probability they continued to live on the remains of Tetty's fortune (for Johnson as yet had no work that we can discern), and the dependent husband may have simply been willing to indulge his wife's whims about living more fashionably than they could realistically afford. They did not remain in Woodstock Street very long. By March they had removed to lodgings at No. 6 Castle Street, near Cavendish Square;[21] whether the move was dictated by economy is unknown. Still cheaper lodgings were certainly available in the older parts of London and in the horrible slums that had spread east along the river, but there was apparently no need to resort to such a drastic move. They were not destitute, and Tetty, who never liked London, might have felt at ease to know that a few minutes' walk would bring her to open fields. Johnson was perhaps happier that his wife be at peace than that he live in the throbbing heart of the city. Two years later, when Johnson was to write to Tetty during his trip to the Midlands, she was still to be found in Castle Street. Whatever hardships they experienced during those early years were insufficient to budge her.

Johnson's first concern in this final removal to London was to get *Irene* produced. Boswell gives us the story that Johnson and Peter Garrick, David's older brother and a schoolmate of Johnson's at Lichfield Grammar School, read through the play at the Fountain Tavern and offered it without success to Charles Fleetwood, the patentee of Drury Lane.[22] Boswell asserts that Fleetwood rejected the play because it lacked a patron, but *Irene* faced many greater obstacles than this simple explanation suggests.

Johnson's lack of success in bringing *Irene* to the stage might be more easily understood in the context of the London theater at that time. An evening at the theater usually comprised a full-length play and an afterpiece, which might be a farce, a pantomime, a dance, or some other minor entertainment. The theaters were run essentially as repertory companies, the main piece changing from night to night. Shakespeare, improved of course, dominated the stage in the late 1730s, followed by such figures as Cibber, Congreve, Farquhar, and Vanbrugh. A season would be filled out with works by Ben Jonson, Wycherley, Susannah Centlivre, and many others.[23] New plays were rare, and their success or failure often depended on a single performance. The system was certainly not favorable to new authors.

The situation was exacerbated by the Stage Licensing Act of 1737, which not only prevented the production of several anti-ministry plays, but also closed down the theaters in Lincoln's Inn Fields and the Haymarket.[24] Only Covent Garden, run by John Rich, and Drury Lane, managed by Fleetwood, remained open. In the years immediately preceding Johnson's arrival in London, the theaters in the Haymarket and in Lincoln's Inn Fields were the primary outlets for new plays. During the last two seasons before the Licensing Act, Fleetwood produced only three new main pieces, Rich none. In the same period, Henry Fielding's company presented nine new main pieces at the New Theater in the Haymarket, including George Lillo's *Fatal Curiosity*; Henry Giffard, who moved his company from Goodman's Fields to Lincoln's Inn Fields in 1736, produced six, three of which were tragedies. When Johnson finally sought to bring *Irene* to the stage, the theaters most open to new works had been shuttered.

After the Licensing Act, Fleetwood became slightly more receptive to new plays but no more encouraging to new authors. From September 1737 through May 1738, only three new productions appeared as main pieces at Drury Lane. The first, *Art and Nature,* was written by James Miller, a popular playwright who had supplied Fleetwood with a new comedy in two of the previous three seasons. (His *Universal Passion* was the only new main piece produced at Drury Lane during the 1736–37 season.) The second was an adaptation of Milton's *Comus*; the third, James Thomson's *Agamemnon. Comus,* revived because of the current surge in Milton's popularity, needed no patron to recommend it. Thomson, well known for his *Seasons,* was a prominent figure in the literary arm of the opposition. Once his play, a political allegory, was licensed, it was guaranteed a large anti-Walpole audience. No new author succeeded where Johnson failed. The situation at Covent Garden was no better: during the same months, Rich produced only one new main piece.[25]

But it was not only the obtuseness or timidity of the managers that foiled Johnson's first attempt in the theater, for he aspired to write tragedy at a time when the public taste had turned to other entertainments. The creative energy of the age was to a large extent channeled into farces, ballad operas, pantomimes, and other small dramatic forms.[26] And with the rising popularity of opera, both Rich and Fleetwood began to emphasize the music and spectacle of their afterpieces at the expense of the more traditional dramatic forms. The theater managers were content to continue with their standard stock of plays, highlighting the novelty of the entertainments presented afterwards. Johnson was seeking to work in the great genre of tragedy at a time when the pygmy genres had overcome it.

Nor was Johnson possessed of either the theatrical background or the artistic temperament to become the great tragedian of his day. His first serious discussions about the theater probably dated back to the winter and spring of 1725–26, passed by the 16-year-old Johnson with his cousin Cornelius Ford, whose conversation was filled with anecdotes of years passed in London in the company of authors. His education continued at the home of Gilbert Walmesley, where Garrick too may have imbibed his early love of drama. But Ford and Walmesley were hardly a substitute for regular attendance at the theater. In temperament Johnson was a tragedian particularly ill-suited to his age. During the 1730s, the pathetic tragedy of Rowe and Otway was in the ascendant, while Dryden's heroic rant was nowhere to be heard.[27] If his mentors counseled the need for pathos, their words could not deflect Johnson's personality from following its own congenial channels. The story of Irene that Johnson found in Knolles's *General History of the Turks* was perhaps more open to pathetic than heroic treatment, for Constantinople was not to be redeemed from Islam by any act of the dramatic imagination: the greatest deeds that could be expected from the characters were rescue and flight. The captivity of Irene provided the author with a situation rife with pathos; and with the introduction of Aspasia, a second fair captive, Johnson doubled that potential. But the pathetic was never Johnson's mode, and his treatment of his heroines becomes an exploration not of female suffering but of the requirements of heroic virtue. He makes the moral case against Irene's apostasy with such authority that even her death, wrongfully carried out though it is, loses much of its motive power: a sense of ironic justice usurps the place of feeling.

Finally, historical tragedy, at least in its heroic form, was moribund in 1738. It managed to sustain itself only by entangling its plots in the rigging of contemporary politics. At least from the time of *Cato*, works in this genre achieved much of their success from their political associations. Thomson's *Agamemnon* and David Mallet's *Mustapha*, both produced between Johnson's approach to Fleetwood and the prohibition of Brooke's *Gustavus Vasa* in 1739, had been sponsored by the Prince of Wales and his coterie. The entire opposition turned out to see Walpole allegorized as Aegisthus in one and as Rustan, Solyman's wicked Grand Vizier, in the other.[28]

But Johnson's play had no easily discernible political position. It was meant to instruct and (we may be sure) to delight, not to be politically contentious. Although the play is not devoid of politics, its pronouncements are vague and idealistic rather than scathingly explicit. Unlike *London* and the two political pamphlets of 1739, *Irene* lacks any direct criticism of the contemporary situation.[29] Thus Johnson was working in an outmoded form and neglected to give his work the one quality that would have guaranteed it an audience—a specific political bias. If, as Boswell suggests, Johnson's play was passed over for lack of a patron, it was probably for lack of a political one.

Irene, it seems, was doomed to fail, for Johnson had understood neither the taste of the audience nor the problems inherent in getting his play into production. The young author, working away at Edial and Greenwich, aloof from the quarrels of Westminster, had probably never considered interlarding his great work with the pettiness of party. In the future he would not be so naive. For his next literary work he used Pope as a model and wrote in a manner that would compel the Town to acknowledge him.

Johnson may have conceived the idea of imitating Juvenal's *Third Satire* shortly after arriving in London in 1737. He carried the texts of Juvenal's poems in his head the way modern men do telephone numbers or stock quotations. As he wandered the streets, amazed by the great bustle of humanity, and talked in the taverns of art and politics, numerous parallels between Imperial Rome and contemporary London would have struck him. Though, as he said later, the manners of Rome were not those of eighteenth-century England, the attributes of the society that revolted Juvenal—rampant poverty and squalor, the haughtiness of wealth, the toadying of parasites, and the preferment of men who feed the lusts of the powerful over men of merit—persisted in the modern metropolis, changes in customs and manners notwithstanding. But Johnson already was engaged on *Irene* and probably gave little serious consideration to the poem.

Upon his return to London with Tetty, Johnson had the expectations of his third night's profits from *Irene* to quell any anx-

ieties about his lack of a current source of income. But with Fleetwood's rejection of the play, these hopes were dashed, and Johnson
was forced to turn away from tragedy and to try his skill in other
fields. He may again have offered someone the Sarpi project, but
the arguments in its favor were certainly no more compelling
than they had been a year before. So he turned to Juvenal.

The advantages of such a project were abundant and obvious.
The subject was clear in Johnson's mind and required neither
much study nor labor. The success of Pope's imitations of Horace
provided a receptive public. Should he acquit himself well as the
English Juvenal, he could become the natural counterpart of Pope.
And if he could use his Juvenalian persona to express some of
the public outrage against Walpole, his work might be cried up
by the opposition. This project, it must have seemed, obviated
all of the naive errors he had committed in writing *Irene*.

Johnson apparently began serious work on the poem during
the first months of 1738. He wrote in his usual fitful manner,
composing many lines at a time, often committing nothing to paper until it was polished. Hours of energy might alternate with
days of inertia. By late March the poem was apparently completed. Johnson now needed a publisher but appears in this case
to have learned an important lesson from his letters to Cave and
his experience with Fleetwood—the frontal attack, the usual
Johnsonian mode, was not always the most successful. He decided to prepare the way for the acceptance of *London* by en-
gaging the good will of a man who could help him.

Before the month came to an end Johnson dropped by St.
John's Gate, the home of the *Gentleman's Magazine,* and presented
Edward Cave with a poem—not his imitation of Juvenal, but a
Latin ode entitled "Ad Urbanum." As editor of the magazine Cave
had adopted the pseudonym Sylvanus Urban, signifying his objectivity and universality. In his pseudonym's implied merger of
the country and the city he was at once rural Englishman and
Londoner, Whig and Tory, merchant and farmer. The name had
received such general acceptance that the magazine's correspondents wrote directly to Mr. Urban. Johnson's address was,
at least in appearances, to the spirit behind the magazine, but
that flattered spirit found physical form in the person of Edward
Cave.

Johnson's poem was occasioned by the magazine wars of the
day. The *Gentleman's Magazine* and its most prominent rival, the

London Magazine, were in a constant battle for prestige and circulation. The *London Magazine* had been modeled on Cave's successful venture and had come into existence a year after its pre-
decessor. From the start the competition had been intense. Since
the two publications were similar in both form and content, they
were reduced to berating one another over trivialities. They
squabbled over which magazine provided more copy for the money
and which was more guilty of plagiarism.[30] In January 1738,
Common Sense, a journal whose essays were regularly excerpted
by both magazines, joined with the *London Magazine* in attacking
the *Gentleman's,* asserting that Cave did not so much abridge its
essays as mangle them. Cave responded with a virulent counter-
attack in his February issue.[31] His readers, inspired by Mr. Urban's pluckiness, sent him a number of poems in his magazine's
defense. Into this situation Johnson entered.

Johnson was not one of the enthusiasts unable to restrain
themselves from praising the magazine. More likely, he visited
St. John's Gate during March, possibly hoping to stir up some
interest in the Sarpi project, perhaps with *London* in mind, and
found out about Cave's intention to publish a number of second-
rate poems in praise of his magazine and himself. What better
way for Johnson to gain a hearing for his projects than to contribute a sophisticated Latin poem that would grace this collection and add respectability to Cave's claims of superiority over
his rivals?

Latin poetry was rare in both magazines, and many of the
Latin pieces that did appear were occasional and reprinted from
other sources. Cave had been aware of the poor quality of his
"poetical article" even before Johnson had pointed it out in his
letter from Birmingham over three years earlier. He tried to attract better poetry by offering prizes. Unfortunately, these brought
little improvement. Johnson's poem, a creditable performance by
the standards of the magazine poetry of the day, would raise the
prestige of the *Gentleman's* by adding a new dimension that its
rival could not easily match. Johnson and his poem would certainly be welcome.

Johnson began his poem with an allusion that was probably
no less obscure in his own day than it is today. The project of
praising Sylvanus Urban brought to his mind the panegyric on
Pope Urban VIII by the seventeenth-century Polish poet Casimir
Sarbiewski. Johnson echoed the beginning of Casimir's poem, re-

peating the Latin vocative "Urbane."[32] But as the praise owing
to a Pontiff differs greatly from that due to a magazine publisher, Johnson quickly abandoned his source, though not its
panegyrical nature.

In Johnson's poem, Urban is praised for his indefatigable labor, and his "learned brow" is crowned with a perpetually green
laurel—this for the man whose "poetical article" had previously
been found defective and whose paper was graced by "low Jests,
awkward Buffoonery, [and] the dull Scurrilities of either Party."[33]
But panegyric could not occupy Johnson's mind for long, and he
regains some of his wonted dignity as he passes from praise to
exhortation. Sensible of the pettiness of the newspaper wars, he
urges Urban to ignore his detractors:

> Linguae procacis plumbea Spicula,
> Fidens, Superbo frange Silentio.[34]

(Be confident and shiver the leaden barbs of a brash tongue with
haughty silence.)

Ironically, as we shall see, by the end of 1738 Johnson himself
had taken over the function of battling the magazine's adversaries and may have even provoked one stage of the confrontation.

The poem closes with praise of the magazine's variety—especially its marriage of the humorous and the serious (*severis lu-
dicra jungere*) and its ability to refresh a tired mind with its useful
trifles (*fatigatamque nugis/Utilibus recreare Mentem*). The praise is
measured and justified, though equally applicable to the *London
Magazine* as to the *Gentleman's*. But Johnson was writing an ode,
and even straightforward compliment had to be embellished. His
last stanza comprises two mythological similes:

> Texente Nymphis serta Lycoride,
> Rosae ruborem sic Viola adjuvat
>   Immista, sic Iris refulget
>   Aethereis variata fucis.

(Thus when Lycoris weaves garlands for the nymphs, the inter-
mingled violet adds to the red of the rose, and thus the many-
hued rainbow gleams with its aetherial dyes.)

The similes point up the signal characteristic of this poem—its
artificiality. Johnson is trying to shine in traditional lights. Though
later he would consider mythological allusions cheap and facile,

he resorted to them here as he did frequently during his early years, whenever he felt the need to be quickly, glibly poetic (it was almost certainly his own facility with such tinsel that led him to value it so little). The poem is unsatisfactory on a higher level, though. The subject cannot sustain the exalted treatment that Johnson gives to it: there is so much pomp for so little reason. To anyone familiar with the magazine and its history, "Ad Urbanum" will appear to come dangerously close to bathos. We can only assume that Johnson had decided to impress Cave and to put him in his debt.

The poem is perhaps most interesting for what it shows us of Johnson's facility for Latin verse. He retained Casimir's Alcaic stanza, one of the verse forms most often used by Horace, but with less of the syntactical complexity seen in either the great Roman odist or his Renaissance imitator. There is no enjambment between Johnson's stanzas. Like Thomson's blank verse, which often seems more indebted to the couplet diction of Pope than the rhythmic periods of Milton, Johnson's Alcaics have a hybrid quality. It is as if he first wrote his typical terse, epigrammatic couplets, and then rendered them in Latin, two per stanza. The poem is constructed like a pile of blocks, one neatly squared off element piled atop another, rather than in the more fluid fashion of Horace. This compartmentalized structure, which might be thought at odds with the essence, if not the prosody, of the classical ode, is typical of Johnson's manner—his hurrying to finish each stanza, counting how many lines were left to be done.[35] Johnson nevertheless does exhibit some of the smaller elegancies of Latin poetry, including balanced phrases, interlocking word order, chiasmus, and the emphatic repetition of key words. Thus, in a poem that was the labor of an hour, perhaps two, he appears to have accomplished more than he really has. His poem is "correct" but not particularly artful in the classical manner, and what dignity it conferred on its subject arose more from the language in which it was written than from the propriety of its sentiments.

"Ad Urbanum" served Johnson well. Cave was flattered and published the poem in the March issue at the head of a page of laudatory doggerel.[36] The way was now prepared for *London*.

Shortly after the warm reception of "Ad Urbanum," Johnson sent his satire to Cave, enclosed in a letter. The letter is not what we would expect of Johnson; it personalizes the flattery of "Ad

Urbanum." He calls Cave "an ingenious and candid man," praises his "generous encouragement of poetry," and distinguishes him from "mercenary booksellers," who pay by the line and know nothing of merit—a particularly ironic comment since late in life Johnson noted that Cave "would contract for lines by the hundred, and expect the long hundred."[37] He also sets up a ruse: the poem is not his own work but that of a friend who "lies at present under very disadvantageous circumstances of fortune." He and Tetty must have run through what money they had, perhaps Tetty's entire fortune, although part of it may have been left behind in Lichfield for safekeeping. It seems an inescapable fact that Johnson marketed his first saleable piece of poetry to meet current expenses.

We must not make too much of Johnson's apparent diffidence in disavowing the poem. He seems merely to have been exploring the avenues of polite contrivance, a common practice among eighteenth-century writers and one raised almost to an art by Pope. The ruse indicates Johnson's uncertainty over how to proceed in his search for recognition. His money was gone, he had little hope for his play, and now he had to sell a poem which he knew to be good but which still lacked a publisher. Courting a man whom he knew at a glance to be his intellectual inferior must have galled him. His famous statement that he "never sought to please till past thirty years old" makes this letter all the more poignant. Only a few years earlier he had been rejected for the position of headmaster of Solihull School partially on the grounds that "he has the character of being a very haughty, ill-natured gent[leman]."[38] Now he was forced not only to flatter and cajole a man who, though good-natured, was essentially a philistine, but virtually to beg for assistance. Since the frankness of his previous approaches to Cave had netted him nothing, this time he would bow and blush. Perhaps for the only time in his career, maybe in his whole life, he hid his pride behind an insincere smile.

This letter was followed by three more documenting the progress of *London* to the press.[39] Cave approved highly of the poem and responded to the "author's" poverty with a "present." Johnson, confident of the poem's merit, was willing to have it printed at his own expense. Cave agreed to back the poem, but suggested that Dodsley be listed as publisher, a move that might increase the prestige of the work. Only the technical problems of designing the exact format remained.

The letters themselves become gradually more familiar in tone and reveal Johnson's assimilation into the society of St. John's Gate. He is introduced to the young poetess Elizabeth Carter, on whom he writes a Greek epigram and who, he says, "ought to be celebrated in as many languages as Lewis le Grand." Now, the young man who only a few weeks earlier had been so eager to please can also express his peevishness by declining unnecessary trips to the Gate, "for it is a long way to walk." Johnson then gets more good news: Cave asks to see *Irene.* The entire future that a short time ago looked bleak is again filled with promise; not only his poem but perhaps also his play has found a publisher. The story ends with the sale of the poem to Dodsley. Approached solely for his name, he was so impressed by the work that he sought first a share of the profits and then the entire property.

Johnson parted with the copyright for ten guineas, a sum that Dodsley was to make many times over in the first few weeks after publication. Although Johnson made an unfortunate habit of undervaluing his literary works, in this case it was not so. Ten guineas was a fair price, especially for the work of an unknown poet, and Johnson himself said that he might have accepted less "but that Paul Whitehead had a little before got ten guineas for a poem; and I would not take less than Paul Whitehead."[40]

London appeared anonymously on May 12 or 13, 1738, within a day of the first part of Pope's *One Thousand Seven Hundred and Thirty Eight.*[41] Whether anonymity was Dodsley's idea or Johnson's remains unknown. In later life Johnson often preferred sending his works to the public without any indication of his authorship, but whether as a young man seeking a reputation he would choose this path seems questionable. Dodsley would have had good reason for insisting on anonymity: he was known to be one of Pope's publishers, and an anonymous satire issuing from his shop, if indeed it had merit, might be thought the work of the great man himself. (Lyttelton apparently thought so in this case.)[42] Such a favorable comparison, even if soon proved false, could only help the sale of the poem. The author might himself be persuaded that he would soon be *déterré.* On the other hand, the undiscriminating crowd might simply ignore the acknowledged work of Samuel Johnson, never bothering to lift it from the bookseller's shelf and leaving his satire unread and himself unknown. Anonymity itself may have been a strategy for securing fame.

Cave, meanwhile, was not slow in seeing Johnson's value as an occasional contributor to the magazine and promptly sought more poetry. He seized upon the Greek epigram on Elizabeth Carter, which combined an elegant compliment with the answer to a riddle that she had contributed to the magazine, as a fine piece for his April issue. Riddles like Miss Carter's were not uncommon in the magazine, for they brought responses by other readers, a situation that Cave always encouraged. But a Greek response to an English riddle was certainly extraordinary; the *London Magazine* could produce nothing comparable in its poetry pages. For once, any claims of superiority would be justified.

The epigram was Johnson's particular forte at this time. He held Martial in high esteem and was justifiably proud of his facility with these short compositions.[43] Whether in Latin, Greek, or English, Johnson's epigrams were like bursts of energy from a brain overcharged with thoughts and images. He could write them on demand and often did. Thus, when Cave wanted poetry for his April issue, Johnson provided more epigrams. First he turned his Greek tribute to Elizabeth Carter into Latin. Then, since Cave was reprinting Richard Savage's first "Volunteer Laureat" in the same issue, Johnson supplied an epigram on the author to append to the poem.

Ad Ricardum Savage, Arm. Humani Generis Amatorem

Humani studium generis cui pectore fervet,
O! colat humanum Te foveatque genus![44]

(To Richard Savage, Armiger, a Lover of Mankind

A devotion to your fellow men burns within your breast; O! may they cherish and protect you!)

Croker did not believe that Johnson wrote "this sad stuff," but his argument, based on the work's insipidity, carries no weight. The very nature of the composition of such pieces makes the occasional jejune one understandable, even expected. The reprinting of the "Volunteer Laureat" was part of an attempt by several of Savage's friends, Cave apparently included, to convince the King to continue his pension. Either this particular matter or the simple hope of a meal may have brought Savage to St. John's Gate, where he might have encountered Johnson. As with the epigram on Miss Carter, a single meeting may have inspired this small effusion. Yet we cannot even be sure that Johnson had met Savage at this time, for he could write an epigrammatical turn on a topic of which he had no personal knowledge. Several months later, for example, Johnson would write Cave that an epigram on Lady Firebrace "may be had when you please, for you know that such a subject neither deserves much thought nor requires it."[45] Johnson apparently knew nothing of Lady Firebrace; he merely spun the verses at Cave's request. In addition, Johnson's epigram on Savage and the two on Elizabeth Carter appear between Savage's poem and two new pieces by "Eliza," as Miss Carter was known to Cave's readers.[46] Johnson's epigrams obviously form a planned tribute to two of Cave's most popular contributors.

The same issue of the *Gentleman's Magazine* contains two more Latin epigrams. "To a Lady who spoke in Defense of Liberty" is definitely Johnson's. Written many years before, it was addressed to Molly Aston, a Lichfield friend in whose company, Johnson later confessed, he once felt rapture.[47] Upon request from Cave for more short pieces, Johnson produced this one from memory. The second epigram, on "Venus in armor," also has a strong claim to being Johnson's, for it is a translation from the *Greek Anthology*, a collection that had engaged his attention while at Oxford and that many years later would occupy sleepless nights as he translated its epigrams into Latin.[48] Although such pieces were but temporary amusements for Johnson, they had an immediate impact on the magazine's "poetical article," adding a tincture of learning and sophistication to the portion of the magazine most in need of such help.[49]

There are no new contributions to the May issue of the *Gentleman's Magazine* that can be positively attributed to Johnson.[50] Early in the month he was probably seeing *London* through the press. After the poem appeared around mid-month, he would have basked in the glory of his triumph, perhaps like the author in *Rambler* 146, frequenting the taverns and coffee houses to hear people talk of his work. Cave printed excerpts from the poem in the poetry section for May and noted it at the top of the register of books for that month; Pope's *One Thousand Seven Hundred and Thirty-Eight* was consigned to twenty-second place.

After the success of *London* Johnson was no longer an outsider. His relationships with Cave and Dodsley had been founded on a solid commercial base, and all had benefited. Johnson had demonstrated a genius not to be found in common writers and had been provided in turn with his first breakthrough into the London literary world. Cave had found a new source of sophisticated poetry for his magazine, and Dodsley had purchased a work that was to sell out within a week. All had gone well for all, and *London* appeared to be a truly auspicious beginning for Johnson: a second edition was called for almost immediately and a third two months later. After many false starts Johnson was finally on his way.

CHAPTER II

THE WORLD OF
THE *GENTLEMAN'S MAGAZINE*

He told me, that when he first saw St. John's Gate, the place
where that deservedly popular miscellany was originally printed,
he "beheld it with reverence."

Boswell, *Life of Johnson*

The success of *London* certainly went far to bolster Johnson's ego,
but his profits from it were by no means great enough to stave
off penury for long. Steady work was needed. He may have toyed
with the idea of living by his poetry, but his nature was not suited
to the constant creative exertion that characterized Pope's slow
craftsmanship. It had taken Johnson over two years, much of it
time of considerable leisure, to write *Irene*. And even if he could
write seventy lines in a day, as he was later to do when composing
The Vanity of Human Wishes,[1] he could not do it every day. The
great outbursts of energy that dot his career, though remarkable
in themselves, are widely spaced and usually pricked on by ad-
versity. He did not write every day; indeed, he probably did not
write every week. Such epigrams as Cave had called on him to
contribute could be done with little thought, no anxiety, and immediate reward—probably a small "present" from Cave and the
applause of Elizabeth Carter. Rather than moving on to new satires or better plays, Johnson threw in his lot with Cave. By June
he was providing substantial assistance in putting out the magazine; by early August he had begun, with Cave's backing, his
translation of Sarpi's *History*. But before we proceed to investigate these matters in detail, we must stop to examine the magazine itself and the first acquaintances Johnson made through it.

At St. John's Gate Johnson became fully acquainted with the
literary underworld, the group that in every age turns out much

of the writing that a contemporary public reads, with both the authors and their work forgotten before the next generation if not before the next sunrise. But Johnson's new milieu was not as grotesque as some have painted it—peopled primarily with starving poets who pawn the books they are to translate or who sleep on "bulks" for want of a lodging. Poverty and irresponsibility were certainly to be found, but so were patient industry and rewarded labor.

Johnson's guide through this underworld, and one of its most curious characters, was Edward Cave himself. He is best known by the two exquisite pictures of him drawn from life by Johnson and Sir John Hawkins.[2] Johnson's sober good sense and sympathy delineate the strengths of Cave's character—the constancy of his friendship, his certain though plodding advancement toward the truth—while Hawkins's natural sourness vividly strikes out his idiosyncrasies.

Cave was a large man, tall and bulky. When young he had been strong and active, but by 1738 that vigor had softened into repose. He was taciturn by nature and a sufferer from the gout. This combination generally kept him seated and silent and often made him appear cool to visitors. His sole interest was his magazine. His method of beginning a conversation was to hand his guest a leaf of the issue then in the press and ask for an opinion.

Cave's sluggish, stolid temperament is the focal point of both portraits. But what Johnson understood to be minute attention to detail and unflappable reserve, Hawkins saw only as obtuseness. Cave was truly a man of business, without pretensions to gentility and thus without need of the grace and tact so highly prized around the tea tables of Augustan England. He once asked an author, probably Hawkins himself, "I hear you have just published a pamphlet, and am told there is a very good paragraph in it, upon the subject of music: did you write that yourself?"[3] He may be defended in this example by considering the frequency with which someone like Johnson would contribute a paragraph or preface to the work of a lesser author; but Hawkins provides other anecdotes that defy such refutation:

> To the proofs above adduced of the coarseness of Cave's manners, let me add the following: he had undertaken, at his own risque, to publish a translation of Du Halde's History of China, in which were contained sundry geographical and other plates.

> Each of these he inscribed to one or other of his friends; and, among the rest, one "*To Moses Browne.*" With this blunt and familiar designation of his person, Mr. Browne was justly offended: to appease him, Cave directed an engraver, to introduce with a caret under the line, *Mr.* and thought, that in so doing, he had made ample amends to Mr. Browne for the indignity done him.[4]

Most modern readers will probably smile at Cave's simplicity and be somewhat put off by Hawkins's strait-laced manner, for the event hardly seems an indignity to us. But the social conventions of one age are not those of another, and Johnson himself might have thought it demeaning had it been done to him. Yet Johnson also would have been the first to forgive the offender. In fact, Cave's lack of tact may have helped ingratiate him with Johnson, for a man will seldom study to deceive who sees simple honesty and good intentions as sufficient to cover over any unintended offense.

In his youth Cave had been considered a promising scholar. He attended Rugby, but several reversals of fortune left him no better than apprenticed to a printer. After earning his freedom and then writing for the Tory paper, *Mist's Journal,* he married and, through his wife's connections, obtained a position with the postal service. He used this position to procure country news, which he sold to a London journalist for a guinea each week. By reversing the process and selling London news to country papers, he soon earned enough money to open his own printing house. He was an indefatigable worker and pressed his staff as he did himself. One of his assistants, Jacob Ilive, complained after leaving the magazine that Cave often kept him working seven days a week to get the magazine out as soon as possible after the first of the month.[5]

Cave was also an ardent projector, and fortunately for him it was his first major gamble, the *Gentleman's Magazine* itself, that made his fortune. In later years he constantly attempted new schemes, but none ever succeeded. His projects were not limited to publishing ventures; he invested a considerable sum, for example, in an experimental spinning machine.[6] But the magazine had been so successful that although his subsequent follies could diminish his fortune, they could not exhaust it.

Cave bore his affluence well: he never pretended to superiority of character because of superiority of fortune. He adorned the doors of his coach not with a coat of arms but with a picture of St. John's Gate, the emblem of his magazine. He was obviously more proud of his accomplishments than of his ancestors. Johnson certainly responded to this combination of pride and unpretentiousness. He never spoke of Cave without great affection, and even when calling him a penurious pay-master he added, "but he was a good man, and always delighted to have his friends at his table."[7] Finally, Cave was a type of man that Johnson always appreciated, one who knew how to get along in the world. Many years later, reminiscing about an old acquaintance of this time, a "metaphysical taylor," Johnson was disappointed to hear that such an intelligent man was not expert in his trade: "I am sorry for it (said Johnson,) for I would have every man to be master of his own business."[8] For all his shortcomings, Cave was indeed master of his business.

Cave began the *Gentleman's Magazine* in 1731, with the idea that it could serve as a digest of the periodical essays and the news various papers printed in a given month. In his Introduction to the first collected volume he states the function of his paper quite directly.

> It has been unexceptionably advanced, that a good *Abridgment* of the Law is more intelligible than the Statutes at large; so a nice *Model* is as entertaining as the Original, and a true *Specimen* as satisfactory as the whole Parcel: This may serve to illustrate the Reasonableness of our present Undertaking, which in the *first* Place is to give Monthly a View of all the Pieces of Wit, Humour, or Intelligence, daily offer'd to the Publick in the Newspapers, (which of late are so multiply'd, as to render it impossible, unless a Man makes it a Business, to consult them all) and in the *next* Place we shall join therewith some other Matters of Use or Amusement that will be communicated to us.

As carried out, this project left little space for originality. The editor merely culled from the weekly journals their most important articles, trimmed them down to their most significant ideas or most controversial points, and presented them without comment. This last point is of major significance; the magazine took no political position. When a controversy heated up in the partisan papers, Cave printed both sides and welcomed any boost that the public debate gave to his circulation.

In the earliest issues, the "Weekly Essays," as the excerpts from the various journals were called, were given the most space, but the magazine also contained a poetry section and a "Monthly Intelligencer." This last department, later renamed the "Historical Chronicle," comprised a great variety of articles: local and foreign news; announcements of births, deaths, marriages, and preferments; occasional listings of stock prices; a list of recently published books; and more. The essays thus provided contemporary opinion; the "Intelligencer," news.

The magazine's format, which may seem simplistic today, was then revolutionary. Newspapers have always been the most ephemeral form of communication, and their fund of concrete detail and contemporary argument—the rags and bones of history—is often crumpled and discarded at the appearance of the next edition. Cave's idea was to freeze history, to provide a compendium of what had been said and done. His readers perceived this, and before his periodical was a year old, Cave had already begun to receive commendations for the impartiality of his work and its value to historians.[9] From the start he had encouraged the idea that the magazine was a reference work, and many readers kept and bound its issues as a chronicle of the recent past.[10]

A large London market was necessary for the success of any periodical publication, and this the magazine must certainly have had. But it seems that Cave was equally interested in distribution throughout the provinces.[11] He was aware of the appetite for London news in the outlying regions, for he earned the money to set up his business by supplying it. The magazine was perfectly suited to appeal to the residents of the countryside, to whom the great abundance of London periodicals would not be readily available. Even though many of the major ones probably had considerable circulation outside of London, it remains doubtful that more than a fraction of what Cave estimated at "200 Half-sheets per Month" would ever reach the market-towns, and none with complete regularity.[12] By culling from this mass the best pieces and most newsworthy events of every month, the magazine provided the countryside with an edited glimpse into London life. To assure distribution Cave maintained a network of rural booksellers throughout England: John Clay of Daventry, for example, distributed at least twenty-five copies of the *Gentleman's Magazine* monthly.[13] The magazine's most significant effect on its time may have been as a means of fully disseminating throughout rural England the news and controversy current in London.

This fact helps us understand Johnson's repeated approaches to Cave and his curious remark to Boswell that when he first saw St. John's Gate he "beheld it with reverence."[14] Besides writing to Cave from Birmingham and Greenwich, Johnson had sought pupils for his school at Edial by advertising in the magazine.[15] He must have been confident of two things: the magazine would have a wide circulation in the Midlands, and good families could be expected to read it. The magazine's prestige was almost certainly less in London, where the essays and newspapers were readily available, but for this young man just up from the country, it remained an epitome of the intellectual life of the city and therefore of the nation. Johnson was not unaware of the magazine's faults—especially its trifling verses and lack of solid, original literary articles—but he welcomed its strengths. The praise of its utility in "Ad Urbanum" was certainly the most sincere aspect of the poem. It should then be of little surprise that he would see with a certain awe the building of brick and mortar that stood on the front page of each issue.

During the magazine's early years it underwent slow but significant change. In 1732 Cave began printing the "Debates in Parliament," an addition that increased the bulk as well as the popularity of the magazine. Publishing Parliamentary debates was not without risk. Cave himself had been jailed, reprimanded, and fined in 1728 for supplying intelligence about Parliament to the *Gloucester Journal.*[16] Yet Cave may have felt that he had little to fear, for the debates printed in the magazine between 1732 and 1738 were not composed by members of his staff, but rather, like the rest of the work, were simply reprinted from other periodicals.

From 1732 through 1736, the debates were for the most part pillaged from *The Political State of Great Britain.*[17] They appeared during the Parliamentary recess, generally from June or July through December, and dramatized the proceedings of the session recently completed. The delayed publication had come to be tolerated, though only grudgingly, by Parliament, for neither House chose to prosecute offenses committed while it was not in session. In 1737, perhaps from fear of prosecution, the *Political State* quit printing debates, and the *London Magazine* took the lead. Cave turned his rival to his own advantage and began copying debates from it.[18] But being dependent on a competitor for such an important aspect of the magazine was a certain sign of inferiority. In order to distinguish his versions from his source (and possibly even as a means of claiming superiority over it), Cave sought corrections and additions from Thomas Birch, who attended the debates on occasion for his own enlightenment or amusement.[19] The risk of Parliamentary prosecution may have seemed less threatening than that of being exposed as the laggard in gathering and publishing Parliamentary information. The next year Cave hired William Guthrie to write the debates for the *Gentleman's*. Thus, it was not until after Johnson had arrived in London that Cave began his own version of the Parliamentary debates.

In January 1735 Cave first included "Original Dissertations" (essays contributed by his readers) in the magazine. There was certainly no remuneration for these works; the chance of publishing one's opinions was the only reward. Since the debates were only published from June to December, the first issues of each year had a large gap to be filled. Rather than just print more weekly essays, Cave decided to increase the variety of his collection by printing the better letters written to the magazine. These also broadened the scope of the periodical by including religious controversies, occasional critical essays, and mathematical problems. Cave thus gave his readers a forum in which to express their ideas and interests.

It is curious that this department first appeared only two months after Johnson wrote from Birmingham offering to send Cave various original pieces. Cave had already begun adding materials from sources other than the periodicals, including a short piece on the beneficial effects of cold baths by Sir John Floyer, a famous Lichfield physician;[20] Johnson apparently perceived the logical next step—articles written expressly for the magazine. He had spent part of his past several years helping out Thomas Warren with his *Birmingham Journal*, and this limited journalistic experience may have encouraged him to try a periodical with a larger market. But Cave had probably already begun accumulating pieces to fill the space vacated by the debates in the January issue. Thus Johnson's offer to fill an occasional column "on reasonable terms" was forestalled by Cave's ingenuity, which resulted in his filling many columns for free.

Of all the departments of the magazine, the poetry section appears to have been the one with which Cave was most willing to experiment. During the magazine's first two years, poetry was gleaned, like the rest of Cave's copy, from the weekly papers, with a monthly installment often limited to two or three pages.[21] But in 1733 he began to accept original compositions, and by late 1734 this department regularly occupied six or seven pages. Readers who sought no more recompense than to see their work in print sent the produce of their teeming brains to Cave, who gratified their vanity. The quality of these offerings is consistent with the amateur poetry of any age, that is, it is virtually unreadable to any age but its own. Cave hoped to balance these jejune pieces with more sophisticated verse. As early as 1733 he tried to stimulate poets of a higher caliber by offering prizes, and in 1734 he appears to have violated copyright by printing a different excerpt from Pope's *Essay on Man* each month.[22]

The prizes for Cave's first two poetry contests, those of 1733 and early 1734, were nothing more than a year's collection of the magazine, and they attracted a response commensurate with the offering.[23] But in July 1734 Cave offered a prize of fifty pounds for the best poem on "Life, Death, Judgment, Heaven, and Hell." As Johnson tells the story, "being but newly acquainted with wealth, and thinking the influence of fifty pounds extremely great, he expected the first authors of the kingdom to appear as competitors; and offered the allotment of the prize to the Universities. But when the time came, no name was seen among the writers that had been ever seen before; the Universities and several private men rejected the province of assigning the prize."[24]

There can be little doubt that Cave had hoped to gain the reputation of a patron of literature (does not Johnson imply as much in his letter offering *London* to Cave?), but even in a venal society such a distinction is not so easily bought. For those who did not define prestige in terms of money—and in Cave's defense, that number is perhaps smaller than one would like to believe—the prize was too small a lure when compared to the possible stigma of being labeled a paid writer for a magazine. Many an author certainly groveled before a Lord only to be rewarded less liberally than with Cave's fifty pounds; but the kind word of a Lord, even if it could not feed one's family, might provide other consolations in a hierarchical society. And to enter the general scramble for Cave's prize, with the possibility of finding oneself rated below an inferior, was a risk not worth taking. Cave had mistaken the temperaments of both poets and scholars, none of whom wished to be associated with the contest. At last he found three unnamed judges who communicated their opinions to Thomas Birch, who then announced the winners in the magazine for February 1736.[25] Several other contests followed, none of which attracted any significant poets, and the problem of finding suitable judges was still plaguing Cave when Johnson arrived.

By 1736 Cave appears to have taken the final step in his attempts to improve his poetry pages—he began to pay Richard Savage for verse. That year Cave printed five new poems by Savage, including the fifth "Volunteer Laureat," all of which appeared simultaneously in the *London Magazine*.[26] Cave also added extracts from "The Wanderer" and revised versions of two other of Savage's early works. Accustomed previously to reprinting matter from the papers or to gratifying his readers by inserting their dissertations or their rhymes, Cave was now showing, apparently for the first time, that he was willing to pay for copy. Within two years he was to hire Guthrie to supply his readers with fresh debates. A change was taking place in Cave's attitude towards the content of his magazine. His movement was glacial, almost imperceptibly slow, but it would ultimately benefit Samuel Johnson.

Through Cave, Johnson was gradually introduced to many of the lesser lights of the London literary world. Cave's acquaintances were primarily the friends of and contributors to his magazine, and these he was quick to bring to Johnson's notice. Hawkins tells of an evening during which Cave conducted Johnson to a Clerkenwell ale-house to meet Moses Browne (a poet of modest abilities who had won first prize in a number of Cave's poetry contests), as well as a few other second-rate scribblers. Hawkins colors the scene with his typical sourness as he sees Cave trying to dazzle Johnson "with the splendor of some of those luminaries in literature who favoured him with their correspondence."[27] But a more benign interpretation may be placed on the scene, for rather than being an example of Cave's dullness, it is more likely an indication of his friendship. To Hawkins, reflecting on the incongruity of the great Johnson being taken to see the author of the "Piscatory Eclogues," Cave appears impossibly ignorant of his companion's abilities. Such an estimation, though, is hardly fair, for Cave could lead Johnson to see without hoping to dazzle.

In fact, Moses Browne probably deserves more respect than either Hawkins or we tend to afford him. The minor poets of any period become the laughingstocks of later generations, for their inanities are no longer disguised by the prevailing though transient assumptions about what constitutes good poetry. But of the numerous would-be writers who frequented the coffee houses, few could boast of as much success as Browne. The young Johnson, a newcomer to the literary world, would certainly have been interested in meeting working authors. Although he expected to rise above such men, he would not have despised them.[28]

If Johnson from his own nature was aware of the dangers of sloth, from another acquaintance he could learn the rewards of industry. William Guthrie, recently hired to compose the original *Gentleman's Magazine* version of the debates in Parliament, was the only professional writer regularly employed by Cave for the magazine in the early months of 1738. He had been at work on Cave's long-in-coming-forth translation of Du Halde's *Description of China* when he was tapped for this additional duty. Guthrie was the archetypal hack writer. His life lacked the pathetic side of William Collins's and the grotesque side of Samuel Boyse's; he never achieved the minor distinction of Thomas Birch, nor did he rise above the limitations of his profession as did Johnson. He remained all his life an author for hire. He managed to write a competent *History of England,* for he was the first author given access to the Parliamentary Journals. But the majority of his labors were anonymous and are now forgotten.

Guthrie could be boisterous, vulgar, and without principle, but he knew Grub Street and he maintained himself by his pen. In his future lay prosperity: having received a pension of two hundred pounds per year for his political pamphlets in favor of the Pelham government, he retained that pension after the accession of George III by switching masters and writing for the Bute government.[29] But the relative merits of party mean little to one who writes for his bread, and Johnson himself referred to Guthrie in terms of some respect: "Of Guthrie, he said, 'Sir, he is a man of parts. He has no great regular fund of knowledge; but by reading so long, and writing so long, he no doubt has picked up a good deal.' "[30] He once told Boswell that Guthrie's life would be worth writing, but this should be no surprise. Insofar as biography is supposed to be instructive rather than celebratory, Guthrie would have made a fitting subject. Much could be learned from the life of a man whose constant application refined his talents and allowed him to survive in a profession that crushed many weaker spirits.

The arrival of Johnson was bad luck for Guthrie. To the May 1738 issue of the magazine Guthrie contributed a curious piece entitled "The Apotheosis of Milton," a dream vision in which the spirits of the poets who are buried or commemorated in Westminster Abbey gather to welcome Milton into their number.[31] It is noteworthy as a rare piece of prose fiction in the magazine, but perhaps more so because it was the work of a writer-for-hire: Cave was apparently willing to pay for more than parliamentary debates. Although Guthrie would continue to write the debates for several years, the few pages that Cave was to allow for original composition were soon to be divided between the magazine's unpaid correspondents and Johnson.

Through Cave, Johnson also met Elizabeth Carter. The young Miss Carter, who would age gracefully to become "the learned Mrs. Carter," the bluestocking of Boswell's *Life* and Pennington's *Memoirs,* was a London phenomenon in 1738. Her poetry in the *Gentleman's Magazine* drew a great response from Cave's readers, and, as we have seen, Johnson himself was incited to poetry by his early encounters with her. She met Cave through her father, the Rev. Nicholas Carter, perpetual curate of the Chapel at Deal and the possessor of several other livings in Kent.[32] He was a fine scholar, adept in Latin, Greek, and Hebrew, all of which he taught his daughter. She worked indefatigably at her studies, her late nights of reading apparently leading to persistent headaches and a weakened constitution. Her age, accomplishments and good nature all suited her to become the wife of an educated gentleman, but she was very shy, and the prospect of one man as a partner for life apparently frightened her. She was from the first inclined not to marry and never did.

Johnson and Miss Carter met in April when he and Cave were discussing the arrangements for printing *London.* She was only twenty, but had already been sending poems to the magazine for four years. Eliza, impressed with her new acquaintance, wrote of Johnson to her father, whose response is as amusing as it is informative: "You mention Johnson; but that is a name with which I am utterly unacquainted. Neither his scholastic, critical, or poetical character ever reached my ears. I a little suspect his judgment, if he is very fond of Martial."[33]

Their most obvious shared interest was poetry—both classical and modern. Johnson had just completed his translation of Juvenal's *Third Satire* and had shown himself proficient at both Latin and Greek verse. She had previously written imitations of poems from several languages—a Horatian Ode, an Anacreontic, and a short piece from the Spanish of Quevedo. She could be pious and thoughtful, as in her long reflective poem on her birthday; gay and trivial, as in her riddles; or "romantic," as in her "Ode to Melancholy."[34] But after meeting Johnson she chose a philosophical theme, "Fortune," and began her poem with an epigraph from the *Tenth Satire* of Juvenal.

This poem takes the form of a miniature "Vanity of Human Wishes." It depicts three characters, each with his own great desire—wealth, political preferment, a coach and four—and each still discontented when the desire is fulfilled. These exempla make up but a small portion of the poem; much of the rest is moralizing. But it is a work not unworthy of notice. Its clear-headed and confident moral tone is similar to Johnson's in his moral essays. It is perhaps a sign of the philosophical and moral kinship of the two young authors.

"Fortune" is of special interest, though, because it begins with the image of man as a hopeless wanderer, lost and confused as to his proper direction. Fortune, she tells us,

> Deludes their senses with a fair disguise,
> And sets an airy bliss before their eyes.
> But when they hope to grasp the glitt'ring prey,
> Th' instable fantom vanishes away.
>
> So vap'ry fires mislead unwary swains
> Who rove benighted o'er the dewy plains.
> Drawn by the faithless meteor's glimm'ring ray,
> Thro' devious paths, and lonely wilds they stray.[35]

This motif, only hinted at in Juvenal's phrase *remota/erroris nebula* (ll. 3-4), was stripped of Miss Carter's pastoral trappings and redone by Johnson with greater compression eleven years later in his version of the *Tenth Satire*.

> Then say how Hope and Fear, Desire and Hate,
> O'erspread with Snares the clouded Maze of Fate,

> Where wav'ring Man, betray'd by vent'rous Pride,
> To tread the dreary Paths without a guide,
> As treach'rous Phantoms in the Mist delude,
> Shuns fancied Ills, or chases airy Good.[36]

The verbal parallels between the two passages are telling—"airy bliss"/"airy Good"; "instable fantom"/"treach'rous Phantom"; "devious paths"/"dreary Paths." Johnson, it would seem, was improving on Miss Carter's poem when he wrote the beginning of his own masterpiece. Whether he himself suggested this motif or contributed to "Fortune" in any way we cannot now determine, but his predilection for Juvenal and especially for the *Tenth Satire* is the poem's obvious inspiration. He had already inculcated that poet's deep insights into human self-delusion in his young friend.

Johnson maintained a lifelong friendship with Elizabeth Carter, for she combined a solid intellect with feminine modesty, qualities that always attracted him; moreover, these were crowned with a religious confidence that Johnson could only admire. Although independent enough to reject all suits of marriage, even those that had her father's definite encouragement, she maintained a traditional sense of a woman's place in society and cultivated, in Pennington's phrase, the "more feminine accomplishments" of needlework and playing the spinnet. Years later Johnson would praise the diversity that made her fit for both conversation and housekeeping:

> Upon hearing a lady of his acquaintance commended for her learning, he said:—A man is in general better pleased when he has a good dinner upon his table, than when his wife talks Greek. My old friend, Mrs. Carter, said he, could make a pudding, as well as translate Epictetus from Greek, and work a handkerchief as well as compose a poem.[37]

One finds in Elizabeth Carter a woman that Johnson would admire—learned, modest, and properly socialized. In 1738 the young Miss Carter had not "lived much in the world," but she impressed Johnson with qualities and abilities that for him had lasting value.

It is also through Cave that Johnson came to know Thomas Birch. Although he is sometimes referred to as an assistant editor of the *Gentleman's Magazine,* or at least as Cave's chief adviser,[38] neither of these titles seems justified. He was never employed by

Cave in any regular function. He lived in St. John's Street, not far from the Gate, and was probably an occasional visitor;[39] but his links to the magazine are in fact quite tenuous. Savage, who in good times probably found little reason to come to Clerkenwell, would communicate his works to Cave through Birch; but in this Birch was assisting Savage rather than Cave.[40] As we have seen, in 1737 Cave asked Birch to supplement the *London Magazine* accounts of the Parliamentary debates, but the very language of the request—Cave's begging the favor of Birch in perusing the speeches—suggests that this was an extraordinary situation. Although Birch might announce the victor in Cave's poetry competition, none of his own work, with the exception of a poem on the death of his wife, ever appeared in the magazine's pages.[41]

Birch had lofty connections; his patron was Lord Chancellor Hardwicke. He was thus an important source to be cultivated, and Cave was not bashful about trying to obtain through him copies of actual speeches delivered in Parliament.[42] But Birch appears to have considered himself of a higher social and intellectual caste than Cave, and there are distinct signs of condescension in his treatment of Cave and his attitude towards the magazine.[43] Birch, it seems, could be approached as a man of taste or as one with privileged information about Parliament, but he would not be enlisted in any regular service for the magazine.

Birch had established himself as a man of letters through his work on the *General Dictionary, Historical and Critical,* a translation, with numerous additions, of Pierre Bayle's *Dictionnaire historique et critique.* His contributions to this work, which in his own day earned him membership in the Royal Society, merit him recognition as one of the fathers of modern biography. Of the almost nine hundred lives added to the new English Bayle, Birch wrote over six hundred. Although these were often merely gleaned from extant printed sources, in a number of cases Birch sought out relatives and friends of his subjects, at times making extensive use of unpublished manuscripts and letters.[44]

Birch's abilities are more difficult to judge than his accomplishments. Horace Walpole called him "a worthy, good-natured soul, full of industry and activity, and running about like a young setting-dog in quest of anything, new or old, and with no parts, taste, or judgment."[45] But Walpole, who in his dilettantish manner was always bothered by the clutter of facts, could not see the value of Birch's voluminous notes and letters. By Johnson's determination, Birch was a great talker but no writer. Hawkins records his remark that "a pen is to Tom a torpedo, the touch of it benumbs his hand and his brain."[46] But Johnson also acknowledged that Birch's fund of biographical and historical trivia was unequalled. Boswell records the following exchange:

> Dr. Birch . . . being mentioned, he said, he had more anecdotes than any man. I said, Percy had a great many; that he flowed with them, like one of the brooks here.—*Johnson.* "If Percy is like one of the brooks here, Birch was like the River Thames. Birch excelled Percy in that, as much as Percy excels Goldsmith."[47]

In addition, Johnson was sufficiently impressed with Birch's achievements as a biographer to compliment him in a Greek epigram that was printed in the magazine for December 1738.[48]

Birch's career is of interest as a foil to Johnson's, and his successes allow us to see Johnson's struggles under a different light. Birch began with less education, weaker parts, and certainly no better prospects than Johnson. As the child of Quakers, he spent his early years in Quaker schools but was barred from the universities. Most of his education was attained on his own through his insatiable reading. His learning was thus spotty, and his Latin only adequate. The lack of a university degree, which had plagued Johnson when he set up his school and which prevented him from entering the law or some other respectable profession, had not hindered Birch. Hard work and perseverance had brought him into association with many of the important figures of the day. His friends included Thomson, Warburton, Savage, and Jonathan Richardson. Although only four years Johnson's senior, he had already made a reputation for himself as a scholarly author and had established himself as a fit companion for the poets, scholars, and connoisseurs of the day. Why should the same not happen for Johnson?

And yet, success, even at Birch's modest level, was to elude Johnson for many years, for a temperamental difference barred him from a similar rise. The contrast is not between industry and indolence, for, as we shall see throughout this study, Johnson could overcome his tendency towards sloth and undertake and accomplish formidable projects. The primary difference was in the willingness of each to court the Great. Although brought up as a Quaker, Birch converted to the Church of England and

without benefit of a university degree took holy orders. Soon after this he obtained the patronage of the powerful Hardwicke
family, and his good relations with Lord Chancellor Hardwicke
and his son provided him with substantial livings for the rest of
his life. Johnson's pride, his principles, or his lack of connections
prevented him from following this route. And even if he wished
to, he would have had little chance of success. Though both men
were fine conversationalists, their styles differed radically. Birch's
talk was anecdotal and, if anything like his letters, quite gossipy.
Such lively chatter is always welcome and easily digested, for it
places few burdens on the listener and poses no threat to him.
But Johnson's conversation was thoughtful and aggressive. His
passion to shine at the expense of his interlocutors would have
excluded him from certain polite circles. His observations in
Rambler 188 were the fruit of experience.

> I question whether some abatement of character is not necessary
> to general acceptance. Few spend their time with much satisfac-
> tion under the eye of uncontestable superiority; and therefore,
> among those whose presence is courted at assemblies of jollity,
> there are seldom found men eminently distinguished for powers
> or acquisitions. The wit whose vivacity condemns slower tongues
> to silence, the scholar whose knowledge allows no man to fancy
> that he instructs him, the critick who suffers no fallacy to pass
> undetected, and the reasoner who condemns the idle to thought,
> and the negligent to attention, are generally praised and feared,
> reverenced and avoided.

The young Johnson, anxious to demonstrate his superiority, would
have been no fitting companion for a young lord, and even a
man who delighted in conversation, as Birch did, might find his
joy lessened by the feeling that talk had become combat rather
than play.

If the differences in style were not enough to separate Birch
from Johnson, there was another source of friction—Elizabeth
Carter. Birch, it appears, was courting her, and Johnson, though
married, must have seemed a rival for her attention if not for
her hand. Eighteenth-century courtship was a social affair, carried on in the presence of family or married friends. Cave and
his wife provided a number of opportunities for Birch to meet
with Miss Carter, and Johnson appears to have been among the
company more than once.[49] Birch could hardly feel at ease in the

presence of the man who had become his beloved's poetic mentor, and one of his Latin letters to her betrays his resentment of Johnson's apparent pedantry.[50] Perhaps because of this, Birch and Johnson were never to grow close, although Johnson would on occasion use Birch as a source of information in his future researches.[51]

This survey of the world of the *Gentleman's Magazine* suggests a picture of life at St. John's Gate unlike that which has sometimes been painted. The Gate has been described by some as little more than a social club, with contributors and friends coming by to chat and smoke a pipe, or as a gathering place for aspiring authors.[52] But there seems little evidence for such conclusions. The actual contributors to the magazine were few and Cave's staff quite small. As long as the magazine remained a digest of other periodicals with the prose and poetry of a few readers interspersed, Cave had no need of authors. During the early years of the magazine, he appears to have handled most of the editorial duties himself while a few trusted subordinates oversaw his presses.[53] The rest of the staff would have been limited to the regular crew of a printing house. Guthrie, the only professional writer employed by Cave for the magazine, could write at least as well at home or in a tavern as in one of Cave's spare rooms; there is no reason to believe that he was often at the Gate. Moses Browne and his brother poets had to be sought out in their natural haunts, the taverns of Clerkenwell. Some of Cave's acquaintances might be expected to drop by on occasion, perhaps Savage in search of a meal or Birch offering a condescending hand, but Miss Carter was entertained at Cave's lodgings adjoining the Gate. We must not expect that a proper, timid young lady would idle away her afternoons around a printer's shop. She was not a paid author, we must remember, but a precocious young poet; she was a friend of Cave, not an employee. Meetings at the Gate itself were probably fortuitous, and Cave's introduction of Johnson to Miss Carter, and perhaps to Savage, was in all likelihood conducted over dinner rather than over proofs. With sheets hung up to dry and Cave sitting immovable in his office, never looking out the window (as Johnson tells us) but with the intention of improving his magazine, St. John's Gate was a less hospitable gathering place than it has sometimes been pictured. The atmosphere there must not be romanticized: Cave ran a press room, not a city desk or a haven for authors.

CHAPTER III

A MINER IN LITERATURE

Of these men it may be said that they were miners in literature, they worked, though not in darkness, under ground; their motive was gain; their labor silent and incessant.

Hawkins, *Life of Johnson*

In the early months of 1738, Edward Cave decided to break from his dependence on other periodicals for Parliamentary debates. By February he had begun to gather his own intelligence from both Houses and had hired William Guthrie to write the original *Gentleman's Magazine* texts.[1] In the following months Samuel Johnson would make his appearance at the Gate, submit "Ad Urbanum" to Cave, and publish *London*. But before the first of the new debates would appear, Parliament would again try to prevent the publication of all such dubious accounts of its proceedings. In his attempt to circumvent the will of the government, Cave availed himself of Johnson's aid. In the process, Johnson moved from being a friend of the magazine to an editor, and his long association with Cave's periodical had its official beginning.

The problems with Parliament arose from the typical overzealousness of the press. In April, one of the newspapers printed the King's response to an address from the Commons before it had been reported from the chair. The House resented this notorious breach of privilege and resolved that the standing order against publishing the proceedings or debates in Parliament be enforced, an action that boded ill for the magazines. The resolution explicitly forbade publishing the debates during the recess, eliminating the means by which the papers had avoided Parliament's wrath in the past.[2] While Cave remained uncertain about what to do, his competition plunged ahead. Parliament adjourned on May 20, and within two weeks the *London Magazine* appeared with a thinly disguised rendition of the debates entitled the "Proceedings of a Political Club." These proceedings were supposedly the product of a group of men who regularly gathered to debate "every grand Question in Politics . . . in the Style and Manner of Parliament."[3] The speakers were denoted by classical names such as Cato, Pompey, and Cicero; thus all demonstrable, if not intended, connection with the actual debates was severed. Although the content of the debates remained the same as it had been before, the government was powerless to prevent their publication. No member of the Commons could claim that his speeches were being related, for the magazine had dropped all stated pretense that its debates provided a record of what passed in the House. The tradition of a free press was already sufficiently strong in England that no prosecution was deemed warrantable. The *London Magazine* had achieved a coup, and Cave was now forced to find some similar ruse that would protect him from prosecution while permitting him to continue the always popular debates. The odd expedient that he settled on was the "Debates in the Senate of Magna Lilliputia."

The June 1738 issue of the *Gentleman's Magazine* begins with a description of the voyage of Lemuel Gulliver's grandson, who sailed to Lilliput to vindicate his grandfather's reputation. There he found that "the Maps of *Lilliput* and *Blefuscu,* and the neighbouring Islands, Kingdoms and Empires, were a perfect Epitome of the Map of *Europe,* and that these petty Regions, with their Dependencies, constitute a Resemblance or Compendium of our great World, just as the Model of a Building contains all the Parts in the same Disposition as the principal Design."[4] The political institutions of Lilliput were also found to correspond to those of Great Britain. The illustrious members of Lilliput's Parliament, with its Hurgos (Lords) and Clinabs (Commons), even bore names similar to their British counterparts: Walelop, Ptit, and so on. The disguise was transparent but effective, for no member of either House was likely to give the public the opportunity for ridicule that would arise from identifying himself as the Urg Pulnub or the Hurgo Castroflet. The letter of the law having thus been satisfied, Cave sent his oddly attired debates into the world.[5]

Johnson's place in all this is difficult to determine. Although the introduction to the Lilliputian debates begins with a straightforward explanation of the resemblances between the great world and the small, its tone changes about half way through, with the author launching satiric darts at both the nation's enemies abroad and its government at home. The rapine and bloodshed brought about by the Spanish and Portuguese colonization of America is directly deplored, as is the venality of politicians, linked here to the Septennial Act. A slightly defter ironic attack is made on the "civilizing" of "remote Dominions" by the transportation of criminals. Such satire is simply not found in the magazine before this time, and its appearance points directly to Johnson.

Yet even if the article has numerous signs of Johnson, it is difficult to be as confident as G. B. Hill that his authorship can scarcely be doubted.[6] The style is by no means uniformly Johnsonian, and although many of the sentiments expressed in the piece, especially those condemning colonialism, certainly accord with his, all do not: it is hardly typical of Johnson to state that the natives who inhabit the colonized lands of the Americas are superior in "Simplicity of Manners, Probity, and Temperance" to their "Degulian" (European) conquerors.[7] Cave, we must remember, already had an author for the debates, William Guthrie, whose first efforts appear immediately following the Lilliputian introduction. Unless Johnson had thought up the ruse, and there is no reason to credit him with this dubious honor, Guthrie would most likely have been given the task of preparing the introduction. A glance at his works shows him to have been no contemptible writer; the basic piece was certainly within his capabilities.

Some form of joint authorship may indeed account for the unevenness of tone and expression that one finds in the piece. If Guthrie had failed to exhaust the article's possibilities, Johnson might then have been allowed to improve it. Johnson, we know, was hired soon after this to revise Guthrie's debates. His reworking of this article, supplementing it with several new paragraphs and, in all likelihood, polishing its general expression, probably brought this curious arrangement about. Guthrie, who had been making his way for some years as a professional writer, would certainly have bristled at the suggestion that his work needed correction; some evidence of Johnson's ability to improve what Guthrie had written might have been needed to prevent bruising his authorial ego. The introduction to the debates probably provided this evidence. In addition, several months later Cave would complain that Johnson had not been making sufficient alterations in Guthrie's texts. He may have been thinking back to this model where a pedestrian original is in parts totally transformed by Johnson's "nervous" style.

In June Johnson's career reached a turning point; perhaps influenced by the introduction to the Lilliputian debates, Cave offered Johnson some form of regular employment as a member of the magazine's staff. But the precise nature and extent of his duties are difficult to determine. Years later Johnson would tell the Rev. John Hussey that he became "the actual editor" of the magazine around midsummer, 1738,[8] a statement that coincides very well with an examination of the issues of the magazine. The several contributions of Johnson that appear through the May issue are all to be found in the poetry section, while from June onwards his hand can be traced in tasks covering many varied aspects of the magazine. Nevertheless, the term "editor" is a broad one and can include many diverse activities, some more significant or rewarding than others.

Johnson by no means replaced Cave, who still maintained a large share of the editorial responsibilities. Hawkins who became one of Cave's unpaid contibutors as early as 1739, stated that Cave retained for himself the tasks of abridging the weekly essays and "marshalling the pastorals, the elegies, and the songs, the epigrams, and the rebuses that were sent him by various correspondents."[9] Nor does it seem likely that Johnson made any extensive contribution to the "Historical Chronicle" at this time. Cave appears to have compiled the weekly essays himself from the papers available to him on the days he performed his regular duties at the post office, and he probably obtained the news for the "chronicle" in the same manner.[10] When it came to his magazine, Cave rarely was inclined to fix what was not in need of repair, and Johnson could add little, if anything, to the conduct of this department. Johnson's editorial duties, then, seem to have been focused on new or original material—correcting the debates, perhaps selecting the best pieces from Cave's correspondents, and writing the odds and ends of copy that would be needed to fill out an issue.

We get a glimpse into some of Johnson's specific duties through a letter he wrote Cave at the end of the summer, probably September, 1738.[11] As one might expect, Johnson little relished the trivial tasks of his editorial role and quarreled with Cave over the assiduity with which he prosecuted his duties. Cave had insinuated that Johnson was not living up to his bargain. In self-defense Johnson responded with a detailed list of his activities.

He began by defending his practice with the debates: "If I

made fewer alterations than usual in the debates it was only because there appear'd, and still appears to me to be less need of Alteration." It is no surprise that Johnson would have found little pleasure in reading over and correcting Guthrie's renditions of the debates and that he would have done little more than correct Guthrie's "Scotticisms."[12] Cave apparently expected more, probably wanting Johnson to redo artless passages and to add material in the manner of the Lilliputian introduction. There are, in fact, few Johnsonian passages in any of Guthrie's debates, and so we must conclude that Johnson restricted himself largely to tinkering with the wording. He approached the speeches not as a contributor, but as a pedant or censor, amending certain infelicities but letting the issues and arguments pass as presented by Guthrie. He may have scrupled at tampering with the arguments, for Guthrie worked from notes, not from his own imagination. According to Hawkins, Cave and one or two of his associates would attend the debates, then "adjourn to a neighbouring tavern, and compare and adjust their notes, by means whereof and the help of their memories, they became enabled to fix at least the substance of what they had so lately heard and remarked."[13] Guthrie would then turn these notes into the speeches printed in the magazine. At this point in his career, when the burden of filling ten pages of the magazine was on other shoulders, Johnson may have been loath to add material, no matter how good, which was obviously unfounded; his distaste for such drudgery would have seconded any moral reservations.

Johnson next turned to a set of verses on Lady Firebrace that Cave had requested. In the September issue appeared six lines "To Lady F[irebra]ce at Bury Assizes." It has been plausibly suggested that the poem was intended to invite a response from a Suffolk poet called Count Bryan, who had contributed a number of short pieces on such subjects as "The Ladies at Bury Fair."[14] This inane poem is one of the few of Johnson's known works that can be thought an embarrassment to him, for the empty conventionality of the verses is exacerbated by the paltriness of the subject. The lines, as usual, are harmonious and the rhymes true, but that Johnson would sink to mentioning "B[rya]n's deathless strain" is almost beyond belief. Yet, this too must be understood in terms of Johnson's new position. As an author for hire, he would have to flatter on command. It is obvious from the letter that such a worthless task disgusted him.

Moving from his role as poet-on-demand to selector of original copy, Johnson assured Cave that a set of "Chinese Stories"
was ready to go to press. In July, the first volume of the Guthrie
and Green translation of Du Halde's *Description of the Empire of
China* was finally nearing completion. Cave sought to puff this
work and so duly inserted a letter in the July magazine, signed
"Eubulus," reflecting on the curious insights into Chinese manners to be gleaned from it. The letter was followed by an announcement that "Some of the *Chinese* Relations alluded to by
our Correspondent we shall take the Liberty of inserting, if we
have room, next Month, and hope they will prove no disagree-
able Entertainment to our Readers."[15] Although Johnson's selec-
tions never appeared in the magazine, his hand may be traced
in the comments on Chinese manners that were intended to whet
the public's appetite.

The "Eubulus" letter is a piece worth looking into, for it helps
illuminate some of the difficulties in tracing Johnson's actual contributions to the magazine. Though only three columns long, the
article has two distinct subjects, as well as two styles. It begins
with a disquisition on the satisfactions to be found in reading
about the manners of different nations, especially of a people so
culturally remote as the Chinese.

> Any Custom or Law unheard and unthought of before, strikes
> us with that *surprize* which is the effect of Novelty; but a Practice
> conformable to our own pleases us, because it flatters our Self-
> love, by showing us that our Opinions are approved by the gen-
> eral Concurrence of Mankind. Of these two Pleasures, the first
> is more violent, the other more lasting; the first seems to partake
> more of Instinct than Reason, and is not easily to be explain'd,
> or defin'd; the latter has its Foundation in Good Sense and Re-
> flection, and evidently depends on the same Principles with most
> human Passions.[16]

A reader of Du Halde, it is pointed out, will experience "each of
these agreeable Emotions." For six paragraphs the writer proceeds in this style, which can with little anxiety be called Johnsonian. But suddenly the style changes—Johnson's characteristic
balance and tendency towards generalization disappear as the
writer pursues a narrative concerning a matter of honor between
two Lords. The letter concludes with a slightly disguised tribute
to Frederick, Prince of Wales.[17]

The Du Halde puff and the accompanying narrative are wholly unrelated in style, content, and purpose; the article has no structural integrity. One may conjecture what happened. Cave decided to print the narrative, perhaps because he thought it interesting, perhaps to please a friend who was a partisan of the Prince.[18] Johnson was then called in to "edit" it. Either he or Cave perceived the possibility of yoking it with a planned advertisement for the Du Halde translation, and the two, bound hip and thigh, were sent limping into the world together. With the addition of the signature "Eubulus," the piece was given the appearance of coming from a reader rather than from a member of the editorial staff. In this puff-cum-narrative, then, we find a work that apparently both is and is not Johnson's, one that has little merit of its own and that might easily be ignored as a piece of the magazine's correspondence. It should serve as a warning of the difficulty of the chase, the uncertainty of the capture, and the questionable value of the prize when one hunts the anonymous Johnson in the pages of the *Gentleman's Magazine.*

Johnson's September letter to Cave provides us with a clue to two more fugitive pieces in the magazine, two letters signed "Pamphilus."[19] As his earliest surviving essays, these deserve some discussion also. The first, which appeared in the July issue, is the answer to one of sixteen political questions posed the month before. Cave, trying to stimulate correspondence from his readers, had Johnson answer one of the "queries" in the form of a letter to Mr. Urban, thereby assuring would-be controversialists that their efforts might find their way into print. Few apparently took the bait.[20]

Johnson's letter takes the form of a dissertation on condolence, eventually focusing on the messages sent the King by both Houses of Parliament on the loss of his wife. It probes the moral responsibility of friends to help ease the burden of sorrow on one who is grieving. In a manner foreshadowing certain harsh statements later recorded by Boswell and Mrs. Thrale, he complains that condolence is generally more ceremony than feeling and does little to aid the sufferer. He cleverly blends his discussion of the true moral obligation that all men share to comfort their fellows, with observations on the artificial appearance of sorrow in many who, by their thoughtless and ill-timed protestations of sharing the grief, extend the pain of the sufferer rather than mitigate it.

The result of this moral disquisition is a censure of both Houses for their extended panegyrics on the late Queen, which could only recall to the King the grief that he had already subdued. But Johnson's dislike for George II is subtly indulged at the end. With a deftly understated twist, he notes that the King might have been made more melancholy by the messages of condolence "had not his Majesty in his princely Prudence, out of his tender Affection to his People, and paternal Regard to their civil and religious Rights, timely discovered a more effectual Remedy." That remedy was Amalie von Wallmoden.[21] Johnson's hint that the King solaced himself for the loss of his wife in the arms of his mistress, reserved as it is until the last sentence and concluding an essay of such high moral tone, is a more effective attack on George than all the blatant gibes of *Marmor Norfolciense*.

The second "Pamphilus" letter is a short essay on the impropriety of the epitaph on Gay's monument in Westminster Abbey:

Life is a Jest, and all Things show it;
I thought so once, but now I know it.

Throughout his life Johnson demonstrated a serious interest in the epitaph as a literary, commemorative, and moral exercise. He touches on all these aspects in the article. But his main intention is to vent his anger that a flippant, irreligious sentiment should be displayed in such a hallowed place. The work's tone is belligerent, and some passages like the following can be construed as presenting an attack on Gay: "Mr. *Gay* has returned from the Regions of Death, not much improved in his Poetry, and very much corrupted in his Morals; for he is come back with a Lye in his Mouth, *Life is a Jest*."[22] The piece seems harsher and more aggressive than Johnson's most censorious criticism. Perhaps he hoped to inspire a rebuttal, but the vehemence and thoroughness of his arguments made any possible defense seem either impious or absurd.

The "Pamphilus" letters are interesting for two reasons—each shows Johnson addressing a topic that he would return to over and over again throughout his life, and each combines the moral seriousness typical of his later essays with a quirk of style: the wry political twist at the end of the first, and the vehemence bordering on belligerence in the second. In neither does Johnson sustain throughout the dispassionate analysis of general nature that was to mark the *Ramblers* and render them unique. The difference, though, may be accounted for in that these essays were written in the guise of personal letters to a magazine, which allow greater freedom for expressing one's passions or prejudices; they are not intended to appear formal literary exercises.

Perhaps the most distressing of the duties that Johnson had thrust upon him in his role as sub-editor was the judging of prize verses. Cave had had considerable difficulty in finding a proper judge for his latest contest, and even if the participants showed little discontent, he knew that long delays in awarding prizes might undermine his desired image as a willing patron of poetry. This contest, Cave's seventh, was first announced in the magazine for March 1736; three prizes—twenty, twelve, and eight pounds— were offered for the best poem on the Divine Attributes.[23] Perhaps the impressive nature of the topic intimidated many would- be competitors, or perhaps it had become known that Moses Browne and John Duick had won most of the significant prizes;[24] in any case, the submissions were few.

The contest was already two years old when Johnson joined the magazine's staff. Cave must have felt that in Johnson, a scholar and poet, he had been supplied with a qualified person to act as judge. But the September letter shows Johnson hesitant to pass sentence:

> As to the prize verses a backwardness to determine their degrees of merit, is nothing peculiar to me, you may, if you please still have what I can say, but I shall engage with little spirit in an affair, which I shall *hardly* end to my own satisfaction, and *certainly* not to the satisfaction of the parties concerned.

Johnson's distaste for this task is not at all surprising. By September he was undoubtedly acquainted with at least two of the contestants, Browne and Duick, and may have feared charges of partiality. His dislike of religious poetry may also have had an effect as he found himself forced to evaluate long, discursive poems on the attributes of God, exercises which he would have thought futile at best. Finally, to determine the "degrees of merit" in works that had little was the sort of task that quickly exhausted Johnson's patience. This task, like many others, may have seemed tolerable when he first decided to become Cave's literary jack-of- all-trades, but as the summer passed, he could not force himself to decide. A duller mind could have chosen without compunction, acting merely to get the job done. A more stalwart mind could have forced itself to do the unpleasant task simply because it was necessary. But Johnson could not act. He never did judge them. In April 1739, three years after the contest was announced, the number of poems in contention was brought to five, perhaps selected by Johnson, perhaps not. The finalists were allowed to choose among themselves. The result was a tie,[25] Browne apparently one of the two winners. Cave never again offered a poetry prize.

By the time the September issue went to press, Cave had reason for discontent with his new editorial assistant. Johnson had been hired to improve the debates, but he appears to have added little of any significance. The "Chinese Stories," which Johnson was slow in delivering, never did appear in the magazine, and the epigram on Lady Firebrace was done with an air of contempt. In judging the contest verses, Johnson balked at a job for which Cave must have thought him perfectly suited, and which Cave would have probably executed himself in a business-like manner if he could have got away with it. Even Johnson's poetic contributions had become scarce. From June through December, only four epigrams by Johnson were printed—the one on Lady Firebrace; a Greek tribute to Birch, which appeared in December; and two more pieces on Elizabeth Carter, Johnson's favorite subject for poetry at this time.[26] Cave's poet had become most unpoetical.

Before leaving this subject, it is worthwhile to take a look at the two epigrams on Elizabeth Carter, for the twin nature of the poems, the first in Latin, the second an English imitation of it, provides us with a paradigm of Johnson's habits as an epigrammatist. The Latin version appeared, unsigned, in the magazine's poetry pages for July:

Ad *Elisam Popi* Horto Lauros Carpentem

Elysios *Popi* dum ludit laeta per hortos,
　　En avida lauros carpit *Elisa* manu.
Nil opus est furto. Lauros tibi, dulcis *Elisa*,
　　Si neget optatas *Popus, Apollo* dabit.[27]

(To Eliza Plucking Laurels in Pope's Garden

　While she cheerfully sports through Pope's Elysian groves, lo, Eliza picks the bays with eager hand. No need for thievery. If Pope, sweet Eliza, should deny you the desired laurels, Apollo will give them.)

The poem supposedly plays upon an incident that took place during a trip to Pope's garden. Johnson, who apparently was not of the company, commemorated the occasion in verse.[28] Soon after the piece appeared in the magazine, Cave received translations from two correspondents, one of whom was Stephen Duck, the thresher poet. Three English versions appeared in the August issue, the last, signed "Urbanus," apparently by Johnson:

> As learn'd *Eliza,* sister of the Muse,
>   Surveys with new contemplative delight
> *Pope's* hallow'd glades, and never tiring views,
>   Her conscious hand his laurel leaves invite.
>
> Cease, lovely thief! my tender limbs to wound,
>   (Cry'd *Daphne* whisp'ring from the yielding tree;)
> Were *Pope* once void of wonted candour found,
>   Just *Phoebus* would devote his plant to thee.[29]

This doublet of poems affords us a glimpse into the way Johnson could approach even a trivial poetic exercise. The Latin version is terse and lean. As in "Ad Urbanum," Johnson resorts to mythology, but in this poem the myth is integrated into the work; a mundane action—the plucking of laurel—is wittily turned into an exalted one—Eliza's achieving recognition as a poet—by Johnson's exploitation of the plant's traditional associations. Yet the mythology is kept to a minimum and only becomes explicit at the mention of Apollo in the last two words. Pope might allow her to pluck a sprig from his trees, but only Apollo can grant "the laurel."

In the translation, all is changed. The terseness of the Latin gives way to elaborate decoration: Eliza becomes "sister of the Muse"; the already conventional *Elysios hortos* are turned into the conventional picturesque of "hallowed glades and never tiring views." (This last phrase seems particularly gratuitous.) The mythological basis of the laurel is no longer reserved, to be opened up suddenly as a spark at the end, but is expanded purposefully as part of the conceit. Daphne herself appears, whispering from the tree. In all of this, the English seems less appealing than the Latin. What the decoration points up, though, is Johnson's determination to do something more in his imitation than merely translate. The witty turn—*Si neget optatas Popus, Apollo dabit*—had already been achieved in the original; to render it literally into

English verse was hardly to write a new poem. Thus the elaboration. Even the turn itself is embellished, if not improved. It is made less explicit, requiring a knowledge of the Latin poem to interpret it: that Pope might deny Eliza some of his laurel is never expressed in the English version; it must be inferred from the original as the act that would be inconsistent with his "wonted candour." But Daphne herself is made to speak the turn, which allows for a new perspective on Pope. The reference to him is no longer distanced and impersonal, but knowledgeable of his genial nature, as might be expected from such an intimate acquaintance of his as the laurel. Both poems are mere trifles, but Johnson's insistence on remaking rather than merely translating the original shows his wonted intellectual vigor, even in trifles. This is typical of the sort of restless energy of mind that caused him to play constantly with ideas and images, forming couplets or epigrams in his head, transforming them, and then usually dismissing them.

Although the September letter cannot be thought to provide an exhaustive list of Johnson's duties, it does suggest that they were largely trivial and by no means constituted full-time employment. That Cave had to send to Johnson by one of his servants and Johnson to write his response indicates that the sub-editor was by no means a daily visitor at the Gate. A few days' work each month would have more than supplied Cave's needs. Guthrie's texts were probably edited as quickly as Johnson could read them; and the rest of Cave's requests, if satisfied at all, would have been accomplished with equal dispatch. If Johnson often found the work distasteful, at least he must have found the pay consoling. The allure of regular income, no matter how scanty, must have been great. The magazine's deadlines could take the place of personal discipline, and the regularity with which he would be forced to review the letters of Cave's correspondents or to turn out a trivial amount of copy would guarantee a steady trickle of shillings.[30]

Few of Johnson's contributions to the magazine through the October issue would have attracted the attention of its regular readers. Perhaps the quality of the writing had improved in some places, but that appeared to be due to "Pamphilus" or "Eubulus," two of the magazine's readers, not to a staff writer. Johnson's traceable contributions were so minor when compared to the great bulk of the periodical that few probably even noticed this slight improvement. In November, however, those readers encountered a work that signaled a major change in the magazine's regular content—the "Life of Father Paul Sarpi."

The short lives that Johnson contributed to the *Gentleman's Magazine* form one of the most obvious links between his early career and his later glorification as "the great Cham of literature." One is tempted to see Johnson in his new position of subeditor as zealous to replace some of the political squabblings of the "Weekly Essays" or the inanities of Cave's correspondents with the moral instruction of biography. But this is to credit policy where circumstance was the key. Over the summer, perhaps about the time that Johnson joined the magazine's staff, Cave agreed to publish his translation of Sarpi's *History of the Council of Trent*, the project that Johnson had proposed from Greenwich over a year earlier. In October Cave announced his plans to publish the work by subscription. A rival translation then being announced, Cave and Johnson decided to use the magazine to advertise their version in much the same way that they had used the "Eubulus" letter to puff the *Description of China*. Since the project was to include Johnson's translation of Le Courayer's prefatory life, the material for an independent article that would give a fine sample of the translator's style was immediately at hand. The "Life of Sarpi" appeared in the November issue not because of Johnson's desire to improve his readers, but as an attempt to attract subscribers to his first major scholarly project. It was even signed "S.J." to make clear that the author of the life was the translator of the forthcoming history.[31]

The life is derived totally from Le Courayer's "Vie Abregée de Fra-Paolo." It is greatly condensed, only about one-eighth as long as the French original. As one might expect from such a drastic reduction in size, Johnson's work is not so much a translation as an epitome, with the translator in some places following his source closely, in others paraphrasing loosely, omitting many sections altogether, changing certain emphases, and intruding a few opinions or reflections of his own.[32] Johnson probably intended to preface the *History* with a full-length version of the life, but reduced his translation to fit the limited space available in the magazine. Thus a tradition of abridged lives was begun.

This interesting and unusual addition to the magazine must

have engendered a highly positive response, for Cave took advantage of another curious set of circumstances to provide his readers with a second biography. Herman Boerhaave, the noted Dutch physician, had died on September 23, 1738, and a long obituary notice was printed in the magazine's "Historical Chronicle" for that month. In November Cave published a letter from a reader lauding Boerhaave and offering one of his unpublished prescriptions for those who "suffer by too a [sic] free a Use of the Bottle."[33] Boerhaave's fame had spread throughout Europe, and both the unusual length of the obituary notice and the letter from the correspondent showed the extent of public interest in his life and works. When late in the year Cave acquired a copy of Albert Schultens's long Latin funeral oration on the great man,[34] the audience was prepared and the materials available for Johnson to reproduce his earlier success. In addition, as the year came to an end, so did the Parliamentary debates. Neither the *London Magazine* nor the *Gentleman's,* though hiding behind the mask of the Political Club or the Lilliputian Senate, was willing to risk printing debates while Parliament was in session. Cave was thus in need of extra copy, and Johnson was given freer rein: instead of being limited to about five columns of the magazine, as in the case of the "Sarpi," the "Life of Boerhaave" was allowed to expand to twenty and was distributed across four issues.[35]

The "Boerhaave," like the "Sarpi," is simply the translation and abridgment of a single source.[36] There must be no mistaken belief that Johnson was here plying the trade of biographer as he did years later. He made no attempt in these works to find fresh information or additional evidence. That he used his critical judgment in selecting and editing the episodes hardly needs to be mentioned. But his additions are few, and many of the moral generalizations that a reader would confidently ascribe to Johnson are merely gleaned from his source. In the 1730s Johnson was a translator and epitomizer, not a biographer. It may be his own sense of this role that led him to praise Birch, a true practitioner of the art of biography, in the Greek epigram of December.

Shortly after "Ad Urbanum" had appeared, the hostilities between the *Gentleman's Magazine* and the *London Magazine* ceased. With the concern over possible prosecution for publishing the debates and the limited space available in the magazines once the debates began to appear, Cave and his competitors turned their attentions away from each other and back to the standard matter of their publications. But in December 1738, the *Gentleman's Magazine* struck with an unprovoked satiric attack on *Common Sense* in the regular Weekly Essays. Cave had taken the offensive and Johnson led the van.

The December attack on *Common Sense* is unlike any of the previous volleys discharged during the periodical war, for it is ironically rather than directly abusive and more mischievous than malevolent. The previous January, *Common Sense* had complained that its essays were hacked to pieces rather than abridged by the *Gentleman's Magazine*'s editors, and with some reason: Cave's radical surgery often reduced an essay in the magazine to half its original length or less, leaving little more than its skeletal argument. In its December attack, the *Gentleman's* justified its policy by printing the entire essay from *Common Sense* for December 2, 1738, bracketing the phrases that would have been omitted in the abridgment.[37] The effect is striking. The first sentence suffices to show the success of the magazine's ploy:

> I am scarce able to express the Pleasure your letter gave me; [for it came to my Hands at a Time that] I really began to fear there was not one of your Branch of our Family left [in the Land of the Living.]

Common Sense had accused the magazine of eliminating "everything that looks like spirit in writing"; the essay as printed shows the editor removing only useless verbiage. The essay is followed by an ironic commentary in which the editor, "S.U.," having dedicated himself to the goddess Prolixity, apologizes for the numerous times he trimmed *Common Sense*'s prose:

> I could not forbear looking back upon my Days of Ignorance, and congratulating myself, that this inestimable Piece was not violated by my *merciless* Hand. How many Delicacies of Expression had I contemptuously expunged! How many beautiful Circumlocutions had I reduced to single Words! How had I *mangled* and *butchered* this most finish'd Piece of modern Rhetoric![38]

The hand is undoubtedly Johnson's.

Whether he had anything to do with the abridgment of the essay cannot be known. He may have come across the copy of

Common Sense already marked for the printer and been struck with the idea of mocking it. But the critical observations themselves contain many definite marks of his style and display the same lumbering irony employed in the political pamphlets of 1739.[39] Johnson's prestige is certainly not enhanced by adding this piece to the canon: the ironic commentary goes on too long and cannot sustain its own weighty humor. Indeed, the bracketed phrases in the original essay plead the magazine's case far more eloquently than the commentary. But quality aside, this piece is significant as an indicator of what lay ahead; for the next five months Johnson was to be regularly engaged in a periodical war that he had helped revive.

Johnson's next blast appeared in the preface to the 1738 edition of the magazine.[40] The preface is a simple exercise in self-congratulation for the magazine's general acceptance by the public, with an accusation that the "Calumnies of our Competitors" were brought on by jealousy of that success.[41] Johnson then turned his attention to *Common Sense:*

> Another Attack has been made upon us by the Author of *Common Sense,* an Adversary equally malicious as the former [i.e., the *London Magazine*], and equally despicable. What were his Views, or what his Provocations, we know not, nor have thought him considerable enough to enquire. To make him any further Answer, would be to descend too low; but as he is one of those happy Writers, who are best exposed by quoting their own Words, we have given his elegant Remarks in our Magazine for *December* at the Foot of p. 640, where the Reader may entertain himself at his Leisure with an agreeable Mixture of Scurrility and false Grammar.

Johnson, probably writing at a feverish pace, did not heed his own declaration that "to make any further Answer would be to descend too low" as he continued his attack for three more paragraphs. Ten months earlier he had advised Sylvanus Urban to conquer his detractors *superbo silentio* (with a haughty silence); now, in the character of Sylvanus Urban, he was pressing the attack, provoking his enemies.

Johnson continued his defense of the magazine in the lead articles for January, March, and May 1739.[42] The first of these, printed in the guise of an anonymous letter to Mr. Urban, differs from the common run of such propaganda. It is a well-balanced attack on the excesses of the party press. Johnson notes that one-half of the publishing world singles out members of the Ministry for a daily panegyric, the other for a weekly satire.

> That Men are never either wholly good or bad, is universally allowed; every Man at some times means well, and most Men are in some unhappy Moments led aside from Virtue. The same Observation may be with equal Justice applyed to Wisdom and Folly. A Fool sometimes stumbles on the Right, and the wisest Man may deviate into Error and Mis-conduct.
>
> For this Reason, to single out any Man for a perpetual Mark of Reproach, or Theme of Panegyrick, to praise or libel by the Week, is a Conduct to the last Degree shameless and profligate, and nothing but long Experience of the Weaknesses into which Men are driven by Party Rage, could make me imagine any Caution necessary against such open and undisguised Artifices.[43]

The censure is distributed evenly, and Johnson avoids any praise of the magazine. By its apparent objectivity, the article seems to be a voice of sanity in the midst of party fanaticism. It reminds the reader of the even-handed manner typical of so much of Johnson's later writings, the clearheaded criticism of the *Preface to Shakespeare* or the calm insight of the moral essays. Yet it was done not in the spirit of simple honesty, but as one of several pieces intended to insult the weekly papers. That Johnson chose to appear as a disinterested correspondent when he was himself among the instigators of the most recent clash bespeaks a disingenuousness not typical of him.

As a result of this article, the *Craftsman* joined *Common Sense* in its war of insults with Cave. In an "Appeal to the Public" in March, Johnson retorted in the typical rhetoric of the dispute, accusing the *London Magazine* of hiring and inciting the weekly papers against the *Gentleman's Magazine*. In the May address "To the Reader," after a short introduction, he printed a "postscript" from the *London Magazine,* letting the insipidity of the style speak for itself as a criticism of the competition.

The dispute with the journals was not confined to such articles. A number of editorial notes appeared in the magazine from January through April, 1739. These were of various kinds, some pointing out solecisms in the *London Magazine* or the weekly papers, others indicating passages or arguments that the journals had pirated from earlier issues of the *Gentleman's*.[44] More im-

portant was a major change in the handling of the "Weekly Essays." Before the December attack on *Common Sense,* the journal
essays were allowed to speak for themselves without comment.
In the first three issues of 1739, this policy is frequently violated
as critical observations sometimes follow an essay. Although not
satiric in the manner of the December observations, they are
equally censorious. In some cases, essays were simply epitomized
with contemptuous remarks by the editor.[45] Yet even in these
editorial intrusions there was an attempt at objectivity, as the *Daily
Gazetteer, Common Sense's* bitterest enemy, received some abuse[46]
and the innocuous *Universal Spectator* was given a lesson on how
Addison would have handled the day's topic. Rather than simply
cutting the articles, Mr. Urban refused to remain silent; he had
become a universal critic.

Johnson almost certainly had a part in this new editorial policy, but the extent of his contributions is difficult to determine.
The remarks in the January issue, especially those on the *Universal Spectator* for January 13,[47] seem very possibly his; those in
February, less so. By March the essays are almost back to their
normal format, with only one obvious insult to *Common Sense.*[48]
One cannot with complete confidence attribute any of the editorial notes or commentaries to Johnson, but neither can one deny
that he influenced or contributed to their content. In all probability Cave maintained much of the responsibility for abridging
the various essays. Johnson may have begun the process of contributing "observations" and may have been responsible for some
of the more radical abridgments and obvious editorial intrusions.
These were not Cave's habits before Johnson's arrival,[49] and the
magazine did not persist in them for long. Cave may have felt
that his long-prized objectivity was being jeopardized. The only
conclusions that can be drawn, then, are general ones: from December 1738 through May 1739 Johnson defended the *Gentleman's Magazine* and abused its competition. The extent to which
he carried that task into the editorial process itself and abridged
or censured or excluded articles is a problem that admits of speculation but not proof.

Although the pieces that Johnson wrote in the periodical war
generally have little literary value, they give a very interesting
view of his uncanny ability to write to the moment. While engaged in a partisan battle for readers, he could censure the political papers for their thoughtless bias. But even beyond that, he
could, in the person of Sylvanus Urban, denigrate the *Craftsman*

and *Common Sense,* the chief political papers of the opposition. Yet the early months of 1739 saw him produce *Marmor Norfolciense* and the *Compleat Vindication of the Licensers of the Stage,* the works that mark his "sudden incursion into violent party politics."[50] While he thundered his abuse against *Common Sense* in the magazine, he sought out its publisher, John Brett, to publish *Marmor.* Perhaps the final ironic twist is that the *London Magazine,* happy to give play to opposition writings, reprinted the introduction, the "Monkish Rhyme," and the English translation from its haranguer's anonymous pamphlet.[51] There is no doubt that Johnson's sympathies lay with opposition, but he carefully restrained them when he put on the mantle of Sylvanus Urban. His willingness to join in the periodical war and write as partisanly for his paper as for his "party" is the greatest indication that he had immersed himself in the world of the London hacks.

From June 1739 to April 1740, there are no pieces in the *Gentleman's Magazine* that can be definitely attributed to Johnson. Frustrated with his position, he apparently left Cave's employ. The period from the appearance of "Ad Urbanum" to this break with Cave is only slightly more than a year; that of Johnson's role as assistant editor even less.

The bulk of pages actually written by Johnson for the magazine during 1738 and 1739 is surprisingly small, certainly not enough to sustain him as a hack writer; few pieces can be traced directly to him, and most provide some sort of particular function for Cave—encouraging the magazine's correspondents, attacking its enemies, puffing the Du Halde, recommending the Sarpi. Only the "Boerhaave" and the "Pamphilus" letter on Gay's epitaph seem to have been written for the sole purpose of adorning the magazine. Much energy has been expended in recent years searching the magazine for pieces to attribute to Johnson. This research is of course necessary to establish the canon, but it also has an insidious effect, for it has long diverted attention away from Johnson's editorial function. He was not brought on to write the bulk of the copy, but rather to oversee the literary aspect of the periodical: to correct the debates, judge the prize verses, encourage correspondents, and improve the poetry pages with an occasional epigram. His ability to generate good copy quickly was gradually put to use, but it hardly seems to have been Cave's primary motive in taking on his editorial assistant.

Whatever other assistance Johnson provided on the magazine
must remain unknown, for editorial contributions are among the
most ephemeral of literary activities. Nevertheless, a careful survey of Johnson's early contributions cannot conclude without
questioning the extent to which his mere presence wrought
changes in the magazine's format. Our investigation has uncov-
ered two obvious changes—the introduction of biographies and
of critical observations on the weekly essays. The first, undertaken because of necessity, was successful and tried again, but at
whose urging, Johnson's or Cave's? The second, although inspired by Johnson's satiric attack in December, was not continued
for long by him. In February or March Cave may have been trying
to play critic himself; by April the magazine was back to its normal state. If Johnson's role is at best tenuously sketched in these
innovations, how is it to be estimated in other, subtler ones?
Mathematical problems become rare in the magazine after 1738.[52]
Cave subsequently decided to print a separate magazine devoted
solely to such puzzles, the *Miscellanea Curiosa Mathematica.* Did
Johnson assert the greater importance of the various literary and
political essays? Who was responsible for abridgments from copyrighted materials? Though quick to appropriate material from
journals and anonymous pamphlets, Cave generally shied away
from large works with an acknowledged author. But not long
after Johnson had begun his labors as assistant editor, Cave began to poach upon the property of the booksellers. In the magazine for November 1738, some "Observations on Lapland" are
excerpted from M. de Maupertuis's *Book of the Figure of the Earth.*
The following April Cave began to print extracts from the recently printed English version of Guillaume Bougeant's *Philosophical Amusement upon the Language of Beasts.*[53] Two months later
the magazine included excerpts from Joseph Trapp's sermons
"on being righteous over-much." But the publishers of this last
work resented piracy and dragged Cave into Chancery Court for
violating copyright. Johnson subsequently wrote a thirty-one article defense of abridgment for Cave.[54] Had he suggested or encouraged this policy, that he later defended it? And who selected
the passages? It had been Johnson's duty to make excerpts from
the Du Halde translation. Was he to do the same for the Maupertuis and the Trapp, or had Cave given up on him and done
it himself? Cave had been slow to innovate during the magazine's
first seven years, yet in the eleven months of Johnson's editorial

service, new ground was being broken in every second or third issue. How is this to be explained? These questions cannot be answered but must be kept in mind if a balanced picture of Johnson's labors for the magazine is to be developed.

As I have already suggested, Johnson's work on the magazine was by no means a full-time responsibility. The greatest part of his early work for Cave was in fact not concerned with the magazine itself, but with two translations. An analysis of these works and of the effort and time devoted to them discovers a backdrop of sustained labor against which the ephemeral work for the magazine must be viewed if one is to get a true prospect of Johnson's first year as a professional writer.

CHAPTER IV

TRANSLATING FOR BOOKSELLERS

They say he is not afraid of the strictest examination, though he is of so long a journey; and will venture it, if the Dean thinks it necessary; choosing rather to die upon the road, than be starved to death in translating for booksellers; which has been his only subsistence for some time past.

Lord Gower to a friend of Swift, August 1, 1739

On August 1, 1739, more than a year after the success of *London,* Lord Gower sought Swift's help in obtaining for Johnson the degree of Master of Arts. In June the Latin Mastership of Appleby School, a post that required an M.A., had become vacant, and Johnson was actively seeking it.[1] One cannot help but be startled by this, for he hated the schoolmaster's life, which amounted to little more than drilling young boys in Latin grammar or listening to slightly older ones construe their Phaedrus. While an usher at the Market Bosworth School, he had written to his friend Edmund Hector complaining of the monotony of his existence: "Vitam continet una dies."[2] Experience had taught him that a schoolmaster might be ill-used by the school's patron, and he could not have been blind to the narrow-mindedness and the brutality that often characterized men whose daily routine included whipping boys for forgetting the mysteries of the dative case. His decision is all the more striking in light of the hopes and expectations excited by the success of *London* and the promising relationship with Cave and Dodsley. But Gower's letter provides an answer: "They say he is not afraid of the strictest examination, though he is of so long a journey; and will venture it, if the Dean thinks it necessary; choosing rather to die upon the road, *than be starved to death in translating for booksellers;* which has been his only subsistence for some time past."[3] The disappointment of Edial and the drudgery of Market Bosworth had not been forgotten, they merely seemed less daunting than the prospect of remaining in London.

Johnson's first year as a writer-for-hire had left him virtually in despair. He had failed in his attempt to establish himself as a man of letters. And Gower's letter appears to strike at the immediate cause of that despair, for after the failure of *Irene* Johnson seems to have concentrated his efforts in making his way by his learning rather than by his imagination. Cave had hired him not primarily as an editor but as a translator. His magazine duties, as I have attempted to show, were too sparse to represent his primary literary responsibilities. His original compositions for this period would fill perhaps thirty of the magazine's double-column pages, and the Life of Boerhaave, itself merely an abridged translation, constituted a full third of that. No man, especially in the underpaid world of the 18th-century hack writer, supported himself on so little copy. Nor is it likely that Cave was lavish in his payment for Johnson's various editorial services.[4] But while his spare hours were sometimes occupied with the trivial concerns of writing epigrams or attacking *Common Sense,* large tracts of time were devoted to two lengthy translations: the previously projected *History of the Council of Trent,* and *A Commentary on Mr. Pope's Principles of Morality or Essay on Man* from the French of Jean Pierre de Crousaz.

That Cave undertook these works, especially the Sarpi translation, is a sign that he did not undervalue Johnson's abilities. Rather, Cave trusted Johnson as he trusted no other writer. He invested a considerable sum of money in each of these projects, and, sad to say, lost virtually all of it. But Cave had something to gain from this partnership as well; what that is can be best understood in the context of the booktrade hierarchy of the day.

In the eighteenth century, booksellers dominated what was simply called "the trade." They were the common holders of copyright; and printers, mercuries, and authors were all dependent on them. In general, the bookseller would purchase the copyright from an author, hire a printer to produce the book, and sell the finished product from his shop.[5] In such a system, the bookseller took all of the risk, for he paid the author and the printer outright. If no one bought the book, his total investment was lost. But he also stood the only chance of great profit. If a work became popular, all of the profits were his: the author received no royalties, and the most the printer could hope

for was the job of printing a second edition. By controlling distribution the booksellers could regulate the profits of all those
dependent on them. An author who wished to retain copyright
might hire a printer to produce his work privately, but he was
at the mercy of the trade for its sale. Printers who might wish to
partake of the booksellers' profits were hampered in much the
same way as authors. Although he might purchase a copyright
and produce a book, a printer had no immediate means of distributing or publicizing his property. For this he was forced to
rely on the rest of the trade.

On the surface there appeared to be a means of circumvent-
ing this difficulty, for under the first rank of copyright-holding
booksellers lay a complex system of distribution, including trade
publishers, pamphlet sellers, mercuries, and hawkers.[6] Trade
publishers were lesser booksellers who would issue under their
own imprints works whose copyrights were held by others. They
would then sell these works on commission. These members of
the trade were generally few, probably no more than five op-
erating in London at any one time.[7] Although an author or an
ambitious printer might have recourse to a trade publisher, he
would not find the road to profit without obstacle. The works
issuing from these shops were invariably in small formats and
were generally expected to be inferior to those brought out by
the major booksellers.[8] In addition, the booksellers took direct
steps to protect their interests. They denigrated works whose sale
they wished to limit,[9] and were not afraid of intimidating printers, the members of the trade most immediately dependent on
them. Writing in the guise of Sylvanus Urban, Johnson noted
their insidious methods:

> Nothing is more criminal in the Opinion of many of [the book-
> sellers], than for an Author to enjoy more Advantage from his
> own Works than they are disposed to allow him. This is a Prin-
> ciple so well established among them, that we can produce some
> who threatened Printers with their highest Displeasure for their
> having dared to print Books for those that wrote them.[10]

A printer who incurred sufficient "displeasure" could find his
business dwindling. And one who printed works not for their
authors but for himself was thought by many booksellers to constitute a direct challenge to their pre-eminent position in the trade
and was thus risking his livelihood. The safest means for a printer

to expand into the retail market was to publish a periodical, the route that Cave had taken to success. He could thus hope for a large sale of his own property without poaching on the booksellers' preserve.[11] Some of the more prosperous printers, especially those having good relations with the booksellers, had begun to purchase copyrights and to distribute their books through the trade publishers; some were even allowed to share in the *ad hoc* partnerships brought together to publish large or expensive works. Nevertheless, the booksellers continued in various ways to regulate the intrusions of printers into their domain, excluding them, for example, from the general sales of copyrights that often occurred upon the death, bankruptcy, or retirement of a copyholding member of the trade.[12]

Cave was no favorite of the booksellers, for his magazine was considered by some, especially the publishers of the weekly papers, an imposition and a piracy.[13] But the success of the *Gentleman's Magazine* had put him above their menaces. By March 1732 he was selling books from St. John's Gate and advertising them in the magazine. These were for the most part ephemera, some apparently vulgar;[14] but in the years that followed, Cave made several attempts to establish himself as a publisher of reputable books.

Cave was obviously interested in moving up in the trade, lured more, in all likelihood, by the profits of the booksellers than by their prestige. The second- and third-rate titles that he had published might augment his profits from the magazine, but they were no substitute for works of larger format and higher price. Established authors, however, were not about to offer their manuscripts to the publisher of a magazine. Cave knew the importance of a bookseller's reputation in marketing a book: he would later suggest to Johnson that Dodsley be the nominal publisher of *London*. If Cave hoped to rival the major figures of the trade, he would first have to establish his own reputation as a purveyor of quality works. This desire to combine prestige and profits would eventually lead him to acquiesce in Johnson's plan to translate Sarpi's *History*.

Cave began this struggle for recognition by joining the consortium of booksellers bringing out "Birch's Bayle," the enormous English version of Bayle's *General Dictionary* translated and augmented by Thomas Birch, John Peter Bernard, and John Lockman. This work had begun to appear serially in March 1733 under the proprietorship of a syndicate headed by Nicholas Prevost, but the competition of a rival translation apparently discouraged the original investors, who abandoned the project after the publication of the first twelve numbers. A new group of sixteen, including Cave, assumed the property, signing a contract with the authors on April 29, 1734.[15] Cave may have been welcomed into the group because of the exposure his magazine could give the project. The *General Dictionary* was advertised monthly in the *Gentleman's* from July through November, 1734, and irregularly thereafter. Nevertheless, for several years Cave was to remain a silent partner, his name omitted from the imprints of the first three volumes. A printer, it seems, might pay his share of the expenses and take his share of the profits, but he did not merit inclusion in the formal list of proprietors.[16]

By the late months of 1735, though, Cave had reason to be solicitous about his inclusion among the proprietors, for he was about to propose his first major independent publication, the English translation of Jean Baptiste Du Halde's *Description of the Empire of China and Chinese Tartary*. The *General Dictionary* was a prestigious work to be involved in, and Cave's place among its proprietors could help legitimate his new undertaking.

In the *Description of China*, Cave chose a work that could, if properly handled, bring both prestige and profit to its publisher. Du Halde's four tomes, compiled largely from the observations of Jesuit missionaries in China, were unrivalled in their detail but perhaps even more valued for their maps, some of the most up-to-date depictions of that portion of the globe then available.[17] The French edition, which had just been published earlier in the year, was selling for ten guineas, a formidable price; Cave offered a translation in two folio volumes for three guineas. He eased even this burden by publishing serially at the cost of a shilling a fortnight. For the text Cave hired two competent authors, Guthrie, whom we have already encountered, and John Green. Green was to prove himself one of the finest geographers and cartographers of the century.[18] Perhaps to ensure that the process of producing the magazine would not interfere with this new project, Cave farmed out the printing to Thomas Gardner.[19] A great deal of care apparently was being taken to produce a work of high quality.

Unfortunately, the project did not proceed smoothly. In order to support the cost of the engravings, Cave required a considerable number of subscribers before he would begin to print. In the delay that followed, a rival translation was announced, which cut into Cave's potential readership.[20] It was not before February 1737 that the fascicles began to appear, at least seventeen months after the initial announcement.[21]

In 1735 Cave proposed the publication of the *Description of China*, hoping for the large profits that could accrue only to the booksellers; by July 1737, when Johnson wrote from Greenwich proposing the Sarpi translation, Cave had experienced little more than the expenses. To take on another such burden with his first creeping along so uncertainly would have seemed madness to Cave. But by the summer of 1738 he had seen *London* and come to respect its author; he had also been rewarded with a fortnightly trickle of shillings as each number of the Du Halde was delivered to its subscribers. The salutary effect of this income must have gone a long way towards convincing Cave to put aside the previous year's doubts. In late July or early August, not long after Johnson took up his editorial duties on the magazine, Cave agreed to publish Johnson's English version of the *History of the Council of Trent*.

The Sarpi translation was to be both a large and a significant work. Its two quarto volumes were to comprise two hundred sheets—one thousand six hundred pages.[22] The immensity of the undertaking makes it clear that Johnson's primary obligation to Cave was not to edit but to translate. His contributions to the magazine, as we have seen, were the work of several hours a week, probably snatched from visits to the Gate; but translation was the appointed labor of many hours at home.[23]

Although we have already examined briefly Johnson's reasons for proposing this translation, a bit more background may help clarify why a young eighteenth-century scholar would seek to make his name by translating the work of a seventeenth-century Italian Catholic priest. Several factors indicate that considerable esteem may have awaited an outstanding rendering of Sarpi's history. This work, growing out of the seventeenth-century struggles between secular states and the Papacy, constituted an attack on the motives and actions of the Catholic Church at Trent and thus provided a powerful weapon for the Protestant states in their resistance to the Counter Reformation.[24] The author had been the architect of and spokesman for Venice's policies in defiance of the Papal Interdict of 1606. At the root of that conflict was the temporal power of the Pope, as the Venetians attempted to protect their republican form of government from inroads by the Papacy. The English were particularly demonstrative in their support; through his envoy, Sir Henry Wotton, James I openly encouraged Venice in its resistance. When Sarpi hesitated publishing his history in Italy, the manuscript was brought to England where it first appeared in print in 1619. Father Paul, by his defiance of Rome, had become a hero to the English Church still struggling to establish its legitimacy. He was so popular in England that both the King and his most celebrated preacher, John Donne, possessed copies of his portrait.

Although Sarpi's reputation waned somewhat in the intervening century as Venice was reconciled to Rome and England was torn apart by its own religious upheavals, for Anglican apologists Sarpi remained a representative of liberal Catholicism seeking the reunion of the Christian churches through reform. With the movement for the union of the English and Gallic Churches espoused around 1720 by William Wake, later the Archbishop of Canterbury, interest in Sarpi was revived. When Father Pierre François Le Courayer, a French scholar attracted by Wake's ideas, was forced to fly to England for writing a defense of Anglican orders, sympathetic churchmen welcomed him, and the Queen herself, always dabbling in matters of politics and divinity, suggested a new French translation of the *History*, a work particularly suited to a disaffected Catholic priest. Le Courayer's work, with its lengthy biography of Sarpi and its extensive notes, appeared in 1736, the year before Johnson's initial proposal to Cave.

Thus, the work that Johnson was now to translate had both a traditional value to the English Church and current notoriety. Cave, as I have suggested earlier, had reason for doubting that a new English version would find a large audience, but he apparently had little doubt about the abilities of his translator. Indeed, in his willingness to support this project Cave seems to have come closer to playing the role of patron than in any of his poetry contests. Although his primary motive was certainly profit, it still cannot be doubted that he was risking a considerable investment so that Johnson might be given the chance to distinguish himself by his learning.

The history was to be no anonymous bit of hack work: Johnson's name was prominently displayed on the proposals. A successful translation would have made him familiar to many churchmen and possibly to the educated public in general. And this further attempt to popularize Sarpi could hardly have escaped the attention of the Queen. The inclusion of his own observations on the history and notes might even have earned him the honorary M.A. that was to be deferred until the *Dictionary* neared publication. A scholarly translation could not rank him with Pope as *London* had, but it could with Le Courayer; and such a comparison would certainly have started him on a career as a man of letters. In the summer of 1738, Johnson was ambitious, and Cave, if not generous, was at least willing to gamble on Johnson's powers and assure him an income. Johnson had come to London "to try his fate with a tragedy, and to see to get himself employed in some translation." The tragedy, so far, had failed; he was now about to try the alternative.

Work on the translation began in early August but progressed slowly. Although Johnson had been the initiator of the project, before long Cave was forced to goad him to work. In the September letter to Cave, Johnson touched on the translation: "As to Father Paul, I have not yet been just to my proposal, but have met with impediments which I hope, are now at an end, and if you find the Progress hereafter not such as you have a right to expect, you can easily stimulate a negligent Translator."[25] By October Johnson had made sufficient progress for Cave to issue a set of proposals asserting that the work was in the press. The first two pages of the translation were included to give potential subscribers a sense of the style and format of the work. According to John Nichols, six thousand copies of the proposals were distributed;[26] Cave and Johnson were casting their net wide.

But coincidence, the least foreseeable of all antagonists, dealt Johnson and Cave a harsh blow from which their project could not recover. On October 20, shortly after the proposals were advertised, a letter appeared in the *Daily Advertiser* from a rival translator claiming precedence in the undertaking.[27] The rival maintained that he had not only the support of many members of the clergy but the approval and the assistance of Le Courayer himself. Yet the *coup de grâce* came not from the rival's arguments but from his name—John Johnson, Assistant Librarian of Archbishop Tenison's Library at St. Martin's in the Fields. "Whether it hath been owing to Chance, or Design," he coyly wrote, "that a Gentleman of the same Sirname with myself should undertake the same Work, I shall not take upon me to conjecture."[28] But he asked that those who had promised him subscriptions would not subscribe to the advertised project. Cave of course could not permit this letter to go unchallenged and, in a letter apparently written by Johnson, responded in the next issue of the same paper that he was the first to issue proposals and was thus guiltless of any impropriety.

> It is generally agreed, that when any Person has inform'd the World by Advertisements, that he is engag'd in a Design of this Kind, to snatch the Hint and supplant the first Undertaker, is mean and disingenuous. But this is not our Case, who are the first Advertisers, and whose Proposals gave Occasion to the Letter.
>
> To obviate any Suspicion that we are indebted for our Scheme to some private Account of Mr. John Johnson's, I am ready to produce the Proposals made to me above a Year ago, and communicated by me to several of the Clergy at that time, which will not only shew the Date of our Design, *but prove* (*since that* is likely to be controverted) that Mr. Johnson's Sirname is no new Acquisition.

The letter concludes with a forceful defense of the project and an apparent determination to carry on.

Cave knew the dangers of a rival, for the *General Dictionary,* the Du Halde, and the magazine itself had all been threatened by competitors. But the prognosis for the Sarpi project was especially bleak, for Le Courayer had already taken a large share of the audience. The poorer clergy and the middle class could hardly be expected to sustain two such projects. But the translation was not abandoned forthwith; in November Johnson was still at work and the early sheets were in the press. Cave received a letter from a subscriber indicating an error in Le Courayer's Preface. He endorsed the letter and sent it along to his press foreman, John Chaney, with a request that he see if the sheets had been worked off.[29] The press in fact had made greater progress than Johnson, for in a letter to Cave written around the twenty-first of the month, Johnson was forced to apologize for falling behind in printer's copy:

> I was so far from imagining they stood still that I conceived them to have a good deal beforehand and therefore was less anx-

ious in providing them more. But if ever they stand still on my account, it must doubtless be charged to me, and whatever else shall be reasonable I shall not oppose, but beg a suspense of judgement till Morning, when I must intreat you to send me a dozen Proposals, and you shall then have copy to spare.[30]

Although no specific text is mentioned here, the Sarpi, then in the press, is almost certainly the work in question.[31] Cave and Johnson were apparently still hopeful of making the project succeed in early December when the "Life of Sarpi" appeared in the magazine.

But optimism alone could not sustain such an expensive undertaking. Before long printing came to a halt. John Nichols asserted that only six sheets were printed off; Hawkins said twelve.[32] Without subscribers Cave hesitated to proceed. As to the rival: John Johnson abandoned his translation in favor of an entirely new history of the Council of Trent but died before sending it to the press.[33]

Much of what we know about the progress of the Sarpi project arises from a single piece of evidence published by Boswell:

I have in my possession, by the favour of Mr. John Nichols, a paper in Johnson's hand-writing, entitled 'Account between Mr. Edward Cave and Sam. Johnson, in relation to a version of Father Paul, &c. begun August the 2d, 1738;' by which it appears, that from that day to the 21st of April, 1739, Johnson received for this work £49 7s. in sums of one, two, three, and sometimes four guineas at a time, most frequently two. And it is curious to observe the minute and scrupulous accuracy with which Johnson has pasted upon it a slip of paper, which he has entitled 'Small Account,' and which contains one article, 'Sept. 9th, Mr. Cave laid down 2s. 6d.' There is subjoined to this account, a list of some subscribers to the work, partly in Johnson's hand-writing, partly in that of another person; and there follows a leaf or two on which are written a number of characters which have the appearance of a short hand, which, perhaps, Johnson was then trying to learn.[34]

This document, which has subsequently disappeared, is frustrating for what it does not tell us—the amount of copy turned in by Johnson, his rate of pay per sheet, the reason for persisting in the work through April when printing must have ceased some time shortly after the new year—but it provides enough information to allow some reasonable conjectures on these subjects.

Johnson, it seems reasonable to assume, was working under a written agreement at a fixed rate of pay per sheet. The existence of a fixed rate can be inferred from the "account" itself: each guinea—the total is in fact exactly forty-seven guineas—would represent pay for a specific amount of copy.[35] Johnson could thus get advances which would then be made up in text, or he could merely accept payment as he brought copy in. That he worked under a formal agreement appears to be a reasonable assumption when one considers the size of the project, its importance to Johnson's career, and Cave's extensive investment. But the existence of a contract can be inferred with more certainty from several comments relevant to the Sarpi translation in Johnson's letters to Cave.

In the September letter, after admitting that he had not lived up to his proposal, Johnson added, "If you find the Progress hereafter not such as you have a right to expect, you can easily stimulate a negligent Translator." Cave's "right" to expect progress may simply be based on the understanding between two gentlemen—that is, if Johnson promised to turn in copy at a certain rate, Cave had a right to expect that he would. Yet it could be a contractual right, and if not, how could Cave stimulate him? Johnson's negligence would result in his not being paid, but poverty would then be the spur, not Cave. Cave could only stimulate him to work by invoking some specific penalty, and such a penalty may be referred to in the November letter. Johnson's statement that he must "doubtless" pay the charges if the presses ever stand still on his account has perhaps been interpreted as simple justice, but this was hardly to be expected. No author, not even a compulsively moral one, would have held himself responsible for the regulation of his printer's business. When the presses stood still in Birmingham for want of copy for the Lobo translation, Johnson was prodded to work by an appeal to his humanity, but he did not, we may assume, pay the printer for his lost time. In the case of the Sarpi, Johnson's dilatoriness appears to have been punishable by Cave, and the two passages from the letters hint at some sort of forfeit to be paid by the author. The contract for the *General Dictionary,* to which, as we have already noted, Cave was a signatory, contained just such a clause. The compilers were to pay fifty pounds if the project was delayed for want of copy.[36]

Johnson's penalty would certainly have been far less substantial, but some such stipulation would have been reasonable. Cave could then expect a steady flow of copy and not have to worry about Johnson's less-than-regular habits interfering with his business.

We can also make some reasonable approximations about Johnson's rate of pay—at least we can set the probable limits within which he and Cave would have agreed. First it must be realized that translation was one of the most poorly paid forms of literary work in the eighteenth century; original composition could command far greater rewards.[37] For *London* Johnson received ten guineas, but for the Lobo translation, a work of four hundred octavo pages, only five. Marjorie Plant has noted that in the sixteenth and seventeenth centuries a translator often had to settle for a few copies of the printed book;[38] and although the booksellers were no longer so tightfisted as that, the few scraps of information that we possess show translators to have been meanly treated in the early decades of the eighteenth century.

In a humorous account of a conversation with Bernard Lintot, Alexander Pope recounts the uncouth bookseller saying that he allowed translators—whom he called "the saddest pack of rogues in the world"—ten shillings per sheet.[39] This figure, though by no means held to in all cases, can be confirmed in some from the scanty remains we have of Lintot's accounts. For the translation of Quintus Curtius's *History of the Wars of Alexander,* published in two volumes in 1714, Lintot paid three authors something more than twelve pounds for a work of approximately twenty-five sheets, about 10s. or 12s. per sheet.[40] Yet Lintot, and others as well, could be considerably more stingy than this. He paid John Digby, one of the translators of Quintus Curtius, a mere forty-five pounds for a translation of Abraham van Wicquefort's *The Embassador and His Functions,* a work of over one hundred forty sheets folio; and in 1742 the widow of Charles Jarvis received from Robert Dodsley a mere twenty-one pounds plus fifteen copies of the printed book in payment for her late husband's translation of *Don Quixote,* a work of over ninety sheets. Digby's actual payment was only about 6s. 6d. per sheet. Mrs. Jarvis received only 4s. 6d. per sheet in ready money, although the sale of her copies of the work may have brought the total to around 10s. per sheet.[41]

Translation from the Greek commanded a higher figure. A Mr. Stephen Lewis of Merton College, Oxford, received £5 7s. 6d.

for a translation of "Aristaenetus's Letters," a work of one-hundred twenty duodecimo pages, or five sheets. And Lewis Theobald received the same amount for his 1713 translation of Plato's *Phaedo,* an octavo work of five sheets.[42] These authors received approximately a guinea per sheet.

Except for the works from the Greek, none of the payments given above significantly exceeds the rate reported by Pope, while at least one falls considerably below it. Thus Lintot's ten shillings per sheet would seem to represent his average payment for prose translation during the second decade of the century, and Dodsley's payment to Mrs. Jarvis shows it to have been at least an acceptable one in the fifth. We can, I think, establish this with some confidence as the lower limit of Johnson's expectations.[43]

The contract for the *General Dictionary* provides us with a probable upper limit. Birch and his fellows were to receive one pound five shillings for each sheet of copy.[44] Their labor—part translation from Bayle, part compilation from standard biographical sources (Wood's *Athenae Oxonienses,* for example), and part original biography based on new research—spanned several types of composition, making their task a slightly more demanding one that Johnson's. Although Johnson was to add observations on the *History* itself and on Le Courayer's notes, similar amplifications were expected from the translators of Bayle. It seems unlikely that Cave would have paid his new translator at a higher rate than he was paying the now-established authors of a major work.[45] Johnson, after all, had a great deal to gain from a successful translation, and Cave was taking all of the risks. The young author was hardly in a position to bargain. If Cave was indeed a penurious paymaster, as Johnson later called him, the range from ten to twenty-five shillings per sheet would certainly encompass his offerings.[46]

The implications that these conclusions, speculative though they are, have on our understanding of Johnson's early career are arresting. Johnson's income of forty-seven guineas must represent payment for a substantial body of work. At a guinea per sheet—a figure more than twice Lintot's and only slightly less than that for the *General Dictionary*—Cave would have paid for nearly a quarter of the *History,* almost four hundred quarto pages. At half-a-guinea per sheet, a rate approximately corresponding with our established minimum, Johnson would have had to accomplish half the work, a staggering amount of lost translation and annotation.[47]

These conclusions will hardly meet with universal approval, for it is difficult to accept that such an enormous amount of Johnson's prose could simply disappear, be converted to waste paper along with the printed sheets. Nevertheless, some adjustment of the commonly held view of Johnson's first year in London is necessary. Forty-seven guineas constitutes a very large sum in payment for translation: either Johnson was given extremely kind treatment by Cave, was remunerated at a level far above that of Birch and Johnson's other contemporaries, indeed, was coddled and cosseted by comparison, or else he worked for his pay as they did, probably producing at least a sheet of translation for each guinea. The first of these possible conclusions is certainly the harder to justify. We have no reason to believe that Johnson held a privileged position among writers-for-hire in 1738. The alternative requires that we see Johnson in his first year as a paid writer working periodically, if not regularly, at an enormous task, turning out copy one, two, three, or four sheets at a time as Cave required or as necessity compelled.

It may be objected that Cave would not have continued to pay for copy that he was not about to print, and that six sheets or twelve, the commonly accepted estimates of the quantity actually worked off, should be thought the extent of Johnson's labors. But this need not be the case. Cave may have been hopeful that the Sarpi, like the Du Halde before it, would overcome all obstacles and that the copy he now accumulated would eventually repay his investment. He might save the expenses of press-time, composition, and paper, yet continue to pay his author as long as hope remained. April 1739 may have marked the end of Cave's sanguineness and thus of Johnson's income.

The contract for the *General Dictionary* provides an alternative explanation. This document permits the proprietors to limit their losses by ceasing publication, but only after providing three months' written notice to the compilers. Thus the authors could not be cut off suddenly from their expected livelihood. This provision was not unique; a similar clause, also stipulating three months as the period of notice, is found in Edmund Burke's agreement with the Dodsleys in 1758 for compiling the *Annual Register*.[48] If Johnson was protected by such an agreement, the curious persistence of his work is made clear: Cave could have decided to curtail printing in late January, but Johnson could continue to turn in copy (probably at a specified rate) for three months. The relations between publisher and author could hardly be amicable in such a situation as the one was forced to pay for what would be of no value to him and the other to earn his subsistence by translating page after page that would never see print; but then, a contract is a contract.

Whether four hundred pages or eight hundred, we can only lament the loss of such a substantial body of work. Of all Johnson's labors before the *Dictionary,* only the Harleian catalogue and the 1745 edition of Shakespeare can possibly compare with it as a scholarly project, and only the Parliamentary debates, a drawn-out effort extending over three years, can rival the quantity of text. Johnson's observations on Sarpi's text and Le Courayer's notes would have told us a great deal about his attitudes towards the Reformation and served as an excellent guide to his reading in Church history. But perhaps what we have lost of most significance in the failure of this work and the disappearance of Johnson's text is a sense of his youthful ambitions. Much of the common discussion of his early career focuses on his position as proto-journalist, his scholarly aims being completely shunted aside. Yet Johnson prided himself on his learning and consciously chose to make his way by it when *Irene* had failed and *London* had left him unknown. The Sarpi was but the first of a series of scholarly projects that he undertook between 1738 and 1746. And let it not be forgotten that it was his scholarship that made him famous: the identity of the "Rambler" was known to only a few, but "Dictionary Johnson" became known to all.

Large project that it was, the Sarpi was not the only translation that Johnson undertook during the last months of 1738. In the hope of catching the tide of controversy and riding it to considerable profits, Cave, possibly influenced by Johnson, turned to two attacks on Pope by the Swiss theologian Jean Pierre de Crousaz as works that might draw an English audience.[49]

Pope's *Essay on Man,* with its mildly deistic slant, had caused little disquiet at home. As Johnson noted in his *Life of Pope,*

> Philosophy and poetry have not often the same readers, and the *Essay* abounded in splendid amplifications and sparkling sentences, which were read and admired with no great attention to their ultimate purpose: its flowers caught the eye which did not see what the gay foliage concealed.[50]

But Crousaz, unable to read English and encountering Pope's work only in its two French translations, saw only the serpent lurking beneath. In 1737 he published his *Examen de l'Essay de Monsieur Pope sur l'homme* at Lausanne, and he followed that a year later with the *Commentaire sur la traduction en vers de Mr. l'abbé Du Resnel de l'Essai de M. Pope sur l'homme,* published at Geneva. Both works had begun to attract attention, but like most controversial books, they were more talked about than read.

Cave hoped to make English texts available while the buzz of dispute was still in the air. He enlisted both Johnson and Elizabeth Carter in the project. Miss Carter would translate the shorter *Examen* while Johnson did the *Commentaire*. In this project speed was more important than style, for other booksellers might have similar plans, and the day would be won by whoever was first in print. The public would be interested in seeing why Crousaz was making such a fuss, but once they had looked quickly into his work, they would just as quickly pass on to new controversies.

Miss Carter was at work on the *Examination* by September, and in the *Gentleman's Magazine* for that month, Cave announced her work as "in the press."[51] Johnson had the Sarpi to busy him and may have made little headway in the *Commentary;* once the trouble with John Johnson erupted in October, he probably concentrated on the larger, more important undertaking so that tangible evidence of its progress might be available. Then, suddenly, disaster struck again. On November 21, Edmund Curll announced in the *Daily Advertiser* the publication of the *Commentaire* translated by Charles Forman.[52] Cave sought Johnson's advice about what should be done, and Johnson's answer has been preserved in an undated letter:

> I am pretty much of your Opinion, that the Commentary cannot be prosecuted with any appearance of success, for as the names of the Authours concerned are of more weight in the performance than its own intrinsick merit, the Publick will be soon satisfied with it. And I think the Examen should be pushed forward with the utmost expedition.[53]

Cave agreed that the *Examination* should be rushed into print, and it was advertised in the *Daily Advertiser* for November 23, 1738. But the *Commentary* still remained a problem. Curll had brought out only the first of Crousaz's four epistles; a translation of the entire book might still be a saleable commodity. Work was not abandoned; Johnson finished the translation and Cave printed it. The book was to be published by Anne Dodd, a mercury who was used by Cave and others as a trade publisher; a unique copy exists with her imprint dated 1739.[54] No advertisement has yet been found to tell us precisely when the work was issued. Cave put the bulk of the edition in storage, where it remained for almost three years. In November 1741, he cancelled the original title page and issued the old sheets under his own imprint.[55]

The Crousaz *Commentary,* though by no means as large or as important as the Sarpi translation, was no slight undertaking. It extended to over three hundred duodecimo pages and included not only Crousaz's text, but also Du Resnel's Preface to his translation of the *Essay on Man,* and a re-translation of Du Resnel's flaccid French couplets back into English. Johnson also added notes that contain an interesting mixture of literary analysis and philosophical discourse and that have the distinction of being some of his earliest published bits of criticism.

Crousaz himself was a professor of logic at Lausanne and, in Johnson's words, no mean antagonist. His philosophical works were well known on the continent, and he had gained a substantial reputation as a defender of Christianity against the onslaughts of rational religion. He championed the cause of free will in both God and man against the "fatalistic schemes" of Spinoza and Leibnitz. His education was grounded in the logic and rhetoric of the late Renaissance, which made him closer perhaps in intellectual background to Milton than to Pope. A pious man whose religion was based on revelation, he distrusted all philosophical systems that were purely rational.

His *Commentaire* attacks the *Essay on Man* on the grounds that Pope's work, though aimed at instruction, expresses certain fatalistic doctrines that might lead away from the practice of piety. Pope, who derived his anemic deism from Bolingbroke—his guide, philosopher, and friend—was certainly no "Spinozist" and could hardly be called an enemy to traditional religion, but in his desire to appear philosophical he neglected to be religious and omitted the place of revelation in his scheme. Crousaz abhorred this cavalier disregard for Christian truth. Philosophy and religion were inseparable in his eyes. Thus, even though the *Essay* was not expressly irreligious, Crousaz found much in it to blame.

Crousaz's attack is fitting for a man of his background: it is virulently disputatious. He berates Pope's philosophical scheme with his entire arsenal of logical and rhetorical weaponry. His objections are not always valid, but at their best they point out the practical moral problems that all theoretical systems tend to overlook. Thus when Pope affirms the general fitness of the universe, Crousaz points out the depravity of many individuals. The Swiss theologian was fearful that in our amazement at the powers of human reason we might forget our own depravity, and in our rejoicing over the perfection of nature, dismiss original sin.

The *Commentary* seems interminable in the reading, for Crousaz's censures are of a piece throughout. The first page of Pope's poem is open to the same objections as the last, and Crousaz had neither the inclination nor the genius to vary his censures or to marshal them in such a manner as to give the appearance of variety. He leads his reader through Du Resnel's French verses, sentence by sentence, piling complaint atop similar complaint, until the reader finds that attention to the argument yields no more enlightenment than inattention.

Johnson's intrusions into Crousaz's polemic are clearheaded and evenhanded. His criticisms of Crousaz generally focus on his querulousness. In his desire to discredit the philosophical system of the poem, Crousaz refused to be pleased. Scarcely any passage, no matter how innocuous, escaped without censure. Johnson despised the excessive subtlety that turned innocent statements into threatening heresies, falling back on the understanding of the common reader to vindicate Pope from small-minded criticism:

> It is a great Misfortune to have too great an Inclination to draw Consequences, and too strong a Desire to search deeper than the rest of Mankind. This Temper is undoubtedly of great use in abstruse Learning, and on some important Occasions; but when carried into the Scenes of common Life, and exerted without any Necessity, only makes the unhappy Reasoner suspicious and captious, shews every thing in a false Light, and makes his Discoveries the Sport of the World.[56]

But Johnson's attitudes towards the *Essay on Man* itself are not so easily encompassed. He was intent on giving Pope his due as a poet; thus he took pains to point out the inferiority of the French version to its English original. Du Resnel's translation was almost twice as long as the *Essay* itself. It lacked the tightness of Pope's expression and often wandered off into illustrations and sentiments not found in the English poem. Johnson was quick to note such flaws as Du Resnel's introduction of "love" into the poem where Pope meant "the passions" generally; this, Johnson says, is "the evident Marks of a *Frenchman's* Genius." On the whole Johnson can be said to have tried to protect Pope from any unjust censures. He railed at Crousaz for attacking Pope when the offensive statements appeared only in the translation.

> I take this Opportunity of observing, once for all, that he is not sufficiently candid in charging all the Errors of this miserable Version upon the original Author. If he had no Way of distinguishing between Mr. *Pope* and his Translator, to throw the Odium of Impiety, and the Ridicule of Nonsense entirely upon the former, is at least *stabbing in the Dark,* and wounding, for ought he knows, an innocent Character.[57]

Yet, in his notes, as in the *Life of Pope* many years later, Johnson showed little fondness for the *Essay on Man* and made no attempt to vindicate Pope's "philosophy" from the objections of Crousaz. And when he found Crousaz willing to accept the principle of a Ruling Passion, he entered his own objection.

> The Author may, perhaps, be conscious of a *Ruling Passion* that has influenced all his Actions and Designs. I am conscious of none but the general Desire of Happiness, which is not here intended, so that there appears equal Evidence on both Sides. Men, indeed, appear very frequently to be influenced a long time by a predominant Inclination to Fame, Money or Power; but perhaps if they review their early Years, and trace their Ideas backwards, they will find that those strong Desires were the Effects either of Example or Instruction, the Circumstances in which they were placed, the Objects which they first received Impressions from, the first Books they read, or the first Company they conversed with.[58]

Throughout the notes Johnson betrays a chauvinistic inclination to place the great English poet securely above his translator and to remove the blame for either nonsense or impiety to the shoulders of a Frenchman when such action was called for, but nowhere is there any hint of a defense of the blithely optimistic philosophy that the poem proposes. Johnson censured the excesses to which zeal led Crousaz, but he did not find Pope's antagonist wrong-headed.[59]

Little is known of Johnson's habits in composing this translation beyond his having written six sheets of it, over a third of the whole, in a single day.[60] The text itself leads us to suspect that he wearied of his task and simply wished it done. Crousaz's commentary on the *Essay*'s first epistle receives frequent notes, often focusing on the inadequacy of Du Resnel's translation. As Johnson progressed, he became more petulant towards Crousaz, but eventually lost interest in him too. The number of notes drops off sharply in the discussion of the *Essay*'s third epistle, and the fourth escapes virtually without comment. Johnson was apparently content to dispense with his own observations so that what had to be done might be done more quickly.

The importance of translation in Johnson's scheme to establish himself as a man of letters can hardly be stressed too much; the Sarpi and Crousaz projects dwarf his contributions to the *Gentleman's Magazine*, and the most significant of those, the "Life of Boerhaave," is little more than an extension of Johnson's role as translator into his subordinate one as magazine contributor. Nevertheless, as I have tried to make clear, the two major translations were not of a piece, and a few useful distinctions may be drawn between them. The survival of the Crousaz, with Johnson's interesting, often acerbic, notes, has achieved for it a place equal to the Sarpi translation in most modern re-tellings of Johnson's life. Its very concreteness—the fact that one can hold it in the hand—gives it a reality that the Sarpi lacks. But for Johnson, as well as for the educated public, there was no comparing the two. Of the Sarpi Johnson would appear to have completed at least forty or fifty sheets, and then he would have been only a quarter done; the entire Crousaz translation consisted of about fifteen. Johnson's name was to appear on the *History*'s title page; the *Commentary* was published anonymously. The Sarpi was to be a standard English edition of an important historical work; the value of the Crousaz depended not on its own merit but on the short-lived controversy over Pope's orthodoxy. The one was supposed to establish Johnson as a scholar, the other to turn Cave a quick profit.

By demonstrating his abilities as both scholar and stylist, Johnson had certainly hoped to overcome the disadvantage that his lack of a degree had placed him at, and although the failure of the Sarpi probably did not rankle so much as the neglect of

Irene, the combination of the two must have been devastating. Yet failure must not be allowed to cloud our perceptions of Johnson's efforts. He did not spend his first year as a paid writer merely piddling and dabbling with whatever trifles Cave might lay before him. Rather, he conceived a practical way of establishing himself in the world of letters and pursued it diligently; he was neither aimless nor indolent. If his labor was not totally regular—and the feat of six sheets of the Crousaz in one day shows that is was not—it was at least persistent. Copy had to be turned out if he was to continue to be paid, and paid he was at fairly regular intervals for at least nine months. The phrasing of Gower's letter, with its powerful Johnsonian resonances—that he would rather "die upon the road, than be starved to death in translating for booksellers"—gives poignant support to these inferences. He had applied himself without result, primarily to the Sarpi, but to the Crousaz as well. He had learned that the world is not so constituted as to readily reward genius and that something so trivial as coincidence could obstruct deserved success. And so during the summer of 1739 he decided once again to try schoolmastering. A schoolmaster's life was one of drudgery and monotony, but it was insulated from the shocks of his recent existence.

CHAPTER V

SAVAGE, POVERTY, AND POLITICS

Lord Graham commended Dr. Drummond at Naples, as a man of extraordinary talents; and added, that he had a great love of liberty. JOHNSON. "He is *young*, my Lord; (looking to his Lordship with an arch smile) all *boys* love liberty, till experience convinces them they are not so fit to govern themselves as they imagined."

Boswell, *Life of Johnson*

Johnson's poverty and his ramblings with Savage have passed from the realm of history to that of legend. Those who know nothing else of his early life can envision in Hogarthian detail Johnson in his ill-fitting great-coat and Savage dressed like a decayed dandy, wandering the streets for want of a lodging and inveighing against fortune and the Prime Minister. But this picture, which exists outside any legitimate historical context, distorts the truth, first by exaggerating Johnson's distress, then by romanticizing his poverty. Once we have adjusted our perspective, we shall still see in these nighttime escapades the powerful attraction of two passionate intellects and the vigorous and manly nature of Johnson's friendships; but much of the rest, especially the hopeless poverty of their days together, will fade from the scene. Truth, it seems, comes in a more homely dress than legend.

The stories of Johnson's poverty are not without foundation. The letter in which he first offered *London* to Cave includes a plea for help, as the author lay "under very disadvantageous circumstances of fortune." It is unbelievable that Johnson would have made such a plea without serious cause. Sanguine hopes for *Irene*'s success may have prompted him and Tetty to live beyond their means for a time. As the remainder of Tetty's "fortune" disappeared, Johnson apparently fell into need. But the ten guineas that he earned from *London* and his subsequent employment for Cave provided him with an income easily sufficient to keep a man and wife above distress.

An exact accounting of Johnson's earnings is now impossible to obtain, but even a conservative estimate provides us with no inconsiderable sum. The Sarpi translation netted him forty-seven guineas; the Crousaz, which totaled about fifteen sheets, probably brought between seven and fifteen guineas more.[1] His miscellaneous services as sub-editor of the magazine earned regular pay but little. The correction of the debates took little time and involved little composition. Individual pieces like the Pamphilus letters and the "Life of Boerhaave" may have earned a supplement to his usual salary, the Boerhaave bringing at most a few pounds;[2] but for the most part Johnson's original compositions were mere outgrowths of his editorial role and may not have merited special pay.

Cave's competitor provides us with a means of determining what editorial services were worth during the middle of the century. In 1755 Edward Kimber was paid only £2 per month for editing the *London Magazine,* and his father Isaac was certainly paid no more for the same task in the 1730s.[3] With Cave retaining many of the editorial responsibilities for himself, Johnson's duties were less than Kimber's and his pay probably no more.[4] Johnson was, after all, earning a considerable income from the Sarpi translation, and Cave was not the man to spoil his laborers with two substantial salaries. A guinea or two a month is perhaps all that Johnson could have expected in his editorial capacity. In the eleven months, then, from July 1738 through May 1739, Cave probably paid Johnson between sixty-five and eighty guineas.[5]

This sum is meaningless in itself to a modern observer, for no fixed multiple can provide a satisfactory conversion to present-day pounds or dollars. But an examination of eighteenth-century wages and prices shows seventy guineas to have been a respectable income. Johnson once fixed the allowance for the barest necessities of life at only six pounds per year.[6] Food and shelter were relatively cheap, and Johnson and Tetty could have expected to spend as little as forty or fifty pounds for an entire year's food and lodging, and this without being contemptible.[7] Tea, though, cost from ten to thirty-five shillings a pound,[8] no trivial sum, and clothing could be very expensive. A suit made of "second cloth," the quality expected of "Clerks in Public Offices," sold for £4 10s. in 1767,[9] perhaps somewhat less in the 1730s. A frugal housewife might make her own clothes, but even then they were not inexpensive, the price of woolen cloth apparently ranging from several shillings per yard for common fabrics to twenty-one shillings for a rich Genoa velvet.[10] Tetty, born into the gentry and concerned about her social position, expected the trappings of her class and thus certainly put a strain on the family finances. A few dresses and an inordinate liberality in brewing tea could consume the better part of an entire year's surplus income. In addition, Tetty generally kept a maid or companion, and although her wages might be negligible, she still had to be fed. Johnson would have found it difficult to reproach Tetty's spending, for her fortune, which survived the bankruptcy of her first husband, had been to a large extent consumed since their marriage, and not only by her trifles, but by his ambitious schemes as well. His scrupulous conscience would certainly have rebelled if he forced her to do without the small luxuries, perhaps her snuff or alcohol, that her fortune would have provided.

Throughout the period of Johnson's work on the Sarpi translation, he can hardly be thought of as enduring poverty. His income was not inexhaustible, nor was his manner of living splendid, but there can be no doubt that he earned a competence. Boswell himself perceived as much. Writing of the period following "Ad Urbanum," he says: "It appears that he was now enlisted by Mr. Cave as a regular coadjutor in his magazine, by which he probably obtained a tolerable livelihood."[11] Boswell knew of the payment for the Sarpi translation and deduced that his added income as editor would have brought Johnson an acceptable wage. This is not meant to deny that Johnson often was penniless, especially in the years that followed, but from August 1738 through April 1739, distress was easily averted by application. Guinea by guinea he made his way through the Sarpi and the Crousaz. As the months passed he became discontented and perhaps felt that the remuneration was in no way equal to the labor, but these are qualitatively different problems from those of poverty and degradation most commonly associated with the period of Johnson's relationship with Savage.

The subject of Johnson's poverty is so closely tied to his friendship with Savage that a change in attitude towards one must inevitably lead to a re-evaluation of the other. All of the available evidence, scanty though it is, indicates that Johnson met Savage at some period after the publication of *London* and that their friendship spanned a single year, one of relative prosperity for Johnson. A hard-working, fairly-well-paid Johnson at first seems to disrupt the traditional scenario, with the "almost incredible scenes of distress"[12] that made Boswell melancholy, but in fact the new picture not only preserves the vividness of the old but gives it an understandable foundation.

Johnson probably met Savage as he met so many other of his London acquaintances—through Cave. Hawkins, whose distaste for Savage's character was made clear in his biography of Johnson, asserted that Savage's misfortunes, "together with his vices, had driven him to St. John's gate, and thereby introduced him to the acquaintance of Johnson." Boswell echoes and expands upon this statement: "As Savage's misfortunes and misconduct had reduced him to the lowest state of wretchedness as a writer for bread, his visits to St. John's Gate naturally brought Johnson and him together."[13] In fact, there is no evidence that Savage at this time was "writing for bread." He was never employed alongside Johnson on the *Gentleman's Magazine;* indeed, his wretchedness was perpetuated by his refusal to seek out such employment. Johnson had found that he could support himself by his drudgery, but there is no evidence that Savage ever attempted to do the same.[14]

Nevertheless, Savage was well known to Cave and had exploited the magazine as an outlet for his poetry and as a minor source of income since at least 1736. In that year five new poems by Savage appeared simultaneously in the *Gentleman's* and the *London Magazines,* the author apparently receiving some small remuneration from both.[15] But Savage's poetical vigor was waning. In 1737 Cave's periodical provided the debut of two more of Savage's poems: the sixth "Volunteer Laureat" and "Fulvia," a poem apparently written years earlier but never published.[16] 1738 saw no new work except the last of Savage's yearly tributes to the Queen. But Cave had sufficient faith in Savage's public appeal to revive his old works as well as debut his new. From 1736 through 1738, nine of Savage's previously published works, including *The Bastard* and extracts from *The Wanderer,* were reprinted by Cave, often with minor revisions by the author. For the new pieces Cave may have been willing to pay a pound or two, perhaps a bit more if he was charitably inclined, but the old ones probably brought little. Cave would have been happy to have Savage's name adorning his poetry pages and may have been willing to pay a number of shillings for the privilege, but he was not accustomed to buying poetry that had already circulated among the public. Thus, although Savage managed to pry an occasional "present" from Cave, he can hardly be said to have written for his bread. Poverty, after all, did not prompt him to labor; sanguine hopes were the constant attendants of his misfortunes. As the *Life of Savage* makes clear, he lived off his friends until they would support him no more; and their forsaking him (if providing a pension can in any way be called that) did not drive him to the magazine in search of work, but to Wales in search of a new set of friends.

Not only is there reason to doubt the absolute distress of Johnson during the summer of 1738, there is also question whether Savage's life at this time was so starkly terrible as it had on occasion been and would soon become again. Johnson himself tells us that at the time of the Queen's death Savage was being supported by a benefactor and that after the last "Volunteer Laureat," which constituted Savage's appeal for the continuance of his pension, "he was for some time in suspence, but was in no great degree solicitous about it . . . till the friend who had for a considerable time supported him, removing his family to another place, took occasion to dismiss him."[17] Savage then appealed to Walpole, but without success. Late in August he received word that he was struck from the list of pensioners. Yet even then he was not without support. During the summer and autumn, he continued to receive the hospitality of various friends. On August 15 he visited Claremont, the seat of the Duke of Newcastle, with Cave, James Thomson, Thomas Birch, and Elizabeth Carter; and he may have been residing temporarily at Richmond with Thomson. Three weeks later he made one of a party that visited Burlington's splendid Palladian villa at Chiswick. Savage's letter inviting Birch to join the Chiswick expedition, dated September 1, gives the impression that he was dividing his time between Richmond and the home of Solomon Mendes at Clapton near Hackney: "I am now going to Richmond & shall scarce be at Clapton till after our seeing the Gardens[,] Mr. Thomson & I proposing to meet the Rest of the Company at Turnham Green." In November Savage was still sponging off Mendes, for on the 13th Birch traveled out to Clapton to dine with him.[18] Thus, even as 1738 was coming to an end, the streets of London had not yet become Savage's permanent home.

Nevertheless, St. John's Gate remains the most likely meeting place of Johnson and Savage. From March through June the campaign to keep Savage his pension was carried on in the magazine,[19] and in August Cave and Savage were together on at least one jaunt into the country. Although for much of the summer Savage may have been lodging out of town with Thomson or Mendes, he may have paid a visit at the Gate as he journeyed between Clapton and Richmond. It seems even more likely, though, that Cave engineered the meeting just as he took Johnson to see Moses Browne and his fellows. Savage, always happy for a free meal, could have easily been lured to Cave's home, where he would have been put on display for Johnson and Miss Carter. A dinner and conversation were magnets to him and could certainly and invisibly draw him to St. John's Gate. In all likelihood, then, Johnson and Savage met during the late spring or summer of 1738 in an atmosphere of conviviality and sanguine expectations.[20] Hawkins's re-imagining of the incident, with Savage driven to the Gate by poverty and despair and there encountering a young author whom he was soon to fascinate, is perhaps what that stiff-necked moralist felt to be the necessary result of Savage's dissipated life, but it accords poorly with the evidence we have.

Removing Johnson from the legions of the sorely distressed in no way challenges the stories of Johnson's night rambles with Savage related by Hawkins, Sir Joshua Reynolds, and Arthur Murphy; it merely forces us to rethink our interpretations of these events. Murphy's picture is the most vivid:

> Johnson has been often heard to relate, that he and Savage walked round Grosvenor-square till four in the morning; in the course of their conversation reforming the world, dethroning princes, establishing new forms of government, and giving laws to the several states of Europe, till, fatigued at length with their legislative office, they began to feel the want of refreshment; but could not muster up more than four pence halfpenny.[21]

As one might expect from Murphy, who had himself been convivial and in debt when an aspiring author, there is nothing maudlin in this description, no need for sighs or long faces. And more important, there is no grand deduction from the events described to Johnson's general financial condition. It was Hawkins who first implied that Johnson was homeless and Boswell who became melancholy at the thought of Johnson's extreme indigence. The stodgy Hawkins must have assumed that no man would wander the streets talking the night away if he had a home to return to, and Boswell, though himself a man of vigorous pleasures and midnight prowls, was unwilling or unable to imagine a young Johnson who was his equal in vigor though his superior in propriety. Neither of these men had the temperament of Johnson and Murphy, and neither understood what he had been told.

Johnson, as we have seen, was no pauper; throughout most of his acquaintance with Savage, his pay was both regular and substantial. Although he had little money for extravagances, he certainly could afford an occasional few shillings for dinner at a tavern and perhaps, if he was then drinking, for a few glasses of wine. Savage treated Johnson like any other companion—the price of his company was footing the bill. And these two could get along on relatively little money, for the diet on which both thrived was conversation.

Similarly we must dispel the idea of the homeless Johnson who wandered the streets for want of a place to go. He and Tetty were settled at Castle Street, living respectably on his income.[22] Their lodgings may have been too small to accommodate Savage decently; perhaps Tetty simply did not want Johnson bringing his friends around, especially Savage, who for all his fine manners would look like nothing but a parasite and debauchee to an angry wife. Savage himself, at least through the fall of 1738, could probably have stayed at Richmond or Clapton when he wished, but the walk to either was long, and it was unsafe after dark. Since there was no place of retirement open to both, and since Johnson was not likely to abandon his companion, the public squares had to furnish what comfort they could.

Johnson and Savage wandered the streets not because they lacked the means to procure a room, but because they cherished one another's company more than sleep. A man who takes his greatest pleasure from conversation will rarely be persuaded to relax his arguments and cease his oppositions merely by the lateness of the hour; and Johnson was of this ilk all his life. When old he kept no more regular hours than when young. Charles Burney recalled many evenings with the Thrales at Streatham where Johnson made a habit of conversing with friends "as long as the fire and candles lasted, and much longer than the patience of the servants subsisted."[23] If Johnson could hardly be persuaded to take to his bed when he sat with regular company, how can we expect him to have retired when he had such a willing companion in Savage? But a more striking analogue to these long nights is found in Johnson's "frisk" with Bennet Langton and Topham Beauclerk during the early 1760s.[24] The two young men woke their middle-aged friend at three in the morning and had no trouble persuading him to join in an all-night ramble, topping it off with a bowl of "Bishop," a mixture of wine, oranges, and sugar that Johnson always fancied. The exuberance of Johnson's personality is evidenced here. Sleep was for him a benign force, but only in a passive way: it did not increase pleasure, it merely put an end to pain. Fellowship, on the other hand, was active; it bound soul to soul. It seems more likely that when Johnson and Savage lamented their few pence, it was more for their inability to get some "Bishop" than for their want of a bed.

Johnson's relationship with Savage did not last long, perhaps a year. At first, while Savage had Mendes and Thomson to shelter him, the two probably met sporadically; but friendship does not need constant togetherness so much as sympathy of mind, and this the two men seem to have had in abundance. The gradual disintegration of each one's circumstances pressed the two closer together and heightened their intensity of feeling. In September Savage had the safety-net of his friends spread below him, while Johnson, though rankled by the annoying tasks of the magazine, had the promise of the Sarpi translation to brighten his future. Johnson could afford to spend on himself and his friend what little money he carried, for any poverty was momentary and easily remedied. A single hard-day's labor could take care of Tetty's needs as well as provide a few more shillings to treat himself and Savage to another night. But as the months passed, Savage's net was withdrawn and Johnson's distant glories proved to be an *ignis fatuus*. The former was reduced to complete penury and forced to lodge in the liberties of the Fleet; the latter was galled by his lack of success.

Johnson's discontent was aggravated by the conversation of Savage. In Hawkins's words,

> They seemed both to agree in the vulgar opinion, that the world
> is divided into two classes, of men of merit without riches, and

men of wealth without merit; never considering the possibility that both might concenter in the same person, just as when, in the comparison of women, we say, that virtue is of more value than beauty, we forget that many are possessed of both.[25]

Savage's experiences, at least in his telling of them, would have gone a long way to convince Johnson that merit was indeed ill rewarded, and his own recent struggles reinforced the lessons of Savage's stories. But their common discontent did not maintain this vague social cast, it found a political focus.

[Johnson] told Sir Joshua Reynolds, that one night in particular, when Savage and he walked round St. James's-square for want of a lodging, they were not at all depressed by their situation; but in high spirits and brimful of patriotism, traversed the square for several hours, inveighed against the minister, and 'resolved they would *stand by their country*.'[26]

These sentiments, recalled years later with an obvious touch of irony, were then passionately felt. In this state of mind, in this atmosphere, in this company, Johnson became slashingly political and allowed his anger and his resentment at felt injustices to overflow into two acid political pamphlets.

In April 1739, as he was finishing work on the Sarpi translation, Johnson tried one more avenue of literature—the satirical pamphlet, a form that Swift had used with impunity to vent his rage. *Marmor Norfolciense* appeared around the second week of May, and was followed two weeks later by *A Compleat Vindication of the Licensers of the Stage*. *Marmor* is a virulent but lumbering attack on the state of the nation, focusing on the moral degeneration of society and the physical despoliation of the land that follow from the presence of a standing army and a corrupt, lascivious monarch. *The Compleat Vindication* is an ironic attack on the stage licenser, who had recently prohibited the production of Henry Brooke's *Gustavus Vasa*, a political allegory both transparent and seditious. In each of these pamphlets we find a Johnson unknown to the readers of Boswell—a rabid, harsh opponent of the ruling government, a critic not only of a party but of the King.

There is a temptation not to take the political pamphlets seriously, for they seem out of place and, to a certain extent, em-

barrassing. They can be condescendingly excused as emotional
outbursts that arose from Johnson's intense relationship with
Savage, or dismissed as hack work filled with cant.[27] Both attitudes are unsatisfactory, for neither admits of a larger context.
Marmor, probably written in April 1739, was done as the Sarpi
project ground to a halt. Johnson had tried three other routes
to literary fame, none with appreciable success: *Irene* still lay in
a drawer; *London,* though winning praise for its anonymous author, had gained Samuel Johnson little more than the certainty
of further employment by Cave; and *The History of the Council of
Trent* was being abandoned. Without the regular income of the
Sarpi translation, another source had to be found. Neither tragedy nor scholarship could be expected to bring immediate income. Another major poem would be the most likely expedient,
but the exertion of such a task may have appeared too great or
the rewards too little. Swift provided a new model. He had shown
that artifice and anger could be used to intensify each other's
effects. Johnson, in obvious imitation of the great ironist, attempted to channel his disgust for the government through his
wit and into art. These pamphlets, then, should not be treated
as mere spontaneous effusions or as political hack work; they were
intended to be artful as well as politically charged. They represent not just Johnson's feelings, but another step in the progress
of his literary ambition.

With these pamphlets Johnson enrolled himself in the opposition, the loose agglomeration of writers and politicians all
united in their hatred of Sir Robert Walpole; and a sense of this
coalition, as well as of the political climate of the day, is necessary
to provide a proper perspective on Johnson's political views and
on the place of his pamphlets in the contemporary ferment. Like
many opposition parties, this one had no universally acceptable
doctrine. What one supported was irrelevant so long as he opposed the policies of the government. Walpole himself was a Whig,
the main survivor of the decade-long struggle for power that followed George I's decision to govern with Whigs and Whigs alone.
All true Tories could thus be expected to oppose this minister,
especially in his support of such traditional Whig measures as the
increases in the national debt and in the size of the army. They
could be expected to rail against "placemen" and to deplore government corruption. But in Parliament Tories formed only a small
minority.[28] Many of the most virulent spokesmen for the oppo-

sition in Parliament were themselves disaffected Whigs, either London merchants like Sir John Barnard, who vigorously attacked Walpole's dependence on the great moneyed corporations—the Bank, the East India Company, and the South Sea Company—or opportunists like William Pulteney and Lord Carteret, whose primary objection to the conduct of the government was that they had no part in it. Such a heterogeneous group could hardly have a coherent, detailed policy based on a commonly accepted set of principles, for no common ground existed. The Tories distrusted Pulteney and his fellows as "outs" desiring to be "in," while the dissident Whigs treated the Tories as an expedient tool to be used to topple Walpole. The opposition was a negative force; it existed primarily to quibble, to obstruct, and to deprecate.

But every opposition requires a program of its own, a set of debating points that embody its attacks on the ministry; and for many decades after the death of Anne, every opposition, regardless of its make-up, had the same one: a mixture of Tory bugbears and Whig catch-phrases that could be readily adapted to attack any government policy.[29] All actions of the ministry were described as attempts to subvert the constitution. A standing army and the great number of placemen in the Commons both gave inordinate power to the Crown, the first by its tendency to encourage arbitrary actions and the second by its subversion of the legislature's independence. All opposition parties thus called for a reliance on the navy as the strong arm of foreign policy and on the militia as the protector of the country; all called for government economies and a reduction in the money paid pensioners and government hirelings; all opposed government foreign policy, whether bellicose or pacific, as destructive of British interests.[30] The exigencies of maintaining and expanding an empire drove all administrations in the same direction, and all those who opposed the government, for whatever reasons, found themselves compelled to adopt these principles. As John Brooke says, "The programme is not to be identified with any group or tradition. It was neither a Whig nor a Tory programme, it was an Opposition programme."[31]

All members of Walpole's opposition rallied around these general and unrealistic principles. All factions could roundly condemn corruption. The Whigs reveled in the rhetoric of freedom; but even the Tories, though generally thought of as sup-

porting the influence of the Crown, could readily deprecate the
abuse of royal power and join in the cry for liberty, for the emphasis of opposition rhetoric was on traditional liberties, those
held by their fathers and grandfathers. Each country gentleman
(the true Tory base) was zealous to protect his prerogatives as
justice of the peace or captain of the militia; his interest was regional, not national. And to the extent that the executive, through
a standing army, made its power felt in the countryside, it in-
fringed on Tory rights. As a result we find Sir Thomas Hanmer
or Sir William Wyndham, prominent Tories both, demanding
limitations on the army and thus on the power of the Crown.[32]
And as the representatives of the landed interest, the Tory country gentlemen deplored the power of the "moneyed" corporations whose interests were served by Walpole's placemen. Tories
felt themselves to be the bulwark of English freedom; it was only
natural, then, for them to equate their loss of influence with the
endangerment of liberty and to see the cause of their decline,
the shift in power from the landed to the moneyed interest, as
corruption.[33]

Thus, the distinctions of Whig and Tory, though real enough
in the eighteenth century, were blurred by the homogenizing
tendency of opposition rhetoric. Opportunistic Whigs could speak
in favor of plans and policies that they would promptly reject were
they once to obtain office, and Tories could echo Whiggish cries
for freedom without a qualm, for their own traditional privileges
were felt to be eroding. The marriage was not a happy but an
expedient one, with all factions railing at the minister in unison,
though not for the same reason.

The literary arm of the opposition was no more homogeneous
and certainly no more precise or rigorous in its principles than
the Parliamentary one. Swift represented the attitudes of the
Queen Anne Tories; James Thomson, David Mallet, and Aaron
Hill were Whig "patriots" directly under the patronage of Frederick, Prince of Wales; Pope, Gay, and Savage defy classification,
as does Bolingbroke, perhaps the most influential political commentator of his day, who called for the abolition of parties and
argued that since the Glorious Revolution there were no more
differences between Whig and Tory.[34] Since these men were not
being confronted regularly with the detailed proposals of specific
pieces of legislation, they could be even more general, more vague,
more unrealistic in their demands than their fellows in Parlia-

ment, and they usually were. And since their ranks included the greatest satiric geniuses in English letters, their attacks could be more imaginative and their lampoons more cutting than even the most caustic remarks offered in debate on the House floor. Differing concepts of the nation's proper direction mattered little to men who all agreed in deploring its present course and who deplored even more strongly its present helmsman: Sir Robert Walpole.

Walpole's reputation has maintained two separate channels: Burke and his followers found in him a master of administration, a man who made government efficient and who made peace rather than war the normal state of the nation; those who look back to the political literature of the era are shown a genius of corruption, a man who used the public coffers to enrich himself and his hangers-on, and whose cynicism is best represented by the dictum "every man has his price."[35] In fact both estimations are largely true, and it was the union of administrative ability and Machiavellianism that raised him above all his predecessors in both power and corruption.

Walpole did not introduce corruption into the government, he merely exploited the weaknesses inherent in the system. The power of the Crown was immense but diffuse, and a mistress might have more influence than a minister in obtaining favors from the King. Walpole sought to consolidate this power by bringing all patronage under his control. By the mid-1730s, hardly a man held a place at court, in the army, in the Church, or in the civil service who did not know himself obliged to Walpole.[36] Patronage itself was not wrong; it was in the nature of a monarchical system. Twenty individual appointments, when secured by as many suppliants, was seen as benign. But Walpole's monopoly of appointments created an army of placemen who were indebted not to the King but to his minister. As many of these men found their way into Parliament, they provided a large voting bloc that was not accountable to various constituencies but to Walpole.[37] His engrossing of patronage was thus seen as subverting the independence of the Commons.

As to his use of government funds both for his own benefit and to influence elections, in these cases too he was merely taking common practice one step further. When Pulteney accused Walpole of appropriating funds for his own use, the minister could respond that he was not the first to become wealthy in office, calling attention to Pulteney's own large fortune, inherited from Henry Guy, who had managed the Secret Service funds under William III.[38] Laboring in the vineyards of the Treasury was generally acknowledged to have its rewards. And it would be extremely naive to believe that at a time when seats in Parliament could be bought more easily than they could be won, the promise of sinecures and the direct use of government funds had never before been lighted on as means of influencing elections. Walpole did not invent corruption, he merely brought his great administrative powers to bear on it; he gave it organization, coherence, and discipline.[39]

But the general hue and cry against corruption went deeper than a hatred of Walpole alone. As Isaac Kramnick has pointed out, the early eighteenth century witnessed a fundamental change in the economic structure of both government and society. The landed interest was losing its long-standing control of government to the awesome power of capital.[40] The traditional social fabric, many felt, was disintegrating. In the *Examiner* Swift had railed against the danger of moneyed men in politics: they produced no goods and paid few taxes; their allegiance was to capital, not to the nation.[41] For Pope the problem was the same: "Paper credit" had lent "Corruption lighter wings to fly."[42] In previous times a man might be bought with a dukedom or an estate, but such grants were impossible to conceal. Money allowed corruption to flourish unseen, and the great Whig schemes for financing the national debt—the Bank and the South Sea Company—were the villains that made paper fortunes possible. Land had become a burdensome way to wealth. Neither crops could grow nor cattle breed with the speed that money could propagate itself. Credit, poorly enough understood by laymen even today when it virtually dominates our lives, at first exhilarated, then nonplussed the age.

If money had become a god, Walpole was its prophet. He had not created the new, degenerate order, but he made it work. He had "screened" the malefactors of the South Sea Company after the bubble burst; he represented the interests of the Bank at court; he bought rather than earned the loyalty of his minions.[43] The minister had embraced the new order, with its great benefits in political expediency. As a result, the government itself had become visible proof that corruption had triumphed.

Opposition to Walpole thus took on a graver aspect. The fervor against him was not merely political, it was moral. This is not to aver that in all cases it was pure and unadulterated; many, including Swift, had hoped to make political gains through toppling the "Great Man," and some, especially power-hungry Whigs like Pulteney and Carteret, did not give a fig for morality, although they constantly played upon its themes in debate. Nevertheless, the great satires of the period, personal and political though they may be, are founded on larger moral concerns. The apocalyptic vision of the fourth book of the *Dunciad,* which had not yet appeared in 1738, arises from the poet's disgust for the venality of the new society.

> Then rose the Seed of Chaos, and of Night,
> To blot out Order, and Extinguish Light,
> Of dull and venal a new World to mold,
> And bring Saturnian days of Lead and Gold.[44]

As Pope himself noted, "Order here is to be understood extensively, both as Civil and Moral, the distinctions between high and low in Society, and true and false in Individuals." All traditional values had been overturned; it was a new, barbarous age. Walpole was at the same time the symbol, the symptom, and the facilitator of the new political order that had accommodated itself to new commercial realities. And both the politics and the economics had the stamp of Whiggism.[45] Thus the "gloom of the Tory satirists" was largely nostalgic, a longing for a social order that was crumbling before their eyes. A sense of dislocation pervaded their work, and well it might, for they were being torn from the security of Renaissance assumptions and thrust against their will into the modern world.

It is in this context of amorphous parties and moral fervor that we must examine Johnson's political writings if we hope to understand his uncharacteristic—"un-Johnsonian," if you will—attacks on the government. Though always a champion of the traditional order, with a far higher respect for a landed than a commercial fortune,[46] he was of all men the least susceptible to nostalgia. He had a clearheaded ability to identify present problems and had little inclination to sentimentalize the past. For Johnson nostalgia was largely cant. But on his arrival in London discontent was in the air, and he imbibed it. Any promising young writer would have felt a strong urge to align himself with Swift and Pope against the forces of corruption. Even Juvenal seemed to join the chorus, for there was little in his denunciations of a degenerate Rome that was not echoed in the weekly papers. To support Walpole would have been unthinkable, for his public image—his dishonesty, his cynicism, his greed, his willingness to sacrifice any principle for private gain—was the essence of "vile Whiggery." Various forces thus converged to drive Johnson into the opposition. And yet all of his political writings are not of a piece: the relationship with Savage and the disappointments of a year's writing for bread seem to have increased his malaise and harshened his tone. A full-bodied contempt for King and government informs the political pamphlets of 1739; the same cannot be said of *London*.

London certainly is an opposition poem: in it Johnson takes a slap at a number of the current opposition bogeymen—the excise, the stage licensing act, the King's trips to Hanover, the venality of pensioners, and so on. Four times he touches on the hottest issue of the day, the government's refusal to take action against the Spanish *guarda costas,* who attempted to stop England's largely illegal Carribean trade. Throughout the poem, Juvenal's censure of Roman venality and hypocrisy is given an opposition cast to bring its moral home more concretely to the reader.

> Here let those reign, whom Pensions can incite
> To vote a Patriot black, a Courtier white;
> Explain their Country's dear-bought Rights away,
> And plead for Pirates in the face of Day.[47]

All the corruption that afflicted ancient Rome was to be found again in modern London. Johnson even indulged in the political nostalgia that characterized much of Bolingbroke's rather fanciful version of English history, depicting the reigns of Alfred, Edward III, Henry V, and Elizabeth as an intermittent series of golden ages—uncorrupt, vigorous, and free.[48] These monarchs had led a strong, unified England; in the current government, faction and self-interest ruled.

And yet, in spite of all the obvious marks of party, the poem is only weakly, perhaps artificially, partisan. Although corruption will show the same face in any century, each age may attribute its spread to a different cause. Thus Johnson could strike home quite successfully when echoing Juvenal's sixteen-century-old condemnations of venality, but his adherence to the *Third Satire* in identifying the main source of corruption resulted in a failure of either political or artistic vision. Juvenal did not foresee the specter of Walpole, nor did he assert the same causes for Rome's ills that the opposition descried for England's. Rome was a city beset from without. As the center of the empire, it drew to itself the educated, the ambitious, and the opportunistic from all the known world, but especially from Greece. The notion that all culture was Greek had given a privileged place to the artisans, sophists, and charlatans of that nation. The manly Roman virtues of justice, temperance, and courage had been vitiated by the spread of Greek manners and amusements. A people that had been enslaved by Roman power was now, weevil-like, attacking from within. In an uncharacteristic bit of slavish imitation, Johnson strained to adapt his poem to Juvenal's realities, substituting French influence for Greek. Although "Thales" notes the corruption of Court and Parliament in the passage quoted above and can "Despise a Fool in half his Pension drest" (1. 73), he rails most vigorously at the "Dregs of each corrupted State," all of whom are supposedly drawn to London. The parallel with Rome here is tenuous at best. Like many of his contemporaries, Johnson may have felt that French manners and Italian amusements (including the "warbling Eunuchs" of the opera) had contributed to the degeneration of hardy English stock, but few would have made foreigners the primary cause of England's present plight; there were far too many indigenous villains. Johnson devoted sixty lines to detailing the vices of the "supple Gaul"—he is a flatterer, a parasite, a toady, a man faithless in all things.[49] But are these not the qualities of the pensioner and the placeman, of Walpole's lackeys? In *London* corruption is largely a foreign disease that has invaded the body politic. Yet opposition rhetoric required that the source of the evil be found within. It was an imbalance of humors that had made the nation venal. Too much Walpole had overtaxed the system, and a little letting of administration blood, combined with a healthier diet, that is, less gold, less luxury, less credit, would restore the balance and bring health to the nation. There was, though, a foreign "invasion" that had subdued Britain, a German one. Its character was different from that described by Juvenal, but at least some of the responsibility for cor-

ruption could have been laid at its door. In April 1738, Johnson
chose to follow his text rather than plunge into dangerous political waters. He would not be so careful a year later.

Johnson's attempt to adhere as closely as possible to the *Third
Satire*, to the detriment of the opposition's political theories, indicates that his allegiance was more to art than to party. He was
more intent on translating Juvenal's work, which he then adorned
with opposition catch phrases, than on remaking it according to
new political realities.[50] One cannot help but infer from this that
his zeal as a "patriot" was far less intense than his desire to shine
as the scholar-poet. The final product is a hybrid, an attempt to
engraft opposition complaints on a Juvenalian stem, with the
common theme of corruption serving to bind the two together.
This is not to say that the poem is not moving, only that its strength
as a political weapon is diluted by Johnson's adherence to an artistic precursor. What power the satire has comes from its more
generalized passages on the dangers encountered and the insults
suffered by a good man in a corrupt world, especially the portrait of the distresses of the poor; and this larger vision it owes
to Juvenal rather than to the *Craftsman*.

In the course of a year, Johnson's attitudes developed a truer,
more consistent antigovernment focus. In May 1739, *Marmor
Norfolciense* appeared,[51] a pamphlet in which Johnson attempts
to combine the artfulness of *London* with a political vision more
directly attuned to opposition concerns. The pamphlet has four
parts: an introduction noting the discovery of a medieval prophecy etched on a stone in Walpole's home county of Norfolk; the
prophecy itself in Latin verse; a translation into English verse,
supposedly done by the discoverer of the stone; and a long ironic
commentary in which a bumbling scholar tries to decipher the
prophecy's meaning. At least three different poses are struck in
the piece—the Merlin-like prophet, whose rough verse abounds
in vivid images; the translator, who brings to his task a wealth of
eighteenth-century propriety and poetic diction; and the commentator, whose absolute faith in the fitness of the government
obscures even the most evident allusion. Although *Marmor* has
been greeted by posterity as a failed work whose only interest
lies in the name of its author, the diversity of its structure betrays
Johnson's conscious artistry and marks the work as a minor *tour
de force*.

If the opposition sentiments of *London* seem formulaic or adventitious, *Marmor* shows Johnson in a sincerer mood. The prophecy, in both its Latin and its English versions, embodies opposition disgust for corruption, but it differs from run-of-the-mill propaganda by omitting such political buzz-words as excise, placemen, and special juries, all of which receive ironic approval in the subsequent commentary. Its larger, more general vision of a disintegrating society heightens the moral tone of the work, and the strangeness of the images and the bluntness of the diction, at least in the Latin, give vent to the author's own revulsion. Although the pamphlet is intended to be humorous, there is a dark cast to the Latin poem that is still evident at times even in the more decorous English version.[52]

The "prophecy" borders on the apocalyptic. A standing army pillages a land that it is too timorous to defend; the French lily spreads over fields that used to be the domain of the British lion; and the Hanoverian horse, in an act contrary to nature and baffling to the ironic commentator, sucks the life-blood of the British lion. The allegory is presented in striking images and harsh language that surprise the unsuspecting reader. The red snakes of the army (*rubri colubri*) devastate the once-rich fields of Britain, defiling all they touch (*Omnia foedantes,/Vitiantes, et spoliantes*).[53] Similarly, the British lion, now turned coward (*ignavus*), watches his sons trampled and tortured, "While he lies melting in a lewd embrace" (*Vetitaque libidine pravus*). To censure the ministry's weak stand towards Spain is one thing, to attack publicly the morals of the King is quite another. There is a recklessness in such a statement that betokens fullness of disgust. The tone of the prophecy differs completely from that of *London*. Cant phrases gave the earlier work its political orientation, Juvenal its moral basis. At the beginning of *Marmor* we have no cant phrases, only a bit of "Monkish" Latin, but sufficiently harsh to show the writer's revulsion.

There is less to be said of the bulk of the pamphlet. The commentary is meant to be Swiftian, but the persona is never developed. He is a foolish pedant, something of a "projector," who suggests that since he cannot fathom the poem, a Society of Commentators should be formed. This allows Johnson to attack pensioners and lackeys, and although the approach may have been new, the topic was old. Walpole's enemies had been hammering away at the same issues for almost two decades; Johnson's irony was not capable of giving such worn-out themes new life.

Although a general aversion for government grown corrupt informs *Marmor,* a more particular occurrence gave rise to Johnson's second political pamphlet. On March 17, 1739, Henry Brooke published a notice in the *Daily Advertiser* soliciting subscriptions for the printing of his play *Gustavus Vasa,* which the licenser had refused to approve for exhibition.[54] The prohibition of *Gustavus Vasa* provided one of those tests of allegiances so necessary in opposition politics. Governing has tangible rewards—pelf and power at the least—opposing does not. Thus any opposition group must derive satisfaction from its own presumed moral or intellectual superiority. Shared indignation and, on occasion, a communal venting of spleen are of no small importance in maintaining party morale. Such an opportunity was provided by the licenser's decision: a man could side with liberty against repression, with idealism against cynicism, with patriots against corrupt ministers. For five shillings he could subscribe to the forthcoming edition of Brooke's play and publish his sentiments.[55] The subscription list provides a glimpse into the opposition's plenty: there we find Sir William Wyndham, the leader of the Tories in the Commons, and the Earl of Chesterfield, the man who had most vigorously opposed the licensing act two years earlier; the "boy patriot" Lyttelton and the Jacobite Sir John Hynde Cotton; Lord Bolingbroke and Mr. Samuel Johnson. Swift, who thirty years earlier had seriously suggested that "a Pension would not be ill employed on some Man of Wit, Learning, and Virtue, who might have Power to strike out every offensive, or unbecoming Passage from Plays already written, as well as those that may be offered to the Stage for the future,"[56] subscribed for ten copies. But Johnson did not stop at subscribing. Incensed at the prohibition of Brooke's play, he set to work on another ironic blast against the ministry. Three weeks after the publication of *Gustavus Vasa,* the literary world was presented with *A Compleat Vindication of the Licensers of the Stage.*[57]

Maintaining the Swiftian vein of *Marmor,* Johnson again created a persona, this one a champion of the government who claims to have employed his pen numerous times in its vindication. He shows himself to be venal and short-sighted, concerned only with personal gain and the maintenance of power. He despises "patriots," whom "neither flattery can draw to compliance, nor threats reduce to submission,"[58] for their obstinate adherence to the principle of liberty and their inexplicable care for posterity. The portrait is drawn more imaginatively than the pedant in *Marmor,* but it still seems grossly handled when compared to Swift's personae.

The *Compleat Vindication* is of interest more for its politics than its art. Liberty is cried up; two Whig "patriots," L_____ and P_____ (probably Lyttelton and Pitt), are lauded for their selfless devotion to the nation's good; the government's attempt to limit free expression is deplored and the liberty of the press is thought endangered. Since an older Johnson was to repudiate all of these attitudes, one is not surprised that Donald Greene labeled the work "Whiggism of the first water."[59]

Nevertheless, we must qualify this judgment. As I have tried to show already, the distinctions between Whig and Tory blur in the ranks of the opposition. That a corrupt administration had endangered various liberties was bruited about by all its factions; thus a staunch Tory could praise liberty with as much reason as the most rabid Whig. We are perhaps surprised to find Johnson praising Lyttelton and Pitt, but that praise focuses on their concern for posterity and their sacrifice of "every flattering hope, every darling enjoyment, and every satisfaction of life to this 'ruling passion.'"[60] Insofar as they scorned Walpole's bribes and abjured places, they themselves had ceased to act like Whigs.

In addition, it did not take Whig sympathies to despise the action of the licenser because the banning of *Gustavus Vasa* was itself a perversion of law. The Stage Licensing Act had passed through both Houses expeditiously, a speech by Chesterfield being the only recorded opposition. Parliament had been easily led in the matter because of a particularly scurrilous and obscene play, the *Golden Rump,* that found its way into Walpole's hands, parts of which he read aloud to the House.[61] The play's licentiousness easily secured Walpole his new law. We must not forget that, as a form of public spectacle, the theater was universally acknowledged to be subject to various restrictions by the Crown. To oppose the act was to deny this prerogative and, by inference, to condone public indecency. But in the banning of *Gustavus Vasa,* the licenser was not protecting the public from obscenity but restricting free expression and stifling dissent. He had refused to explain his decision, and the law provided no avenue of appeal. Arbitrary power had been wielded against an Englishman; what greater portent of doom could there be?

If we understand the term "Whig" as Johnson certainly did—

as describing a man whose prejudices run towards personal liberty and societal and governmental innovation rather than towards subordination and tradition—Johnson had no Whiggism
in him and put none in his pamphlets.[62] The cries for liberty in
the *Compleat Vindication* arise not from a desire that Englishmen
be given new freedoms and that the traditional order be modi-
fied, but rather that their long-held freedoms be maintained
against arbitrary authority. Corruption was eroding the traditional framework of society, and Johnson, along with many other
Tory members of the opposition, was engaged in a fundamen-
tally conservative attack on the new order. His zeal was not for
innovation but for the reinstitution of a government that deserved the honor and respect of its subjects. With the triumph
of liberalism, the modern world has come to see a contradiction
between liberty and subordination that did not exist for most men
of the eighteenth century. True liberty is now perceived to be
antithetical to a hierarchical society, but for Johnson and many
of his contemporaries, fundamental freedoms were thought in
no way at odds with the class structure. The law was the securer
of individual rights, and the social order, with its myriad and
complex interrelationships, was the template from which the law
was drawn. When law itself was abused, as it had been in the
banning of Brooke's play, the social order was in danger of
subversion. The author of *Marmor* and of the *Compleat Vindication* did indeed fear for liberty and was willing to stand with
L____ and P____ in defiance of a corrupt regime; but he was
no Whig.

　　In 1738 and 1739 Johnson was brim full of vigor and zealous
to help bring about a government of good men. In the years that
followed, his ardor cooled as he realized that corruption was not
limited to one party nor virtue to another. The scramble for places
after Walpole's fall was a sure sign that more than one scoundrel
had taken refuge under the banner of patriotism. And the merchants who had demanded war with Spain had shown how the
pursuit of national honor could become the high road to wealth.
The villains of 1739 had turned out to be less mercenary than
the heroes. Johnson gradually concluded that English freedom
had never been in danger; it appeared to have a momentum of
its own and could not be easily deflected from its course. If anything, it was tending to expand too rapidly, giving encouragement to those who could not distinguish between liberty and li-

cense. Government was a necessity, and a strong minister unafraid to use the power of the Crown was best. Insofar as weakness threatened stability, it was a greater enemy of the pubilc good than was graft. The dread of corruption had been supplanted by a craving for public quiet. As Johnson looked back, he realized that Walpole had merely governed in the name of the King, and if he enriched himself and his supporters, he did little more than those who had preceded him. But, more important, he had maintained peace and encouraged commerce, providing for all Englishmen the dual blessings of order and plenty; thus, he had governed well. Virtue might be desired in a minister, but it is not to be expected—not when power is at stake.

One more current of Johnson's thought must still be remarked on if the picture is to begin to approach its true complexity: Jacobitism. There should be little doubt that Johnson's sympathies at this time lay with the King across the water, and much of the venom of *Marmor* may be attributable to this allegiance. That work does not call openly for the toppling of the Hanoverian dynasty, but it is, nevertheless, distinctly Jacobitical.[63] Johnson focuses his disgust on the British lion, who, *pravus et ignavus*, presides over the polluted land. In the commentary he adds a scarcely concealed criticism of the succession: the commentator notes "how common it is for intruders of yesterday, to pretend the same title with the ancient proprietors, and having just received an estate by voluntary grant, to erect a claim of 'hereditary right.'"[64] The Hanoverian "intruders" may have the estate, but they only "pretend" to the title. This was sedition, as was the earlier slur against the King; only a fool would have written such stuff without an honest conviction, and Johnson was no fool. The frustration of a series of literary failures, the long talks with Savage, and the "indistinct and headstrong ardour for liberty which a man of genius always catches when he enters the world"[65] combined to blur his vision and prompt him to publish what few others openly spoke.[66]

This is not to suggest that Johnson would have actively supported King James's cause. Indeed, his preference for order had probably long since made him acquiesce in the *de facto* kingship of the Georges. The Pretender might be honored as the legitimate claimant to the crown, but to throw the nation into turmoil to restore him would be to hazard public chaos for the sake of a principle. The danger overbalanced any possible gain.[67] But even such luke-warm Jacobitism could only have increased his opposition to Walpole, who in all his perceived corruption would seem a fit minister for a depraved monarch.

The political pamphlets proved the last major exertion in Johnson's first sustained venture into literature. Through May 1739, he seems to have had a hand in editing the magazine—his last blast in the periodical war appeared that month—but all trace of his style disappears after that date, not to be found there again for nearly a year.[68] The great experiment of coming to London to make his way by his literature had ended in total failure. All effort appears to have ceased. There are no more pamphlets, no more translations, no poems, no tragedies. June and July were certainly months of anxiety for him. All major sources of revenue were gone. The few shillings he might have earned helping Cave, if indeed he continued to give undetectable assistance after May, were certainly not enough to support Tetty in her accustomed habits. Tetty's capital, if any still remained, would again have had to support them. Savage was at the low ebb of his fortunes, living in the liberties of the Fleet and preparing to fly to Wales. Johnson's temperament is not so inscrutable that some reasonable conjectures cannot be drawn. Failure had led to depression, depression to indolence, indolence to poverty. In the last month before Savage's departure, Johnson may indeed have been as miserably poor as his friend, a situation that could only have cemented their relationship ever more firmly. Finally, when in July Savage exiled himself to Wales, Johnson too sought some less precarious mode of living than translating for booksellers. Soon after, he left for Leicestershire to press his application in person for the vacant mastership of Appleby school while Tetty remained in London.[69] The final decision was delayed for several months because of a dispute among the governors, and Johnson lingered in the Midlands, returning to Lichfield and visiting his old friend John Taylor at Ashbourne. When in mid-December the position was finally granted to Thomas Mould, "a founder's near kinsman," Johnson still lingered.[70] London, the source of hope two years before, now offered little but drudgery. Finally, in January he heard that Tetty had injured herself. Six months after his departure, fraught with guilt, he dragged himself away from the leisurely pace of Midlands society, back to an ailing wife and the labor of a hired writer.[71]

CHAPTER VI

RESISTING FATE

No man but a blockhead ever wrote, except for money.
                                                    Samuel Johnson

Johnson had spent six months in the Midlands without work. Money was again a cause for concern. With Tetty's capital rapidly disappearing, if not totally gone, they would again soon be in need. On the last day of January 1740, Johnson and his mother mortgaged the family house on Market Street in Lichfield to Theophilus Levett for eighty pounds.[1] That same day Johnson wrote a conciliatory letter to Tetty in London, promising her that their "troubles" would never separate them more and assuring her that he had seen nobody in his rambles that did not confirm his esteem for her.[2] Their financial problems were at least temporarily alleviated by the mortgage, as Johnson promised to send Tetty twenty pounds within a week. Whether his mother's problems in maintaining the bookshop had precipitated the sale of the house or whether Johnson's own distresses were the cause, he nevertheless shared in the gain and could only have felt heightened distress that his efforts in London had not prevented the family's divesting itself of property. Nor could he have derived much comfort from the knowledge that no further expedients existed to save him if he were to fail again. But the letter continues with cause for hope. David Garrick had ingratiated himself with several of the actors at Drury Lane and extorted a promise from Fleetwood to produce *Irene* at the start of the next season, if not before.[3] With ready money and new prospects of success, Johnson returned to London, probably within the next month.

Johnson's portion of the mortgage money apparently provided him with a brief period of ease, for he does not seem to have rushed back to St. John's Gate. He may have tried to press his case with Fleetwood or to find another project like the Sarpi, for the magazine contains no indications of his presence in any editorial capacity before April and no works definitely attributable to him until the June issue, when the "Life of Blake" appeared.[4] The earliest and most tantalizing hints of his presence appear in the weekly essays for April, which contain sneering glances at the *Craftsman* and *Common Sense* reminiscent of the periodical war of 1738–39.

> The *Craftsman* of the 26th, also attacks the *Gazetteer* Writers upon a Point we waved taking Notice of. The Disputes of these Authors turn upon the Abilities and Virtue of their Patrons, not without large Digressions as to the Modesty, Decency, and great Use of their own Writings; about which they differ as far as the East and West. We shall not attempt to reconcile them: We have already experienc'd that *Veritas Odium parit*.

> . . . [*The Craftsman's*] Paper of the 19th is taken up with a Project from a Correspondent, the Plan of which, he says, he stole from *Machiavil*, relating to the Power and Politicks of a *Prime Minister*; a Theme pretty well exhausted.

> *Common Sense* of the 5th is nothing but an Allegory, under the Notion of a Quack, reflecting on the M_____. That of the 19th contains farther Extracts from the *State of the War, &c.* a Subject we have often taken Notice of, and shall again in a proper Manner.[5]

The haughty tone of these remarks calls to mind Johnson rather than Cave, who rarely intruded opinions into his summaries; it was Johnson who gave the magazine a supercilious air. Nevertheless, a momentary shift in editorial tone is hardly incontrovertible proof that Johnson had resumed his old station.

By the next month, however, he appears to have been back at work correcting the debates. In the debates of May 1740, the Hurgo Toblat, in the nondescript style typical of Guthrie, states his intention to list the expenditures squandered on a foolish foreign policy over the past eighteen "moons." But the editor interposes:

> Here the noble Hurgo, with that Accuracy and Distinctness which is hereditary to him, gave a Detail of the Particulars he proposed; but as the Sums which he mentioned would make a

very odd Figure, if specified in our Language, and as the Names
of many Places, Countries, Commanders, &c. would be quite un-
intelligible to us, we make no doubt but the Reader will pardon
us if we omit them, and proceed to the Conclusion of the Hurgo's Speech, which was as follows.[6]

Guthrie's figures may have proved inaccurate or his account con-
fusing, so the unwieldy material was excised to facilitate the flow
of the argument. Such trimming had been Johnson's task a year
before; its application here, in a distinctly Johnsonian period,
provides the first certain indication of his return.

That same month Johnson was also to be found helping Cave
turn out another abridged translation, *The History of Tahmas Kuli
Khan, Shah, or Sophi of Persia.*[7] Like so many of Cave's productions, this book was supposed to capitalize on the current notoriety of its subject. The military exploits and barbaric cruelties of
Nadir Shah, or Kouli Khan, were recounted regularly in the
"Foreign History" section of the *Gentleman's Magazine,* where his
soldiers are said at one point to have slaughtered three hundred
thousand inhabitants of Deli.[8] When a French account of the Shah's
life reached London, Cave, perhaps in conjunction with Wilcox
the bookseller,[9] hired a translator to turn it quickly into English.
But, as happened with almost comic regularity, Cave found his
project in competition with another translation. With speed of
production now an important concern, the project was cut back.[10]
The often inaccurate geographical and historical accounts of Persia were omitted and Kouli Khan's life epitomized, thus reducing
the original French work of two-hundred pages to a slim English
pamphlet of thirty-five. Cave was apparently unwilling to invest
heavily in another doubtful project. The short biography was
rushed into print and given the first place in the magazine's register of books for May.

Johnson's part in this work is difficult to establish, for although the *History* contains some decidedly Johnsonian passages,
many paragraphs—in some places whole pages—are so badly done
as to make Johnson's sole authorship highly unlikely. Another
translator had probably been engaged some time earlier, with
Johnson brought in merely as editor and given the task of reducing the work's bulk and preparing it for speedy publication.
In the process he apparently condensed some portions of the
text, excised a good deal more, and interpolated some of his own

reflections. The result is another hodge-podge work in which passages of Johnsonian balance alternate with flaccid, inexact prose.[11]

By June Johnson was ready to resume his role of occasional contributor to the magazine. The trivial wages to be earned correcting the debates were certainly insufficient to sustain him; more substantial projects had to be found. The most obvious offering was another biography, a continuation of the series that had been so well received over a year earlier. The political situation directed Johnson and Cave to their next subject. During the months that Johnson had been away from the magazine, the opposition had succeeded in forcing the ministry to declare war on Spain. But Walpole had no stomach for this war, and none of his colleagues proved capable of assuming command. Admiral Vernon, who had been one of the most persistent voices in the Commons for action, had been sent to the West Indies in command of a small fleet and took Porto Bello with only five men-of-war.[12] His success increased the public clamor for a more aggressive posture towards Spain. To catch the martial spirit of the nation, Johnson and Cave agreed on a life of Admiral Robert Blake, whose daring exploits against the Spanish and Dutch ninety years earlier would feed the public hunger for tales of sea battles and British heroics.

The "Life of Blake," like Johnson's previous lives, was derived from a single source, in this case Birch's biography of Blake in the *General Dictionary*.[13] Johnson made effective use of Birch's extensive notes as he wove a narrative from the *General Dictionary's* double-structured text; but he did little more than condense, reorder, and rephrase. The life filled seven pages in the June issue of the magazine and was sufficiently popular for Cave to reprint it as a fifteen-page pamphlet later that year. In addition, Cave turned to Johnson for more naval exploits. The next and perhaps most appropriate subject was Sir Francis Drake, whose fame rested largely on his harassment and plunder of Spanish shipping in the Indies. In July Johnson contributed a paragraph announcing a forthcoming life of Drake,[14] the first installment of which appeared in the magazine for August 1740, to be continued in September, October, December, and the following January.

The "Life of Drake" represents some minor progress for Johnson as biographer. For the bulk of his narrative he again relied on a single source, a collection of four seventeenth-century pamphlets, each relating one of Drake's voyages to the New World, entitled *Sir Francis Drake Revived.*[15] But there are indications in the text that he also made use of Richard Hakluyt's *Principal Navigations, Voyages, and Discoveries of the English Nation,* and possibly of Nathaniel Crouch's *The English Hero.*[16] Nevertheless, the work also exemplifies the irregular character of Johnson's journalistic pieces, for it is noticeably unbalanced and oddly clipped at the end. The first two installments, nearly half of the entire life, never get beyond the first voyage, explaining in considerable detail the successes, frustrations, and dangers encountered by Drake in his privateering expedition of 1572.[17] Johnson then dutifully turned to the second pamphlet, giving a detailed epitome of Drake's voyage around the world. His condensation was still long enough to fill the magazine's allotted space for three months. But with the completion of the second voyage the decision was made to end the piece quickly; either Johnson could no longer sustain the interest to go on, or Cave feared that his audience had had enough. The remaining adventures had neither the charm of novelty nor the compelling force of immediacy. In January 1741, as the last installment was going to press, the ill-fated expedition to Cartagena was launched, and the public was anxious for reports of real rather than memorialized victories. Thus the rest of Drake's life was compressed into less than one page of the magazine. His third voyage to the West Indies is superficially related; his service against the Spanish Armada, "far more memorable, but less necessary to be recited in this Succinct Narrative," receives one sentence; and his last voyage is reduced to a single paragraph, half of which is Johnson's own reflections on his subject's death.[18]

The "Life of Drake" is perhaps the most interesting of Johnson's early lives, for it allows us to see the author confronting stories of natural wonders and alien peoples about which he knows no more than his readers except through the perspective of the original narrators. Johnson seems to abandon much of his wonted skepticism as he relates the mechanism by which flying fish remain aloft, the size and speed of a South American "ostrich" (actually a rhea), and the bearing capacity and surefootedness of the llama (quaintly referred to as a Peruvian sheep). He is similarly interested in recounting the skill of native craftsmen, for example, how those living near the Straits of Magellan make watertight canoes out of tree bark sewn together with sealskin thongs, while certain South Sea Islanders hollow out tree trunks for the same purpose.[19] But when his source reflects on human nature in its savage condition, Johnson is unafraid to interpose. The best example occurs in his rendering of the second pamphlet, *The World Encompassed by Sir Francis Drake,* whose author appeared certain of the innate goodness of savage man and treated the vicious attacks upon Drake's party by several tribes as reprisals for the cruelties of the Spaniards. No friend to Spanish colonialism, Johnson at first largely echoed his source, noting that although the manners of the Patagonians before the arrival of the Spanish cannot be known, "the Slaughter made of their Countrymen, perhaps without Provocation, by these cruel Intruders . . . might have raised in them a Suspicion of all Strangers, and by Consequence made them inhospitable, treacherous, and bloody.[20] But in the source, all Indian vice seemed to be attributed to this single cause. Finally, on encountering a tribe described as "of a tractable, free, and loving nature, without guile or treachery,"[21] Johnson could no longer maintain his calm. Neglecting his source's characterization of the natives, he described the Indians' nakedness and their crude shelters; then he launched into a tirade against those who equate savagery with innocence and civilization with corruption.

> Such is the Condition of this People, and not very different is, perhaps, the State of the greatest Part of Mankind. Whether more enlightened Nations ought to look upon them with Pity, as less happy than themselves, some Sceptics have made, very unnecessarily, a Difficulty of determining. More, they say, is lost by the Perplexities than gained by the Instruction of Science; we enlarge our Vices with our Knowledge, and multiply our Wants with our Attainments.[22]

Such reasoners, Johnson tells us, have imposed upon themselves through the unjust comparison of two men of differing inclinations: "The Question is not whether a good *Indian* or bad *Englishman* be most happy, but which State is most desirable, supposing Virtue and Reason the same in both." This attack on the cant of savage innocence is what we expect from Johnson, and it represents the most vigorous critique of a source that we find in the early biographies. He was not about to abdicate his judgment merely because he was appropriating someone else's facts.

The chief attraction of Drake's adventures, for both Johnson and his audience, was their novelty, that hungered-after quality in Johnson's concept of the voracious, ever-questing mind. The lives of Sarpi, Boerhaave, and Blake offered material for commonplace observations on the peace that is to be gained when diligent study is accompanied by piety or on the difficulties that fortune can present to any man, whether priest, doctor, or admiral; but the life of Drake made possible larger speculations about the uniformity of human nature and the just distribution of happiness and misery throughout the world. It is not surprising, then, that Johnson, unwilling to pass over native customs for the sake of hurrying on with his narrative, protracted his account of Drake's circumnavigation. The glimpses of the little-known worlds of the Americas and the East Indies appear at least as important to the author as his hero's exploits. When the various situations of man had been considered, and little remained but to recount more sea battles, Johnson did not hesitate to bring the life to a hasty conclusion.

In November 1740, while the "Life of Drake" was still being published piecemeal, word reached London that the young genius Johann Philip Baratier had died at the age of nineteen. During the last two years of his life Baratier had corresponded with Elizabeth Carter, who had been brought to the German prodigy's attention by a family friend living at Canterbury. Soon after the young man's death became known, Miss Carter informed Cave of a series of letters written by Baratier's father to his acquaintance in England recounting the progress of his boy's education.[23] The letters provided original material available to no one else, and from them Johnson was to weave his next biography, achieving a minor coup for the *Gentleman's Magazine*.

The "Life of Barretier" (Johnson chose an alternative spelling) appeared in the magazine for December 1740 and February 1741. As the life itself makes clear, for biographical material Johnson relied totally on the fond, fatherly accounts in the letters, generally doing little more than translating what the elder Baratier had written. Not totally trusting scholarly reputation, Johnson looked into Baratier's translation from the Hebrew of the *Voyages de Rabbi Benjamin,* noting the penetration of the young scholar and the maturity of his judgments. But research ended here.

The paucity of material led Johnson to fill out his work with reflections on education and other such relevant topics, and the obvious partiality of the letters brought about some questioning of the father's interpretion of events; but these observations could not save the work from appearing sketchy. This early version of the life has few dates, and although the succession of events is clear, whether one followed hard upon another or was delayed for a considerable time is not often discernible from the narrative. Johnson was undoubtedly hampered by omissions in the letters, which were never intended as a source for a detailed biography, but the scarcity of information did not hinder him from proceeding. A Birch would have written François Baratier seeking dates and details; Johnson was content to rely on what he had before him.

Herein lies the difference between Johnson the popularizer and Birch the antiquarian scholar. Johnson's talent lay in analysis rather than investigation, in questioning the assumptions or attacking the credulity of the original writers, rather than in fixing dates or numbering publications. And when he chose to comment on or to differ with his source, his appeal was not to newly discovered facts but to common experience. His insights into human motivation and his staunch determination to see mere men where others might see heroes provided the basis for his commentaries. These, of course, are the actions of the moralist, not of the historian. Thus his early lives exist outside the pale of scientific or inductive biography, then in its infancy, and outside the great movement towards the maturation of historical studies generally. Even though the "Life of Barretier" is based on original, unpublished material, it cannot be called researched, and so is not distinguishable from Johnson's other early biographies. Nevertheless, Johnson was not insensitive to the work's weaknesses. When over a year later François Baratier sent Miss Carter a more detailed biography of his son, Johnson seized upon this new source to flesh out his account, almost doubling its length. The additions, really in the form of long notes expounding upon statements in Johnson's original version, were inserted in the magazine for May 1742.[24]

We must not conclude from this series of biographies that Johnson had finally and willingly accepted the role of hack writer, for his contributions through most of 1740 are so sparing as to leave even less evidence of his activity than before his departure for Appleby. Upon his return he probably resumed many of his duties as sub-editor of the magazine, including the correction of Guthrie's debates; but these duties, as we have seen, were often trivial and easily dispatched. His original contributions, though often longer than those of his previous year with Cave, are fewer in number. From May through November, 1740, we find the "Life of Blake," three installments of the "Life of Drake," an "Epitaph on Claudy Phillips," and a few miscellaneous advertisements, notes, and paragraphs[25]—hardly the output of a man slaving for bread under the harsh eye of a close-fisted bookseller. Early in 1739 Johnson had been producing nearly as much text for the magazine while also carrying on two translations. And if we consider Johnson's habits of composition, the two lives were probably done during several great outbursts of activity, not segment by segment as they appeared in the magazine. Each of the pamphlets from which the "Life of Drake" was derived was probably tackled individually. Thus the first would have provided copy for August and September, and when that had been used up, Johnson would have turned to the second. If such was his practice, and it seems likely that it was,[26] he would only have been called upon for original copy about three times in seven months.

Johnson, it seems, was avoiding complete absorption into the magazine. By November Guthrie apparently had had enough of writing debates, for Cave was left without copy for the upcoming issue. But Johnson shunned both the labor and the pay that composing the debates promised. Desperate for copy, Cave turned to his competitors, printing slightly revised versions of the *London Magazine*'s debates.[27] It seems highly unlikely that Cave would have opened himself to a charge of plagiarism had he found his young man-of-letters willing to take up the task. We can only assume that Johnson was not, and with reason. To take over the debates was not to join the magazine but to surrender to it, to see one's creative energies dissipated in a labor that excited little applause and that would have to remain anonymous for both the safety of the author and the credibility of the material. Throughout the summer and fall of 1740, then, Johnson appears to have been resisting his fate. If Fleetwood could be trusted to live up to his word, *Irene* would reach the stage by October.[28] Until that time, Johnson may have been confident in his expectations for his play or may have been meditating other projects; he certainly was husbanding his talents. Journalism was still a stopgap providing a steady monthly income of perhaps a pound or two,[29] with an occasional larger payment for special contributions. Such

work might tide him over until his play should earn him recognition or a more substantial undertaking should present itself.
Unfortunately, the play was to remain unproduced, and no new
project would be found.

It was Johnson's fate to be drawn completely into the obscure,
anonymous world of Grub Street. *Irene, London,* and *The History
of the Council of Trent* had all failed to lift him from its shadows
while impending poverty maintained its unremitting downward
pressure. The *Gentleman's Magazine* offered the surest promise of
income, and so it was ever deeper into the magazine that Johnson was carried. If we may judge from the extent of his contributions, his descent was gradual, beginning with an increased load
in December 1740 and culminating in his acceptance of the burdensome task of writing the debates the following July.

The *Gentleman's Magazine* for December 1740 contains not only
the continuation of the "Life of Drake" and the first installment
of the "Life of Barretier," but also Johnson's first major miscellaneous contribution since his return from the Midlands—an "Essay on Epitaphs."[30] The essay expands upon the general principles laid down two years earlier in his attack on the impropriety
of Gay's inscription. Here we find a particularly good example
of Johnson's disciplined criticism as he ascertains the proper
function of funerary inscriptions and then measures the practice
of various writers against his freshly defined rules of the art. An
epitaph, he suggests, should make the reader think of mortality
rather than art; thus, "Heathen Mythologies" are found totally
unsuited for the commemoration of a Christian life, and the un-
polished sincerity and unashamed piety of the "Monkish Ages"
are preferred to the stylized classicism of "more enlightened
Times." When details of the subject's life are recorded, the truth
is never to be violated, though vices are not to be commemorated; and whenever possible, private virtue, "which . . . may
admit of many Imitators," should be stressed. Many of the qualities of the mature criticism—the attempt to establish the true
nature of the art form, the demand for thought and the dispar-
agement of mere decoration, the subordination of a hollow classicism to the search for common humanity—are found in this
brief piece, which should take its place as Johnson's first fully
developed critical essay.

Even debates appear to have received extra attention from
Johnson this month. The November debate on "the Encouragement of Seamen to enter the [King's] Service," one of those pla-

giarized from the *London Magazine,* was concluded in December. Although the November debate has no signs of Johnson's style, the first two paragraphs of its continuation in December do have a Johnsonian ring.[31] The debate then relapses to the earlier, nondescript style. The same issue, though, contains an original debate on "Navy estimates." This short piece, only seven pages, bears noticeable signs of Johnson's style and should certainly be entered into the canon as his first debate.[32] Thus, in the December 1740 issue of the magazine, one suddenly finds four pieces of original composition by Johnson, his most extensive contribution to any monthly number up to that time. For the next four months he was to maintain this increased output.

In the 1740 Supplement, Cave reverted to pillaging the *London Magazine* for his debates, but in place of the standard two-page preface to the collected volume, Johnson provided a single self-congratulatory paragraph, followed by a five-page essay "On the Acta Diurna of the Old Romans." Although showing definite signs of his editorial hand, this article can hardly be considered totally Johnson's own. It begins with a series of observations on the utility of news sheets and their appearance in such diverse cultures as ancient Rome and China. The succeeding two paragraphs provide a concise history of the Acta based on numerous classical sources, all dutifully cited in the footnotes. Ten fragments of Roman news are then rendered into English and glossed with explanatory notes. The essay concludes with two paragraphs that reflect satirically on the excesses of modern journals and point out the greater regard paid by the Romans to the rites of a false religion than by contemporaries to those of a true one.

The introductory paragraph is undoubtedly Johnson's;[33] and the sudden shift in tone towards the end of the essay—from historical objectivity to a humorous gibing and then to a sober reflectiveness—again suggests his hand. But the exact provenance of the body of the work is far more difficult to establish. Henry Dodwell's *Praelectiones Academicae* appears to be the ultimate source of both the Acta and brief history. Dodwell printed the Latin fragments, along with an introduction and annotations, in an appendix.[34] The essay in the *Gentleman's Magazine,* though showing signs of indebtedness to Dodwell, is by no means derived totally from his work.[35] Since Johnson was not likely to scour Cicero, Tacitus, and Suetonius for additional material when Dodwell alone had provided more than sufficient information for such an essay, it seems likely that he made use of an intermediate source; but the nature of that source—whether in Latin, French, or English, whether previously published or merely sent to the magazine by one of Cave's correspondents—and Johnson's precise treatment of it remain undetermined.[36] It is not clear whether Johnson translated it, abridged it, or merely reprinted it, adding his own introduction and conclusion. Nevertheless, this preface, though a trivial matter for Johnson to assemble, points up once again the improvement of the magazine's intellectual character whenever such projects were handed over to Johnson.

With the beginning of the new year, Cave tried again to free himself from his dependency on the *London Magazine* for the Parliamentary debates. He had materials for at least one more original debate on a topic of continuing interest: the navy's powers of impress. The problem of obtaining experienced seamen to man the fleet was virtually insurmountable, for most detested the harsh discipline and meager wages of the navy and fled the docks and bank-side taverns as soon as a press-gang was mustered. Merchants compounded the problem by hiding sailors who had signed on to work trading vessels. Various expedients had been proposed, none with much success. On February 5, 1740, the Commons had debated the merits of registering all seamen to facilitate locating them in time of need. Lord Gage had sent a copy of his speech on this bill to the *London Magazine* in May; Cave appropriated it for his June issue,[37] adding a note that a complete debate on the topic would soon follow. The promised debate did not appear, but seven months later the topic was particularly apposite. On January 27, 1741, the ministry brought in a bill to allow constables to search the premises of anyone suspected of hiding seamen. The opposition was furious at such an affront to liberty, and so the impress was again the subject of controversy. Cave sought an original rendering of the previous year's debate, and Johnson supplied it in the form of a short, self-contained piece of ten pages, the only debate in the January issue.[38] But even if Johnson was willing to write an occasional debate, he was not yet ready to present his neck to this burden on a regular basis. In February Cave returned to the previous expedient of raiding the *London Magazine* while Johnson provided him with a debate of a different kind.

At the end of the debates in the 1740 Supplement, the editor added a note that the magazine would publish "the Substance of the most important Debates that have happened in the Parliament of *England*, before the Commencement of our Magazine, beginning with a remarkable one in the Protectorship of *Cromwel*."[39] This was to provide Johnson's next major journalistic task. In February appeared the first half of the "Debate between the Committee of the House of Commons in 1657, and O. Cromwell, upon the Humble Petition and advice of the Parliament, by which he was desired to assume the Title of King," an extremely free rendering of an obscure political pamphlet of 1660 entitled *Monarchy Asserted To be the best, most Ancient and legall form of Government, in a conference had at Whitehall, with Oliver late Lord Protector & a Committee of Parliament.*[40] In a prefatory paragraph, Johnson noted that the editors had intended "to insert [the original] in our Magazine without Alteration; but we found it, upon closer Examination, by no Means adapted to the Taste of those who expect Entertainment and Instruction at the same Time; or require, at least, to be improved without unnecessary Labour."[41] To fit the "Debate" to the taste of the time, Johnson completely rewrote the pamphlet, preserving nothing but the tenor of the arguments. Such drastic action, though, was needed, for as Johnson noted in his short preface, the original is "so ungrammatical, intricate and obscure, so full of broken Hints, imperfect Sentences, and uncouth Expressions" that it could appeal to few but antiquaries. The pamphlet itself appears to be the edited jottings of one of the participants in the original conference, with all the errors and absurdities that arise from an auditor's hurried scribblings. It was Johnson's task to digest the one-hundred-plus pages of stunted arguments and run-together sentences and to fashion from them a new, more palatable work, one not just abridged but improved.

To accomplish this end, Johnson largely ignored the structure of the original. He reduced the numerous individual speeches by the members of the committee to two long discourses, each one followed by a response from the Protector. He eschewed the chaotic succession of arguments in the original, marshalling them in a more reasoned manner and listing in the margins of the magazine the names of the speakers responsible for each.[42] He embellished some arguments and ignored others, at times relying less on the text than on his own sense of the question to guide him. Of all the speeches, only Cromwell's first major response is rendered at all closely. Johnson condensed some of his points and added to others, but the original order of the arguments was maintained. Nevertheless the rugged, informal diction of the speech, which was perhaps more indicative of the Protector's character than were any of his arguments, is lost in Johnson's balanced phrases. Yet in this polishing, we must remember, Johnson took great pride. To supplant the harsh phrasing of seventeenth-century Commonwealthmen with the measured cadences of a more reasonable time was to bring art to bear on rude nature. To write in such a manner was not to distort the original but to improve it, to take that which is obscure and to shed light on it.

The Cromwell debate possesses none of the inherent interest of the early lives or the "Essay on Epitaphs," but of all Johnson's early "hack" work, this piece is one of the most impressive. The abridgment of a biography, with its simple narrative structure, was a far simpler task, and even the Parliamentary debates, which called for more fertility of imagination, placed fewer demands on the author's judgment. Yet the Cromwell debate will remain an unread piece of Johnsoniana, and perhaps rightly so. Even in 1741 the subject was largely one of antiquarian interest, its relevance to the contemporary political situation at best oblique.[43] The debate was most likely an attempt to "preserve" a curious but forgotten piece, much in the manner suggested by Johnson seven years earlier in his first letter to Cave. But his attempts to suit the work to the public taste robbed it of any authority. Thus the obscurity of the matter deters the common reader, while the sacrifice of the authentic to the elegant repels the modern antiquary.

The Cromwell debate, which was sufficiently long to be divided between the February and March issues, was followed in April by the translation and radical condensation of the Abbé de Guyon's *Histoire des Amazones Anciennes et Modernes*. In the resulting "Dissertation on the Amazons," Johnson reduced the Abbé's three-hundred page book to less than twelve of the magazine's columns. Following his normal procedure, he condensed and paraphrased freely, perhaps emphasizing what interested him most.[44] Little in the work is noteworthy; it stands primarily as an example of Cave's decision, perhaps influenced by Johnson, to provide his readers with glimpses into some of the more curious or sensational works then being published in France.[45]

During the five months from December 1740 to April 1741, Johnson contributed five different types of work to the magazine: one biography and part of another, a critical essay, two short

Parliamentary debates, the condensation and "preservation" of a long-forgotten political pamphlet, and the translation and abridgment of a recent piece of scholarship. In this period, his compositions never filled fewer than six pages of an issue, and they expanded to as many as eighteen pages in January. Never before had he written so much and with such regularity for the magazine. He would appear to have become a regular contributor, but in May his articles stopped. Room had been made for Johnson's essays and abridgments, at least in part, by the reduced coverage of the Parliamentary debates during the winter months.[46] But a new season of debates was soon to be called for. The session just ended had included several major disputes, including a well-orchestrated and nearly successful attempt to banish Walpole "from his Majesty's Presence and Councils for ever." Cave's readers expected full coverage of the proceedings.

These and other political matters usurped the place of Johnson's offerings. The King prorogued Parliament on April 25 and called for new elections. With the end of the session, Cave ran two "Lords Protests"—signed statements detailing the minority opinion on various questions debated in the upper House—in the April issue. Since the Protests had already appeared in pamphlet form, Cave eschewed both the Lilliputian machinery and the traditional expedient of dashes to disguise the Lords' names.[47] In the May issue, election results, followed by more Protests, displaced the debates from their traditional lead position. That month Cave also printed a "Summary of the Charge against Sir R. W.," the abridgment of an opposition pamphlet setting forth the alleged foreign-policy blunders of Walpole's administration.[48] The debates, news from Admiral Vernon in the West Indies, and the weekly essays filled the remaining available space. The June issue was similarly crowded. There was no room for lives or critical essays, but there was a place for Johnson, one that for the moment he chose not to accept. Cave had decided to reinstitute his own version of the debates. In May he printed an original debate on the Lords' "Address of Thanks to the King," which was continued in the June issue. The style is not Johnson's. Cave had pressed someone into service, but we do not know whom; perhaps Guthrie had returned, perhaps Cave wrote it himself.[49] But one point is clear: Johnson was not yet willing to take on the regular burden of turning out speech after speech.[50]

Johnson's ability to earn a livelihood by writing miscellaneous pieces for the magazine was obviously limited by Cave's needs;

so long as the magazine's format remained constant, those needs were few and irregular. When war fever was high, the weekly essays had been significantly cut back to make room for the "Life of Blake" and for one or two installments of the "Life of Drake," but the essays formed one of the most important aspects of the magazine's *raison d'être*; the concept of a "magazine" as a repository of a month's news and fugitive pieces demanded that the essays remain well represented. Cave could slight them from time to time, but not continually. Also eligible for pruning were the miscellaneous articles submitted by readers or derived from other sources. Johnson's own work, of course, fit under this very general rubric. But Cave courted the goodwill of his readers and may have hesitated cutting them off completely for Johnson's sake. If Johnson was to earn a substantial regular salary, he would have to fit himself to the magazine. And what Cave needed most was fresh debates.

By July 1741 the attempt to oust Walpole had already received extensive coverage in the magazine: there had been the "Summary of the Charge," an answer to that pamphlet, and a Protest on the same topic. But Cave had not yet provided his readers with a debate. Moreover, the *London Magazine* had stolen a march on its competitor, beginning its account of the Walpole debate in May. Another pedestrian rendering of the same arguments could not be very satisfying to the magazine's readers, but a new version of the material, digested and reworked in the manner of the Cromwell debate, might help Cave reassert the superiority of his periodical. Again he turned to Johnson.

The lack of better prospects and, most likely, the need for a steady income compelled Johnson to acquiesce, and not this time for another isolated debate, but for a whole series. With his assumption of the debates in July 1741, Johnson's role in the magazine expanded in other ways as well. The next month his hand was for the first time to be found extensively in the "Historical Chronicle." For two years Johnson had intermittently offered the magazine his services as sub-editor and as occasional contributor; during part of that time he had written full the gaps left by the seasonal contraction of the debates, but never had he dominated the magazine as he was soon to do.

CHAPTER VII

THE PARLIAMENTARY
DEBATES

He nevertheless agreed with me in thinking, that the debates
which he had framed were to be valued as orations upon questions of public importance.

Boswell, *Life of Johnson*

One can hardly approach Johnson's Parliamentary debates without a desire to echo Burke's famous outburst on the works of
Bolingbroke—Who now reads them? Who ever read them
through? They have become little more than a source of anecdote—the social Johnson proudly admitting to a small gathering
that it was he, not Pitt, who wrote like Demosthenes; the scrupulous Johnson, uneasy before his death for having "imposed
upon the world"; the politically biased Johnson, making sure that
the "Whig dogs" did not get the best of any argument. The debates themselves are lost in the archness, the poignancy, or the
verve of Johnson's recollections; the difficulties and the magnitude of the task are ignored. What of the ambitious young man
confronted with the Sisyphean labor of filling twenty double-columned pages every month, yet even in anonymity driven by a
passion to excel? Of this we hear nothing, for Johnson was loath
to call up memories of pain and struggle. And even Johnson's
own recollections about bias must be interpreted with an eye to
both the texts themselves and the situation in which he worked,
for he came to the debates as a hired writer whose publisher had
made political neutrality one of the canons of his magazine. A
biased debate was a violation of editorial policy. Cave, we may
assume, would not have tolerated blatant lapses. Thus, the anecdotes of this period, colorful though they are, may cloud more
than illuminate the true nature of Johnson's accomplishment.

We can only assume that Johnson's first attempts at writing debates were based on similar materials and possessed the same doubtful authority as Guthrie's work. Cave would certainly have provided his new author with as much information as he provided his old one. For the publisher of a magazine, the Parliamentary session that lasted from November 1740 to April 1741 was no different from those that preceded it. The regular spies were employed and the standard materials compiled to provide as realistic a basis for the new debates as possible. When Johnson accepted the burden, then, he certainly found himself provided with facts and arguments; only the weaving of the actual web of debate remained.

The extent of these materials is hard to determine, but anyone acquainted with the difficulties of taking detailed minutes during a heated or a complicated discussion will suspect them to have been sketchy and cryptic. In addition, since taking notes in either House of Parliament would be construed a breach of privilege, a "stranger" would have to be discreet in his activities. The vigilance of the doorkeepers may have been diminished by a few covertly passed shillings, but even so, the task required circumspection. Cave's note-takers and memory-strainers might secure a list of speakers, a slapdash digest of the arguments, and a number of key phrases or images, but probably little more. Such, it would seem, was the skeleton of a debate provided for Guthrie as well as for Johnson; Cave's author added sinew, organ, and flesh.

Because of these materials Johnson's debates were often fairly accurate with respect to the order of speakers and the basic substance of the arguments, but they were rarely faithful to individual expressions.[1] That William Pulteney was out-maneuvered by Sir Robert Walpole in his attempt to give the final speech on the matter of Walpole's ouster, Johnson makes clear in his version, but the speeches attributed to Pulteney and Walpole have little authority.[2] Occasionally Johnson anchored a speech in reality by including a speaker's actual phrase or curious argumentative twist, but even such concessions to "truth" became submerged in the great roll and swell of his periods.[3] Thus even when rooted in Parliamentary events or echoing an authentic sentiment, Johnson's debates were still in large part "the mere coinage of his own imagination."[4]

And yet, even these "slender materials" were not always available to him. "Sometimes," Boswell relates, "he had nothing more communicated to him than the names of the several speakers, and the part which they had taken in the debate."[5] But scant information was hardly a hindrance for Johnson, for his method of composition would have made highly detailed accounts a burden. The debates, Hawkins tells us,

> were written at those seasons when he was able to raise his imagination to such a pitch of fervour as bordered upon enthusiasm, which, that he might the better do, his practice was to shut himself up in a room assigned him at St. John's gate, to which he would not suffer any one to approach, except the compositor or Cave's boy for matter, which, as fast as he composed it, he tumbled out at the door.[6]

Johnson told John Nichols that when composing the debates, "three columns of the Magazine, in an hour, was no uncommon effort, which was faster than most persons could have transcribed that quantity."[7] When seized by such a creative frenzy, one does not stop to check a fact or examine an outline. To follow a source requires that it be kept constantly in mind; to write from one's own head, an exhilarating though sometimes disastrous adventure, frees an author to rely on his own store of idea and argument. As mind is more, so labor and danger are less. For Johnson, with his perpetual flow of argument, the normal materials provided by Cave were an abundance of information; when that little was not available, he would have prided himself on his ability to carry on undismayed.

We must beware, though, of equating rapidity with carelessness, for there is nothing slovenly and little that can be called ill-conceived in these works. In the delay between the Parliamentary event and its report, Johnson had countless hours to store up arguments and expressions—perhaps with whole speeches and rebuttals warring in his head—only committing them to paper when copy was needed. The debates often show a thoughtfulness and a range of considerations unlikely to have been called up extempore. Although the debates are not all of a piece, some more firmly anchored in fact than others, we may assume that for the most part Johnson consulted Cave's notes and plotted the course of his arguments before setting to work; but once work was begun, he pursued his track at a headlong career without pause for refreshment or hesitation at the fear of a wrong turning, lest momentum be lost and the author be confronted again with the difficulty of starting out.

That Johnson brought unparalleled fertility of mind to this labor has never been disputed, but the extent to which the debates are artful has been.[8] Sir John Hawkins maintained that Johnson captured the specific character of each speaker, distinguishing "the deep-mouthed rancour of Pulteney" from the "yelping pertinacity of Pitt,"[9] two vivid and telling epithets that seem to have been derived more from Hawkins's own political prejudices than from a careful reading of the debates. Most readers, I think, would agree that if the speakers are individuated at all, it is only in the most general way. Pitt and Lyttelton are always zealous for liberty, and Sir John Barnard, a London businessman, always protects the interests of his fellow merchants, a class of citizens that Walpole distrusted and despised. Bishops, who rarely speak in the Lords' debates, abhor vice when they do. General Wade thinks like a soldier and Walpole like a practical politician. Chesterfield is distinguished by his sarcastic gibes against the Ministry; although wit may glimmer occasionally in the invectives of various other opposition haranguers, only Chesterfield makes it an integral part of his attack. But even here we have nothing more than a "character"—the debater as man of wit—rather than a true portrait of Chesterfield, for the wit is in Johnson's manner, not in his Lordship's. Each speaker conforms thus to a type. As G. B. Hill notes, "His parliamentary speakers have scarely more variety than the characters in *Irene*."[10]

At this most general level all distinctions end, for in style all the speakers merge. Sir John Barnard provides a fine example. Hawkins, who certainly had heard him speak at public assemblies if not in Parliament, declared he "had a stile little better than an ordinary mechanic," abounding in jargon and "vulgarisms"; yet in Johnson's debates he was made to speak "in language as correct and polished as that of Sir William Wyndham or Mr. Pulteney."[11] And both Wyndham and Pulteney were compelled in the pages of the *Gentleman's Magazine* to abandon their characteristic strengths as orators, whatever they might have been, and to adopt in their stead particularly Johnsonian elegancies. Even the Urg Carnewoll (Velters Cornewall), a Tory back bencher whose defense of Herefordshire cider adds an unusual note of humor to the Mutiny Bill debate, speaks in the measured periods of the best Johnsonian orator:

The Cyder, Sir, which I am now rescuing from contemptuous Comparisons has often exhilerated my social Hours, enlivened the Freedom of Conversation, and improved the Tenderness of Friendship, and shall not therefore now want a Panegyrist. It is one of those few Subjects on which an Encomiast may expatiate without deviating from the Truth.[12]

The *res* is Cornewall's, the *verba* Johnson's. Whether Chesterfield attacks with sarcasm or Walpole justifies with expediency, the same balanced phrases and tendency towards generality inform the style. The texture of the language is the same throughout. As a result, Johnson's speeches lack the significant detail that would serve to distinguish between speakers of a similar type.

In many cases, then, the speeches are truly interchangeable, for the prevailing types in the Commons debates are often nothing more than opposition and ministry politicians and in the Lords debates, Lords. Sandys, Gybbon, and Pitt always castigate the ministry. In the best of circumstances, when a speaker is shown in all his individuality, with his own quirks of expression, his own cadences, and his own solecisms, one political haranguer is not easily differentiated from another; when all must voice their fears or sneer their contempt in Johnson's homogeneous style, every trace of individuality vanishes. Johnson may have given more "general ideas" to Pulteney as a speaker of high reputation, but on the whole his speeches differ little from the outbursts of his fellow "patriots." A reader opening a debate at random will find himself hard pressed to determine much more than the party of a speaker.

Within the Lords the speakers are even more difficult to distinguish than in the Commons, for Johnson tried to maintain a dignity of address that he perceived as intrinsic to the House. All are orators of the same stripe. Lord Hervey leads the opposition to the Spiritous Liquors Bill, the administration's attempt to increase revenues by replacing a heavy, regularly flouted tax with a lighter but collectible levy; but his long opening speech, which denounces the bill as an attempt to raise money by encouraging vice and debauchery, differs from the supporting speech of the Bishop of Oxford only insofar as one is an introduction to the Lords' objections and the other an elaboration of certain details. In style, tone, and argument the two blend together as if parts of a single speech. It should not have been difficult, one hopes, to distinguish between Pope's "Sporus" and Bishop Secker, especially since one was affected in his manner, the other preach-erly;[13] but in the *Gentleman's Magazine,* styles blurred. There is one voice to be heard throughout the entire debate, and it be-longs to none of the actual debaters.

This uniformity of style, the stately movement from clause to clause, sentence to sentence, speech to speech, results in the lack of what G. B. Hill called "the tart reply" in Johnson's debates. Confrontations occur, but without the angry sputterings and un-considered retorts that burst from men who feel themselves in-sulted. The most famous passage from the entire corpus is one such exchange between Pitt and Horatio Walpole in which the Prime Minister's brother taxes his adversary with the youthful folly of preferring "sounding Epithets and splendid Superla-tives" to "Justness of Argument, and an accurate Knowledge of Facts." This evokes perhaps the harshest reply in all the debates:

> The atrocious Crime of being a young Man, which the hon-ourable Gentleman has with such Spirit and Decency charged upon me, I shall neither attempt to palliate, nor deny, but con-tent myself with wishing that I may be one of those whose Follies may cease with their Youth, and not of that Number, who are ignorant in spite of Experience. . . .
>
> Much more, Sir, is he to be abhorr'd, who, as he has advanced in Age, has receded from Virtue, and becomes more wicked with less Temptation; who prostitutes himself for Money which he cannot enjoy, and spends the Remains of his Life in the Ruin of his Country.[14]

Pitt's vituperative innuendo, reflecting perhaps even more on Sir Robert than on his brother, is clear, but his anger seems muted. In this speech as elsewhere the control of the periods masks the vehemence of the response. Passion, we must remember, dis-dains formality, and anger abjures balanced phrases. Thus the heat of Johnson's speakers often appears dissipated before it can be fully expressed. This is not to say that the debates are totally without drama, only that Johnson was more zealous than the members themselves to maintain a decorum befitting members of Parliament.[15]

The debates, then, are not realistic: the speakers are not dif-ferentiated by oratorical mannerism, regional dialect, or occu-pational cant; nor does Johnson seek to capture the multifarious nature of a Parliamentary debate, with its occasional inane speeches, irrelevant arguments, and somniferous speakers. His debates have an even surface and a pompous style (in the positive, eighteenth-century sense of the term) such as no real gathering of men ever did or could sustain. But this, at least from Johnson's perspective, was hardly a fault. Both his temper and his artistic sense ran contrary to the sort of novelistic re-creation of the Parliamentary milieu that a modern reader might fault him for ignoring. The debates were never intended to be either detailed records of fact or particularly realistic fictions. Johnson had no interest in amusing his audience with one man's stammer or another man's "vulgarisms." He could only have learned these peculiarities by long attendance at the debates themselves, a great effort that would have yielded little reward. Only once had he entered the gallery of the House of Commons,[16] and it was not inertia alone that kept him away. He certainly felt no need to ape the styles of the men he would hear, for his own style could by no means depress and in most cases would greatly enhance the reputations of the members. He could express their sentiments more elegantly than they could themselves, and he could hone their reasonings and marshall their arguments with an eye to the overall effect of the debate.

Writing before the ultimate triumph of the novel, Johnson was exempt from the modern prejudice for realism. One only has to consider *Rasselas,* "The Vision of Theodore," and the many fables and allegories in the *Rambler* to understand that realism was not Johnson's mode, even when creating his most artful fictions. Significance, he felt, resided in the general rather than in the particular. The "truth" of the debates, that is, the general import of each speech and the conceptual framework underlying each position, would not be better elucidated by sharper confrontations or more colloquial speakers; truth lay in idea, and so expression could be usurped by the author for the purpose of putting idea in the most compelling form. And this required art. To limit the consideration of the debates' art to matters of dramatic tension or the discrimination of speakers is to judge Johnson's efforts by standards that for him did not obtain.

That the debates took their particular form as a result of conscious art and not of Johnson's inability or unwillingness to gather sufficiently detailed source materials can be inferred from his treatment of *Monarchy Asserted.* He disdained that pamphlet's antiquated language and haphazard structure, even though both reflected closely the original debate; he chose not to excerpt and edit the work's clearer passages, but to refashion it completely. He imposed his own order on the inchoate mass, respecting arguments more than speakers and preferring clear expressions to authentic ones. This practice was paralleled in his handling of the Parliamentary debates, where he frequently subordinated the actual to the essential. For verisimilitude, the order of the speakers was followed as closely as possible and particular phrasings occasionally woven into the new fabric, but for the most part, the work was subject to the invention, diction, and arrangement of the author. In other words, Johnson brought to the task not the instincts of the modern-day reporter but the *techne* of the classically educated rhetorician.

Rhetoric today is a devalued art. The term itself has come to signify obfuscation or empty flourishes and is most commonly heard as a synonym for political cant. But in an age before tape recorders and other gadgets for seizing upon the flux of time, art was the only preserver. And art not only records but transforms. Just as a sculptor gives new life to a subject, insulating it from the thousand shocks and infinite imperfections of mortality, so the rhetorician takes facts and arguments, not available only to himself but often dispersed through a community, and molds them into a discourse. The actual floor debates merely provided the basic material of which the magazine's versions were Johnson's artistic distillation.

Such an attitude required neither specious nor complicated justifications, for Johnson's approach was that of the ancients. The Greek and Roman historians adorned, and in some cases larded, their works with speeches never delivered, in styles often alien to the supposed speakers. This is not to suggest that Johnson or any of his contemporaries thought history was to be written in the manner of Livy, merely that, given the task of writing debates, Johnson had a series of classical precedents before him. Thucydides himself sought not to capture the actual words spoken at Athens or Sparta, but rather to relate "what . . . was called for by each situation."[17] Johnson, who never spoke or wrote without trying to excel, would have found in the practice of the ancient historians a means by which art could legitimately be brought to bear on an undertaking that might otherwise be dismissed as mere hack work.

In Johnson's hands, the speech, often composed according to

classical rhetorical divisions, became the basic unit of thought. A man who spoke miscellaneously to the House was liable to find his utterances pared down to a single topic in the magazine.[18] In other cases, arguments apposite to the debate but never uttered in Parliament might be attributed to men who had participated but who had spoken on other matters: such a practice, abhorrent to the modern historian or journalist, was easily justifiable under the larger demands of Johnson's rhetorical art. We must not forget that to value a speaker's real words, in all their paltriness, over a rhetorically perfected distillation of his meaning is a modern prejudice.[19] It is to value the shell of a nut so greatly that it can never be cracked to get at the meat. It is to disdain the truth of art and to glorify the truth of "fact." Thus the rhetorician has given way to the stenographer just as the oil portrait has succumbed to the photograph. And in all of this what is constantly neglected is genius. The factual materials presented Johnson were sifted, weighed, and sorted, then recombined and, if need be, supplemented to form a more orderly, more artistic, and, to many an eighteenth-century mind, truer whole. In doing this Johnson merely adhered to classical practice. Thucydides reported the Melian Dialogue on the basis of no more information than Johnson possessed for most of his debates, and even in his most imaginary flights Johnson went no further than Livy.[20]

All of this is not meant to imply that the debates are a neglected masterpiece, but merely to vindicate Johnson from charges of inaccuracy or carelessness. His primary "fault" was that neither his artistic temperament nor his journalistic methods were particularly modern. He was in fact not a failed Parliamentary reporter but a consciously artistic controversialist. We must not assume that Johnson was writing for the ages when he hurriedly penned these debates, but we must reject any suggestion that their primary failing is a deficiency of art. Their generality, with the emphasis not on the speaker but on what was called for by each situation, is the essence of Johnson's art. It is folly to think that Johnson might have written the debates otherwise had he spent more time in the Commons gallery or been given more detailed accounts of the proceedings.[21]

Johnson's debates certainly are flawed; the demands of journalism often vitiated the aims of art. Many of the debates are quite long and therefore unavoidably repetitious. But wearying length and excessive repetition, both in the nature of parliamentary convocations, are to be shunned by the careful rhetorician. We can have little doubt, though, that Johnson sometimes extended his speeches when nothing new remained to be said, merely because more speakers had to be accommodated and more pages of the magazine filled. Nevertheless, he commonly produced sophisticated discussions of timely issues that still can engage thoughtful readers. The real drama of Johnson's debates is not to be found in personal confrontations but in the testing of ideas. The issues are those that confronted eighteenth-century legislators, and Johnson brings them, rather than the men who debated them, into focus.

Before proceeding, though, we must lay to rest the question of Johnson's supposed bias, for he is hardly to be taken seriously as the arbiter of the age's intellectual disputes if he slanted his accounts and distributed genius and obtuseness according to party. To most readers the debates seem even-handed, and the question of bias would probably never have arisen except for a flippant remark made by Johnson long after he had concluded writing them. When praised for his impartiality, he demurred: "I saved appearances tolerably well; but I took care that the WHIG DOGS should not have the best of it."[22] But this statement, with all the marks of Johnson's brusque humor, is not quite so patent as it might appear. Which "Whig dogs" did he have in mind? Sandys, Pitt, and Carteret were no less Whigs than Walpole and the Pelhams, and Johnson knew a Whig when he saw one, whether in office or out. But let us assume that Johnson still maintained his opposition sympathies and that the "Whig dogs" were to be found in the ministry; Walpole himself, then, should be the chief butt of Johnson's subtle malignity. Yet from his handling of the Great Man, few, I think, would infer bias.

Johnson enters into Walpole's arguments with remarkable objectivity. He puts on the guise of the practical politician with surprising ease and wears it with unexpected comfort. In the seamen's debate, one of Johnson's earliest and only the second one in which he portrayed Walpole,[23] we find an intelligent minister intent on manning the fleet, first by offering a premium to volunteers, then by the impress if inducements should fail. The opposition, concerned about any infringement of English liberty, deplore impressment as singling out one group of men for slavery. But Walpole has no concern for their abstractions. The nation is at war and must have sailors. There may be other ways to get them, but none so cheap and none so sure as the impress. His answer to the carping of the "patriots" is not to deny that liberty will for a small group of men be suspended, but to assert the duty of all citizens:

> The Power of searching for Sailors, however it has been represented, is far from setting them on a Level with Felons, Murderers, or Vagabonds; or indeed from distinguishing them, to their Disadvantage, from the rest of the Community, of which every Individual is obliged to support the Government.
>
> Those that possess Estates, or carry on Trades, transfer Part of their Property to the Public; and these ought, by Parity of Reason, to serve the Public in Person, that have no Property to transfer. . . .
>
> Every Man, Sir, is obliged by compulsive Methods to serve his Country, if he can be prevail'd upon by no other. If any Man shall refuse to pay his Rates or his Taxes, will not his Goods be seized by Force, and sold before his Face? If any particular Methods are proposed for obligin[g] Seamen to contribute to the publick Safety, it is only because their Service is necessary upon more pressing Occasions than that of others; upon Occasions which do not admit of Delay, without the Hazard of the whole Community.[24]

Although to a modern reader Walpole might appear to exalt property unconscionably by bringing it onto a level with human liberty, to much of Johnson's audience such a comparison would have been far less odious. Few men of the day would have denied that civil society existed in large part for the protection of property; nor would they have quibbled with the idea that each man must contribute to the public good according to his means—at least, no man would deny that his neighbor should so contribute. One need only look to the works of Adam Smith or Edmund Burke to glimpse the esteem in which property was held in that century.[25] Although Walpole's ideas may seen unpalatable to a more egalitarian twentieth-century audience, the Great Man should by no means be thought here the butt of Johnson's subtle satire, for how is a man being mocked who merely repeats the commonplaces of his society? In fact, Walpole's argument from duty and expediency is largely unanswerable from a realistic eighteenth-century perspective. A nation that refused to maintain an extensive navy in times of peace had no recourse but compulsion if it was to man its fleets speedily in time of war. Walpole knew this, as did those members of the opposition who came to power after his fall and who continued for the sake of expediency a practice so injurious to English liberty.

In a subsequent speech on the same bill, Walpole is made to clarify the argument from necessity; in the process he shows a truly Johnsonian sensitivity to the uncertainties of political action:

> Every Law which extends its Influence to great Numbers in variou[s] Relations and Circumstances must produce some Consequences that were never foreseen or intended and is to be censured or applauded as the general Advantages or Inconveniencies are found to preponderate. Of this kind is the Law before us, a Law enforced by the Necessity of our Affairs and drawn up with no other Intention than to secure the publick Happiness and produce that Success which every Man's Interest must prompt him to desire. . . .
>
> That the Bill will not remove every Obstacle to Success; nor add Weight to one Part of the Balance without making the other lighter; that it will not supply the Navy without incommoding the Merchants in some degree; that it may be sometimes evaded by Cunning, and sometimes abused by Malice, and that at last it will be less efficacious than is desired, may perhaps be proved; but it has not yet been proved that any other Measures are more eligible, or that we are not to promote the publick Service as far as we are able, though our Endeavours may not produce Effects equal to our Wishes.[26]

The speaker knows both the complexities and fallibilities of human institutions; he has no naive belief that men will offer to do their duty to their country without some form of constraint.

But Johnson did not stop at representing Walpole as a practical man with a reasonable purpose; perhaps relying on one of Walpole's actual statements in the debate and certainly expressing one of the minister's well-known personal sentiments, Johnson allowed his speaker to vent his spleen at London's merchants, who, with their unanimous voice decrying the Spanish depredations, had hounded him into a war he had sought to avoid and who now bemoaned the harm done to private shipping by the seizure of sailors. The real Walpole apparently despised this class for their clamorous opposition to his government, Johnson's Walpole for their avarice.

The Merchants, Sir, who have so loudly complained of the Decline of Trade, the Interruption of Navigation, and the Insolence, Rapacity and Cruelty of the *Iberians;* the Merchants who filled the Nation with Representations of their Hardships, Discouragements, and Miseries, and lamented in the most public Manner, that they were the only Body for whom the Legislature had no Regard, who were abandoned to the Caprice of other Nations, were plundered Abroad and neglected at Home. The Merchants, after having at length by their Importunities engaged the State in a War, of which they have themselves certainly not the least Pretensions to question either the Justice or Necessity, now, when by the natural Consequences of a naval Armament, Sailors become less numerous, and Ships more difficult to be equipp'd, contract in private with such Sailors as they are inclin'd to employ, and conceal them in Garrets hired for that Purpose, till the Freight is ready, or the Danger of an Impress is past, and thus secure their own private Affairs at the Hazard of the Public, and hinder the Operations of a War, which they, and they *only,* sollicited.[27]

Indeed, what is Walpole here but a man beset by inconsistent and small-spirited opponents, and what are the merchants but Whig dogs?

In this debate as elsewhere, Walpole hardly seems vile. He is consistently pragmatic; necessity rather than principle directs his policies. This may be construed as a fault by some, but if it be so, it is a fault that is carried without blush by a speaker who portrays himself as committed to his country's good.[28] His reserve often contrasts favorably with the passionate speeches of his enemies. Nor is the debate on the Seamen's Bill unique. As Donald Greene has noted, in the Commons debate on Walpole's ouster, Johnson called up all of his dramatic powers in order to portray the minister much more sympathetically than the facts warranted.[29] But in the depiction of Walpole in general, as in the debates as a whole, there are few scenes like this last, where a humble minister defends his name and his honor more than his policies, and few passages so personal as the attack on the merchants. On the whole the character is lifeless; Johnson's Walpole is not so much the Great Man as a disembodied voice enunciating the rationale of the government's policies.

But if Walpole is not damned from his own mouth, he is definitely flayed by his enemies. Their strident harangues fill page after page with denunciations of corruption. Their concerns are all moral and theoretical, and one can hardly doubt that principle is on their side. Their arguments may on occasion appear merely obstructionist, but the more important the debate, the greater the appearance of sincerity.[30] Nevertheless, even the most vituperative attacks must not be considered conclusive in their effect.

Opposition zeal, even if pure, at times seems excessive. Sandys and Pitt despise Walpole's blunders and abhor his corruption, but in their attacks, error and evil begin to blur; one finds no motives for the minister's willingness to sacrifice British honor or for his drive to cut back English liberties. Walpole is raised to a caricature of vice and corruption: not only are his policies inept, his soul is cankered. This, of course, had long been the contention of the opposition; Johnson's speeches merely embody the virulence and venom of the *Craftsman*. But vehemence alone rarely convinces an intelligent audience; it merely serves as an outlet to dissipate the pent up frustrations of the "outs." And as Donald Greene has pointed out, neither Johnson's Sandys nor his Pitt was above demagoguery.[31] Johnson did not hesitate to fire off intense volleys of savage rhetoric, but one can hardly imagine him believing that by raising the pitch of opposition voices or by larding the speeches of Pitt and Sandys with *argumenta ad populum*, eloquent though their indictments might be, he slanted a debate in their favor.[32]

Johnson's treatment of Lyttelton—a man whose Whiggism he seems to have disliked, yet who is reflected on favorably in the *Compleat Vindication*—demonstrates the ambiguity with which Johnson could handle opposition Whigs. In the debate on the Seamen's Bill, Lyttelton is shown to be full of zeal for the right. His arguments are by no means insignificant, nor are his expressions flaccid. He balks at the impress because "cruel and oppressive Measures can never be justified, till all others have been tried without Effect." And the crucial attack on the motives of the government is put into his mouth:

> Necessity, absolute Necessity, is a formidable Sound, and may terrify the weak and timorous into Silence and Compliance; but it will be found upon Reflection, to be often nothing but an idle Feint, to amuse and to delude us, and that what is represented as necessary to the Public, is only something convenient to Men in Power.[33]

But his speech gradually becomes entangled in the web of abstract liberty, and he ends with a comparison that most readers must have thought excessive:

> I hope we shall unite in defeating any Attempts that may impair the Rights which every *Lilliputian* boasts as his Birth-right, and reject a Law which will be equally dreaded and detested with the Inquisition of *Iberia.*

Johnson here may have been indulging his spleen, and if so, it was at the expense of an opposition rather than a ministry Whig.[34]

The problem of determining Johnson's prejudice is aggravated by the resignation of Walpole, which occurred before Johnson had been at his task for a year. The Whig deck had been reshuffled, and the resulting hands looked quite different. Hervey was turned out of his place and joined his old enemy Chesterfield in opposition. Carteret, now Secretary of State, made peace with the Pelhams. Pulteney was rewarded for years of obstructionist speeches with a seat in the Lords, and Sandys, the new Chancellor of the Exchequer, was to be heard opposing a Place Bill and censuring Pitt for his attacks on Carteret's foreign policy. The ease with which these men adapted their principles to their places made manifest the unscrupulous Whiggery that Johnson so despised. Even those Whigs who remained in opposition, especially Pitt and Chesterfield, did so not for fear of being tainted by the touch of the Pelhams but merely for lack of a place in the new administration. Johnson, we may be sure, saw before him a great array of Whig dogs.[35]

The new political alignments had little evident effect on the debates. The new opposition attacked from principle and the new ministry justified from expediency. Thus Carteret, who had long criticized the "exorbitant exactions" of Walpole's administration, supported the Spiritous Liquors Bill, with its promise of increased revenues, while Hervey, a steadfast supporter of Walpole's taxation schemes,[36] could only revile its pernicious tendencies. Yet this situation may have presented Johnson with an ironic structure that allowed him to remain objective in his arguments while still demonstrating, at least obliquely, the unprincipled behavior of his speakers. Carteret, whose speeches are some of Johnson's most eloquent, provides the most obvious case. He was the primary accuser in the Lords' debate on removing Walpole, where he asserted that the minister's corruption was so great and his power so extensive that no case could be made against him until he was stripped of his control of the public purse, for by this he purchased the silence of his contemptible lackeys. But after the Great Man's fall and his own accession to power, Carteret screened his old antagonist, opposing the Commons' attempt to indemnify against prosecution all who would bring forth evidence. His legalistic arguments against this immunity, often compelling in themselves, grate harshly against his earlier accusations. Although he had previously seen government funds scattered like seed in the weedy patch of Walpole's supporters and had suspected the determinations of the Commons under Walpole's control "to be influenced by some other Motives than Justice and Truth," he could now find no specific crime of which the old minister stood accused[37] (this in spite of the fact that an unsuccessful Parliamentary candidate from Wendover had admitted receiving five hundred pounds of Treasury money from one of Walpole's aides to further his candidacy[38]). It did not take a very cynical observer to see that Carteret's arguments, sound though they might be when abstracted from political realities, were prompted not by a care for an Englishman's rights but by a political deal. For anyone who could remember previous debates, vile Whiggery was displayed without the objectivity of the debates being compromised.[39]

Finally we must realize that the form itself demanded a certain objectivity. The Parliamentary forum did not call for the baring of souls but for the exchange of arguments. Thus for each speaker Johnson provided a public face, no more; it was not within his province to demonstrate sincerity or hypocrisy. This inherent objectivity certainly worked to Walpole's advantage. The monstrous visage depicted by his enemies shattered the minute it was forced to speak. The betrayer of his country, the corrupter of innocence, the buyer of votes, and the purveyor of honors had no public voice. When confronted with the task of giving this agglomeration of evils a tongue, Johnson was forced to demythologize it. The zeal of the opposition and the pragmatism of the ministry were their appropriate postures, and if Johnson occasionally indulged his own dislikes, as he may have done in the case of Lyttelton, it was not by demonstrating hypocrisy, which of course could not be shown without vitiating the speaker's argumentative stance, but by allowing the speaker to exceed the proper limits of his characteristic attitude. Hypocrisy, though not an irrelevant consideration for a citizen trying to determine which political faction is in the right, was irrelevant to the rhetorical form of the work. It was incumbent on the speakers themselves to challenge the sincerity of their opponents, and this Johnson permitted them to do.[40] But he did not distort their public presentations of themselves. If Carteret is insincere, it is not to be divined from any one speech, but from a comparison of several, each of which represents his position at a different time.

The fairness of the debates can hardly be disputed. Most are so perfectly balanced that the reader's prejudices rather than his critical acumen determine the victor. The apparent truth or falsity of an argument, and therewith the success or failure of a speech, depend here as in all political disputes on the assumptions of the hearer or reader—that is, on his party. Those who today find Johnson's debates skewed reveal more about their own "party" than they do about Johnson's art.[41] His integrity, his sense of the task before him, and the form of the work itself all insisted upon objectivity, and his zest for arguing ensured that no point would go unchallenged.

As I have already suggested, the true drama of Johnson's debates is in the testing of ideas—the pushing of one argument to its logical end, and then the attempt to undercut it from a different perspective. In doing this, the debates provide an excellent introduction to man's political nature. They are intensely political, but in the best sense of the term. They grapple with the ambiguous nature of the common good and demonstrate the complex problems inherent in governing a "free people." Although the topics permit abstract disquisitions, Johnson never lets ideas tyrannize over human affairs. Principle is always measured against practice, and well-intentioned proposals are analyzed for their workability. An aura of the fallibility of all human enterprise lingers around these works as they elucidate the multiplicity of "truths" on which opinions are founded. The assurance of one speaker is mocked by the complacence of his opponent. Those who speak as if confident of the truth are always encountered by antagonists equally confident of other truths. In the interplay of debate we find men maintaining arguments that their opponents believe themselves to have refuted, and asserting as undeniable, propositions that their antagonists reject as specious or absurd.

From a tangle of Whiggism, Toryism, idealism, and pragmatism, the decisions must be made that will direct the nation.

Of the disputes Johnson preserved, some have lasting significance, others do not. The age-old fear of a standing army has been quelled on both sides of the Atlantic; similarly, the course of English history has, with only beneficial effects, vested the executive power in a "Prime Minister," a creature abhorrent to Johnson's contemporaries. But many issues that seem interesting merely as glimpses into a distant time elicit arguments still apposite to modern disputes. A modern reader may initially look with condescension on the politicians of a world long departed, one apparently much simpler than our own. Some of their practices, like the impressing of seamen, seem hopelessly unenlightened. But the questions raised in the seamen's debate—Can the country afford to raise military salaries to attract qualified men? Can forced service ever be reconciled with a free society? Are the inequities within the system of conscription sufficient reason to abandon it?—have been heard by twentieth-century visitors in the galleries of modern senates. In the debate on an "address for papers," the opposition seeks access to secret documents on the conduct of the war while the ministry demurs because of national security.[42] Such disputes rest upon the fundamental problem of a free society, the struggle between governmental authority and individual liberty. But this problem is never completely resolved; only temporary accommodations are made. In each generation the problem reasserts itself, taking a new form that arises at least in part from the reigning intellectual fashion; but the root conflict persists, and the arguments that serve faithfully in one age will, with some superficial modifications, continue to do so in the next.

When Johnson's legislators turn to matters of economics, their discussions are governed by mercantilist principles exploded later in the century by Adam Smith and thus may seem either naive or ill-informed. But even here there is something for the modern reader. In the debate on the Corn Bill—an attempt to embargo grain during the war with Spain—the members of the Commons weigh the potential damage done to the British and colonial economies against the immediate benefits of causing short-term hardships to the enemy.[43] The arguments on both sides, simple though they may seem when put in their homely eighteenth-century dress, are the same ones that have been tricked out in a

modern vocabulary and adorned with graphs and statistics in order to influence East-West trade in the second half of this century. Let it be remembered that modern economic theories have
not eliminated such debates, for the matters that concern all senates, whether ancient or modern, are political in essence rather
than scientific.

Perhaps the most important feature of the debates for a modern reader is their human scale. As one views such disputes, government becomes demythologized; it is shown to be nothing more
than men of different backgrounds and prejudices struggling to
make their society function in its own best interest. The problems
of political choice, we discover, do not always require recourse
to "experts," but are perhaps best solved by the thoughtful deliberations of well-meaning men.

Although the debates are free of any obvious editorial moralizing, the situations that Johnson was to depict and the issues
he was to confront were replete with lessons of their own. The
conflict between ideal visions and practical solutions dominates
many debates. The role of government as the guardian of morality becomes the primary issue in the debate on the Spiritous
Liquors Bill. Are the people in fact ungovernable in their private
habits? Can a law which the people as a whole despise ever be
enforced? Should the universal sale of alcoholic spirits be sanc-
tioned and taxed, thus enriching or impoverishing the treasury
in direct proportion to the vice of the citizenry? Elsewhere Johnson turns to the limitations of government—the gulf between the
legislators' intentions and a law's actual effect. The debate on the
Mutiny Bill arises from an attempt by the citizens of Ledbury to
exploit an ambiguity in the language of a law. Before they can
take any reasonable action, the members of the Commons must
decide "whether this Law is disobeyed, because it is misunderstood, or only misunderstood by those who had resolved to dis-
obey it."[44] In the debate on "trade and navigation," the Lords
confront the folly of passing laws either that cannot be enforced
or that leave discretionary power in the same hands where it has
long existed, thus making a new law superfluous.[45] By calling
such annoying problems to the attention of his readers, Johnson
never allows the zeal for ideal solutions to eclipse practical considerations.

Nor do Johnson's debates ignore the compromises that stern
reality can force upon a man of principle. The Duke of Argyll's

speech on the "state of the army" provides a fine example. Although an act had been passed late in 1740 to augment the army, Argyll, one of the first men in the military since the days of King William and an experienced and highly successful campaigner, opposed the traditional means of raising troops—the creation of new regiments. He preferred instead to have new recruits dispersed among existing companies, a step that would save the government the expense of commissioning new officers. One does not expect a military man to use fiscal responsibility as an argument for diminishing the relative strength of the officer corps, the source of all discipline and steadfastness in battle. Nevertheless, the army could still be sufficiently disciplined, Argyll argued, with fewer officers, and the new men could be trained more expeditiously by being interspersed among seasoned troops. These arguments, though, were merely extenuations; they implied that the changes would not do the nation irreparable harm. But the alternative might, for under Walpole's administration corruption governed all appointments, and connections rather than proven valor or personal merit determined military preferments. Johnson made Argyll's disgust manifest:

> To gratify the Leaders of the ministerial Party, the most despicable Triflers are exalted to an Authority, and those whose Want of Understanding excludes them from any other Employment, are selected for military Commissions.
> . . . For we have seen, my Lords, the same Animals to-day cringing behind a Counter, and to-morrow swelling in a military Dress; we have seen Boys sent from School in despair of Improvement, and entrusted with military Command; Fools that cannot learn their Duty, and Children that cannot perform it, have been indiscriminately promoted.[46]

For Argyll, then, a diluted army was to be risked rather than allow Walpole to burden the nation with more of his personal dependents, men who could neither be readily disciplined by their superiors nor be expected to conform to the military code. An interest with the minister destroyed subordination. Thus the Duke did not choose his position for its obvious merit; rather he rejected the alternative. His choice lay not between good and bad but between a lesser evil and a greater. Such is often the nature of political choice.[47]

One of the most compelling effects of the debates is the sense they give of the dignity of political dispute. Although speakers often question the motives and revile the characters of their opponents, Johnson still maintains the appearance of well-meaning men in conflict. Every speaker, regardless of party or public reputation, whether Walpole or Pulteney, Hervey or Pitt, urges his position for the public good. If the debates are in any way idealized, it is in this: they do not depict what is self-serving and mean in politicians. Johnson's legislators, like their flesh-and-blood originals, hid their insincerity. If they were scoundrels, they concealed the fact behind the veneer of patriotism. The reader was left to conclude as he would about motives. But by shifting the focus from motives to arguments, from speakers to issues, Johnson was able to provide complex yet clear discussions of timely questions. That the debates "do not read like speeches that had ever been spoken"[48] is of no consequence, just as it is totally irrelevant that they teach us nothing of Pitt's oratorical style or of Walpole's demeanor. For Johnson's contemporaries they provided a sense of the issues of the day, filtered through the mind of a highly intelligent observer. For this there may be no better source.

Insofar as two-and-a-half centuries have dulled the popular interest in these disputes, Johnson's debates understandably remain unread. This lack of an audience helps clarify for us the distinction between Johnson's hack work and his literature. It is not that the first is badly done, for the debates, as I have tried to show, were accomplished with a great deal of intelligence and a considerable portion of art. But hack work will generally attempt to fulfill a narrow need for a specific time—that is, it will suffer from temporality. If the debates reveal something about man's political nature, that achievement is incidental rather than fundamental; their primary purpose remained the depiction, at length, of current quarrels over current problems. Art will seldom triumph totally over such parochial intentions. Even so, art can exist in some limited way, providing a heightened truth for a work's immediate audience and leaving a glimmer of its effects for future generations.

CHAPTER VIII

THE EDITOR

A very diligent observer may trace him where we should not easily suppose him to be found.

Boswell, *Life of Johnson*

On September 9, 1741, only two months after Johnson began composing the Parliamentary debates, Cave wrote to Birch asking whether the Society for the Encouragement of Learning would be interested in purchasing *Irene*. Johnson was offering not only the copyright, but "whatever advantage may be made by acting it."[1] The play was his only remaining literary property, his only immediate hope for escaping Grub Street, and he was willing to part with all rights to it. In trying to sell it off he was perhaps acknowledging that his original plan had failed utterly, accepting at least for the time being his role as a writer for hire. He had indeed committed himself to Cave as he never had before. For the next year he would labor regularly under Cave's yoke, and the signature of his style is to be found throughout the magazine; the debates, of course, formed the colossus of his journalistic achievement, but he also left numerous diminutives bearing their maker's mark scattered throughout the periodical—in editorial notes, original articles, journalistic accounts of foreign wars, notes on foreign books, and at least one abridged translation. The frequency, extent, and visibility of his contributions prove him to have been more completely involved in shaping the content of the magazine than he had been during the previous several years. But trivial undertakings could not long hold him. By the autumn of 1742, as other projects offered greater challenges and perhaps more considerable rewards, his interest in journalism flagged. And although he steadfastly maintained his monthly production of Parliamentary argument and counterargument, he gradually divested himself of his lesser duties, until by the end of 1743 the rhythmic patterns, tell-tale diction, and characteristic inversions of his prose were to be found in the debates alone. But during the intervening two years the magazine made its first significant strides towards becoming not just a miscellany for the average Englishman, but a journal worthy of the attention of the learned.

During the last six months of 1741, as Johnson settled into the rhythm of turning out debates, he contributed few original pieces to the *Gentleman's Magazine*. In the issue for July, in which Johnson's uninterrupted series of debates began, there appeared "A Panegyric on Dr. Morin," on the whole a sentence-for-sentence rendering of Fontenelle's *Éloge de Morin*.[2] Two months later Johnson contributed a short piece entitled "The Jests of Hierocles," translated extracts from the φιλογελως (or *Facetiae*) of Hierocles, a sixth-century grammarian, to which he added a short introduction and notes.[3] There was then a hiatus until March 1742, during which his only original piece was another formulaic preface, to the collected issues of 1741. This scarcity of formal essays is deceiving, though, for besides his assumption of the debates, the last half of 1741 and the early months of 1742 saw a considerable expansion of Johnson's editorial duties.

The most obvious of his new contributions are to be found in the small summaries of foreign affairs included near the end of each month's "Historical Chronicle." The "Foreign History" had long comprised letters and dispatches relating the political machinations and military adventures of European monarchs and middle-eastern potentates. During 1740 the bare dispatches began to be woven into narratives, providing a continuous account from month to month of continental affairs.[4] There is no hint of Johnson's style in these early pieces, and there is no reason to presume that he edited them. But in the magazine for August 1741, the issue immediately following Johnson's first regular contribution to the Parliamentary debates, we find a new voice in the "Foreign History," a discursive one, not content to recount troop movements but determined to evaluate and explain policy and motives. On the reported butchery of a great many Chinese by the Dutch in the East Indies he reflects:

> It is scarcely to be supposed that it was not equally practicable to have expelled, as to have murdered them, and in Christian or Human Breasts, it might have been expected that Compassion

would have over-balanc'd the Sense of any slight Apprehensions
of Danger.

But what cannot Cruelty commit, inflamed by the Lust of
Money and Dominion; the Account of the Spoils of the *Chinese*
is sufficient to raise a Suspicion, that other Motives than that of
Self-Preservation contributed to this dreadful Havock, of which
we yet have no Relation but from those that made it.[5]

Both the cadence of the periods and the character of the reflections immediately put one in mind of Johnson.

But just as in most of Johnson's other editorial duties, his contributions to "Foreign History" were irregular, varying from issue to issue. Although he appears to have occasionally composed
an entire article, extracting the essences of various materials and
fashioning from them a short essay, he appears more often to
have merely polished what another had compiled, often adding
an introductory paragraph or interpolating a moral reflection.
Nor did his enthusiasm last long. Donald Greene has discerned
some marks of Johnson's style in the eight consecutive installments from August 1741 to March 1742. After that Johnson's
contributions became either less regular or less evident. His style
appears only sporadically in this department over the next nineteen issues of the magazine and then disappears completely.[6] We
must not forget, though, that Johnson "corrected" Guthrie's debates for at least fifteen issues of the magazine, yet left few discernible signs.

Another section of the "Historical Chronicle" in which Johnson seems to have taken an extensive part, if indeed he was not
its originator, was "Foreign Books." This department was first
added to the magazine in November 1741 and ran intermittently
until September 1744. These articles are generally little more than
listings of various books published on the continent, with an occasional sentence of commentary. It seems likely that such a compilation would have been inspired by Johnson, for in later life
he several times suggested undertaking a review of foreign scholarship.[7] From his earliest correspondence with Cave, Johnson
proved himself interested in raising the intellectual level of the
magazine, and although there is little in the way of "review" in
the brief notes that were appended to select titles, the lists still
served the highly useful function of announcing to English readers the productions of foreign authors.

Each monthly installment was a haphazard collection. Some titles were probably recent imports to be found in the bookstalls of London. Others were the personal acquisitions of Cave's friends, such as the life of Baratier sent to Miss Carter by the deceased youth's father.[8] Still others had not yet made the trip across the Channel, but were probably noted from advertisements. One such example is the entry for *Davidis Arnoldi Conradi Cryptographia Denudata,* which is given the following terse Johnsonian reflection: "The natural Curiosity of Mankind to discover what is industriously hidden from them, cannot but procure a favourable Reception to *the Art of Decifering.*" But the editor of "Foreign Books" had never seen the work. Two months later he announced that "we have received from our Correspondent in *Holland Davidis Arnoldi Conradi Cryptographia* . . . and finding it very curious, shall give our Readers a Translation of it."[9] The list, then, was not evaluative, but enumerative: it did not purport to select the best works of foreign scholarship, merely to list what came to the editor's attention. It was a compilation rather than a review of foreign books, and its editors had no need of deep insight or critical acumen.[10]

This department of the magazine followed the characteristic boom-and-bust syndrome of Johnson's editorial undertakings. "Foreign Books" appeared monthly from November 1741 through May 1742, and with only two omissions through the rest of the year. It then went into serious decline, appearing only four times in 1743 and twice in 1744.[11] The frequency of "Johnsonian" observations also declined, although not the frequency of commentary in general. By 1744 the entire concept had changed; in the two installments that appeared that year, the list of titles was replaced by the epitome of a single work in a style that is clearly not Johnson's. A feeble attempt was being made to keep the concept of a foreign book section alive; but without Johnson's interest or energy, it was not viable. Yet even in the period of Johnson's deepest involvement he can hardly be thought of as the author of "Foreign Books," for the enumerative nature of most of the installments prevents us from assigning "authorship" to anyone. There is no reason to believe that even in a single installment, all the entries were the work of one person. Johnson's contributions were frequent and fundamental, especially early on, but he was just one of several compilers who gave the department its varying character. And it is not so much the occasional observations sprinkled throughout various articles that demonstrates Johnson's most significant contribution, but the simple fact that the magazine bothered to compile such a list at all.

Beyond "Foreign Books" and "Foreign History," we find few traces of Johnson's style in the "Historical Chronicle." He was perhaps responsible for a note encouraging contributions to the building of the Devon and Exeter Hospital, for an introductory sentence to the account of Walpole's resignation, and for the commentary on a "flying Warlike Machine";[12] but for the most part Cave or his regular compilers continued their monthly duties with little need of Johnson's services. His direct stewardship may have been limited to those aspects of the "Chronicle" that he seemed particularly well-fitted to improve; nevertheless, his counsel may have been pervasive and general.

Outside the "Historical Chronicle" Johnson's editorial responsibilities appear to have remained much as they had been before. On occasion he added a headnote or supplied a disdainful reflection on the periodical papers, but with no greater frequency than in the past.[13] As we shall see, after August 1742, Johnson became involved in several projects, the most significant of which, the Harleian catalogue, took him away from Cave's workrooms for long periods. From that time his editorial work, although perhaps consisting of regular and prescribed duties, was probably accomplished during irregular appearances at the Gate. A Johnsonian "Foreign History" in one issue but not in the next probably resulted from the conjunction of a fortuitous arrival and an immediate need. From his earliest days in Cave's employ Johnson may have aided in selecting and editing the contributions of Cave's correspondents, but even in this his help may have become difficult to rely on. Nevertheless, debates still had to be done, and when this need brought Johnson to the Gate, Cave could have readily pressed him to select a month's poems or shorten an excessively long essay. There were, we may be sure, a number of silent contributions that Johnson made to the magazine even in 1743, a period of few obvious pieces beyond the debates, but the exact nature and extent of these is beyond discovery. There is, though, one area where we find Johnson developing a surprisingly strong interest, even to the point of arrogating to himself the role of universal commentator, and that is the field of economics.[14]

The focus of the magazine's attention, as well as the nation's, was the woolen trade. Woolen manufactures, the principal component of English overseas trade, had been hurt badly over several decades by French competition. This was particularly galling because the English believed the French woolen industry to be dependent on high-grade English or Irish wool.[15] Although exporting raw wool had long been forbidden, the depressed state of the industry in England increased the pressure on sheep raisers to find illegal markets. As smuggling grew, the mercantilist wisdom of the day sought for solutions in tighter restrictions on trade. The magazine, in the natural course of its affairs, began to mirror the general concern.[16]

In October and November 1740, Cave printed extracts from a pamphlet entitled *The Consequences of Trade,* a call for the public adoption of a scheme by Samuel Webber to prevent smuggling by the mandatory registration of raw wool. The pamphlet appeared largely without comment, but in the January 1741 issue of the magazine, a note was added at the foot of the table of contents attacking one of its assertions. In the ensuing months, a controversy arose between the magazine and the supporters of Webber's scheme, with Johnson contributing the magazine's lengthiest defense. But nothing definitely attributable to Johnson at this point could be called economic commentary; he merely countered the challenges of Cave's adversaries as he had done two years before.[17]

The circumstances involved in publishing another pamphlet at the end of 1741 elicited from Johnson his first significant economic commentaries. A year earlier the Commons had become enraged when one William Cooley distributed at the door of the House a pamphlet entitled *Considerations upon the Embargo of the Provision of Victual,* a notorious attack on Walpole and his administration insinuating that the embargo on the exportation of Irish cattle had been precipitated not in hopes of starving the French and Spanish in time of war, but in order to enrich certain "Contractors for Provision for the Publick" and through them certain "great Men." Cooley and two printers were committed to prison for producing and distributing "a malicious and scandalous Libel, highly and most injuriously reflecting upon a just and wise act of his Majesty's Government."[18] When Cave reprinted the entire pamphlet in the magazine for December 1741, Johnson intruded into the text a series of "remarks" set off in italics refuting many of the pamphlet's contentions.[19]

The pamphlet was a useful inclusion in the magazine, for it

provided the subject of Johnson's Parliamentary debate "on a seditious paper," which appeared in the 1741 Supplement, and it added counterpoint to the debate on the Corn Bill, which was reported in the magazine for May and June, 1742. The remarks themselves may have served a dual purpose. First, they added fresh insights into the year-old controversy. The embargo had been intended to prevent Irish grain and beef from feeding Spanish and French forces. The pamphleteer had argued that it would result in a slight inconvenience to the enemy, but an "extravagant loss" to Ireland and the colonies. Johnson could discuss the pamphleteer's speculations in terms of the war's actual progress: "the Event has since seem'd to justify the Measures which are here examin'd. The *French* fleet is well known to have returned from *America* without Effect for want of Provisions; and it is probable that the long Inactivity of the *Spanish* Squadron may be imputed to the same Cause."[20] Second, an attempted refutation might screen Cave from any charge that he was propagating a libel: the Commons might bridle at seeing a condemned pamphlet given greater circulation than ever before, but they could hardly complain if the printer included a systematic attempt to refute it. Nevertheless, policy may have had nothing at all to do with the inclusion of the remarks, for we cannot rule out the simple possibility that Johnson was annoyed by what he read and determined to confute it.[21]

Johnson's remarks on the embargo pamphlet tell us surprisingly little about his economic views. From these remarks we can readily deduce that he had no love for the Dutch or their passionate belief in the primacy of trade, but the majority of his observations are political rather than economic. He frequently provides common sense explanations of the motives of the government in response to the pamphleteer's innuendo. To the question why Walpole should seek an act of Parliament to proclaim the embargo rather than rest on the royal prerogative, Johnson responded: "The Reason might perhaps be no more than the Desire which is natural to every Man, of avoiding the *Odium* of an unpopular Act, at the Approach of a new Election."[22] Nor was he afraid to assert the government's right to impose economic hardship on Ireland for the sake of the conduct of the war. Johnson brushed aside his author's lament of the "deplorable ruin" to be visited on Ireland with the insensitive reflection that "Provinces are sometimes laid waste, that they may neither shelter nor supply the Enemy."[23] Sovereign authority is not to be questioned, not even on the grounds of a general distress; this is a theme that years later Johnson would return to when other overseas "provinces" were to complain of the motherland's economic controls.

Soon after Johnson's critical analysis of the embargo pamphlet, the magazine showed renewed interest in the woolen trade. Although Cave had long since stopped sparring with Webber, the public controversy over what to do about the exportation of wool had not abated. Numerous projectors had offered alternatives to Webber's scheme, and the country was now faced with a surfeit of pamphlets on how to proceed. For the February issue Johnson attempted an overview of the entire problem, providing one of his most interesting editorial accomplishments, as well as the most sophisticated discussion of economic matters to be found in the magazine up to that time.

The *Gentleman's Magazine* for February 1742 devotes seven pages to the analysis of four schemes for preventing the exportation of wool, three differing greatly from Webber's, one attempting to fine-tune his original plan. But rather than merely abridging the several pamphlets, Johnson broke each one down into its constituent parts and crafted from these a more instructive and clearly organized whole.[24] First he epitomized each scheme separately and with little comment. These he followed with a list of the "Causes of the Declension of the Woollen Trade," comprising observations gleaned from the four pamphlets under consideration. Next he added a series of "Objections to Mr. Webber's Scheme," also extracted from the pamphlets. To each of these last two sections, but especially to the objections to Webber, he added notes, set off from the extracts in italics. By this three-part structure he managed to compress the essence of four lengthy pamphlets—their authors' solutions to the problem, their estimations of its causes, and their objections to the best-known proposal on the topic—into the compass of five and a half pages of the magazine. But Johnson was not yet finished; he added his own observations on each of the four schemes, along with seven provisions "which seem necessarily to be required in any Plan that shall be offered for this Purpose." The whole is a triumph of organization, clarity, and incisiveness.

Johnson's interest in the wool trade did not end here, although this was certainly its fullest flowering. In the next issue of the magazine Cave printed an abstract of a fifth scheme, this one "prepared by the Commissioners for Trade, and laid before Parliament," to which Johnson added sixteen critical observations.[25] These observations, extending to nearly three columns in the magazine, provide his most detailed critique of any single plan. After a ten-month hiatus, Johnson returned to the wool question in January 1743, abridging two pamphlets—*The Grasier's Advocate* and *An Enquiry concerning the Importation of Irish Cattle*—and intruding commentary. At this point Johnson disappeared from the forefront of the debate.[26]

In all his observations on the wool trade, Johnson offered no challenge to the mercantilist ideas of his day.[27] In his dissection of the schemes for preventing the exportation of wool, he merely examined the probable success of the various proposals. Each projector had suggested a plan by which the government would intervene in the mercantile system—by taxes on raw wool and bounties on exported cloth, by extraordinary price supports, by an excise, or by a registry. Johnson avoided any analysis of the underlying economic principles of each scheme; he merely considered its practicability.[28] Although he showed great perspicacity in his observations, his approach was largely that of a thoughtful layman: he used the most convincing arguments and calculations of each of the authors to illuminate the limitations of the others; he demonstrated no independent stock of fact or theory. Nevertheless, his analyses show a mind alert to the myriad complications of an economic system, to the inescapable fact that the easing of pressure on one segment of the economy is liable to increase pressure on another. His last remarks, those on the two pamphlets of January 1743, are acutely discerning in this manner. But perhaps the most curious aspect of all his reflections is that the one scheme to receive his unqualified support—that the Irish be encouraged to breed cattle rather than sheep and to sell their beef to foreign markets[29]—seeks to regulate the quantity of wool indirectly by forces within the marketplace rather than by direct government control. I am not here suggesting that Johnson was a prophet of free trade, merely that when given the task of analyzing schemes for governmental intervention, he could find none without objection.

In fact, like his remarks on the embargo pamphlet, Johnson's commentaries on the wool trade tell us much more about his political views than about his understanding of economics. Of the seven provisions that he suggested be made part of any scheme to prevent exportation, only one is expressly economic—that bounties be offered to lower the price of English cloth at foreign markets—and one other regulatory—that no wool be conveyed in sea-going vessels. The rest relate to the administration of the scheme: that a time limit be set; that oaths be avoided except in the case of prosecution; that the people choose the enforcing officers through their parishes; that some means be found to regulate the conduct of the patentees; and that heavy fines rather than death be the penalty for offenses.[30] The first shows a man wary of experimentation, the last one who hates cruelty; the rest bespeak a distrust not of governmental authority generally, but of its local manifestations. He will not have merchants daily tempted to perjure themselves, nor will he permit the townsman to be tyrannized over by a stranger who obtained his potentially lucrative post by bribing a corrupt patentee. In short, the horrors of the excise were to be avoided. Johnson made this explicit in his rejection of the scheme presented by Joshua Gee in his *Impartial Enquiry into the Importance of our Woollen Trade:*

> This Scheme approaches more nearly to a probability of Success than either of the former, though it is defective in not providing a Repayment of the Duty on Wool for that Cloth which is carried to foreign Markets. . . .
> The chief Objection to this Scheme is, that it must be executed by Excise, that it must reduce innumerable Multitudes to a State of Slavery.[31]

Such alarmist rhetoric at first seems out of place amidst Johnson's carefully reasoned reflections; but if the response is not a reasoned one, that is because the question of imposing an excise was beyond reason. An excise permitted the invasion of a man's property without evidence of wrongdoing: this was no affront to abstract liberty but a direct assault on individual rights. The lesson of Walpole's ill-fated excise scheme of 1733 was clear, fresh, and lasting in Johnson's mind: Englishmen despised the exciseman's surveillance far more than they desired a distributed tax burden or regulated trade.[32] Perhaps the dominant theme of Johnson's observations on the wool trade is that when government regulation finally comes, it must be benign.

As we have seen, the great expansion of Johnson's editorial duties—his "Foreign Histories," the beginning of "Foreign Books," and the most extensive of his economic commentaries—occurred between July 1741 and June 1742. These twelve months, almost totally devoted to the magazine, also saw Johnson's last major outpouring of miscellaneous pieces. During the spring of 1742, as the number of pages given over to the debates decreased in its normal yearly cycle, Johnson again filled out the several issues. In March he contributed an essay on the recently printed memoirs of the Duchess of Marlborough and the first installment of a translation of *Cryptographia Denudata* ("The Art of Deciphering"), one of those unusual subjects that could seize his imagination.[33] In April he added "An Account of the Life of Peter Burman," the abridged translation of a Latin funeral oration; in May, the supplementary notes to the "Life of Barretier"; and in June, an "Essay on Du Halde's *Description of China*," comprising in large part abridgments and paraphrases of select chapters from Cave's long-delayed project.[34] But just as his editorial contributions slackened with the coming of summer, so did his miscellaneous essays. Although installments of the *Cryptographia* and of the Du Halde essay continued to appear through September, Johnson ceased offering any new works in June.

For the next eighteen months Johnson wrote little prose, beyond the debates of course, specifically for the magazine: the only notable pieces include the prefaces for 1742 and 1743 and an essay on the Crousaz-Warburton controversy intended to call to public notice Johnson's translation of the *Commentaire*, which Cave had re-issued late in 1741, and copies of which must have still been cluttering his warehouse in the early months of 1743.[35] Johnson, it is obvious, had lasted only a year as the magazine's mainstay. Although he would continue the debates at least through the end of 1743, by the end of summer 1742, he had little time to devote to anonymous letters to Mr. Urban. He had turned to other things.[36]

This is not to say that no other Johnsonian pieces appeared in the magazine for 1742 and 1743. Cave was not so foolish as to have such a talented friend writing miscellaneous pieces for other projects and not make some use of them. Late in 1742 Cave printed two Johnsonian compositions done with other ends than the magazine in mind. In November Cave himself had published an edition of Thomas Sydenham's works,[37] for which he

had enlisted Johnson to write the life of the great English physician. Cave then inserted the life in the December magazine. In
the fall of 1742, Johnson had begun to compile a catalogue of
the Harleian Library for the bookseller Thomas Osborne. Cave
also seized upon the published proposals for this work, which
consisted largely of Johnson's "Account of the Harleian Library,"
and inserted them in the same issue.[38] In each case the appearance of Johnson's piece can be seen as an attempt to stimulate
interest in a publishing venture while also allowing Cave to bring
more of Johnson's excellent prose to his readers.

In addition, Cave appears to have solicited Johnson for more
poetry, but the translator-biographer-cataloguer was unwilling or
unable to rouse himself to fresh composition. In July 1743 he
submitted four poems to the magazine, all done years before,
though revised now for publication.[39] Prolonged badgering appears to have been the only way to stimulate Johnson to write
verse at this time. During the period of his most extensive involvement in the magazine, from December 1741 through December 1743, only one freshly penned piece of his verse appeared in its poetry pages, a translation into Latin of Pope's verses
on his grotto; and this, which appeared three months after the
quartet of early poems just mentioned, is prefaced with the apol-
ogy that it was "the casual amusement of half an hour, during
several solicitations to proceed."[40] Although it is always dangerous to postulate some form of intellectual or creative paralysis,
the facts here seem to indicate some such problem. One can point
to *London,* Johnson's only truly successful literary attempt to this
point, and wonder why he did not return to Juvenal. Dodsley,
now a friend and not a mere business acquaintance, would certainly have been willing to publish more satires "by Samuel Johnson, the author of *London.*" But Johnson's poetic energy was apparently sapped, perhaps by the debates, perhaps by the
psychological burden of his continued anonymity, perhaps by fear
that he could not live up to the promise of his earlier poem.
Whatever the cause, Johnson was no longer striving to be a poet.[41]

Three of the shorter prose works of 1742–43—the review of
the memoirs of the Duchess or Marlborough, the reflections on
the controversy between Crousaz and Warburton, and the "Life
of Dr. Sydenham"—deserve extended consideration, not because of their art (although Boswell was certainly right to call the
piece on the Duchess's memoirs "a masterly performance"), but

because of the circumstances of publication or the quirks of authorial temperament that render each in some manner unsatisfactory.

The essay on the *Account of the Conduct of the Duchess of Marlborough,* perhaps the finest short piece Johnson wrote for the *Gentleman's Magazine,* comes to us with a curiously weak and apparently hurried ending. This excellent work, with its reflections on the necessary distrust of those who would regulate the world's opinion of their own actions and its thoughtful commentary on the Duchess's characterizations of William, Mary, and Anne, moves smoothly through its generous allotment of seven columns of the magazine. But the essay comes to a sudden halt with the following reflection:

> The inferior Characters, as they are of less Importance, are less accurately delineated; the Picture of *Harley* is at least partially drawn, all the Deformities are heighten'd, and the Beauties, for Beauties of the Mind he certainly had, are entirely omitted.[42]

The essay appears to end carelessly, with an afterthought supplying the place of a conclusion.

Those who read this piece without a thought to the exigencies of periodical publication will perhaps feel that Johnson took insufficient care of the endings of his compositions, but this is to ascribe to hurry or negligence what was the result of editorial rigor. Johnson did not disdain concluding; rather, his essay was trimmed. The table of contents for the March 1742 issue of the magazine, which may have been printed before the essay itself, or at least was not corrected to reflect changes in content, lists several subjects to be covered on the essay's last page: "Of Mr. *Harley,* afterwards E. of Oxford, Mrs. *Masham,* and *Jack Hill,* &c."[43] The brief reflections on Harley are all that remain of this material in the essay's truncated form. To help elucidate his commentary, Johnson appended numerous excerpts from the *Account* in the form of notes, and these, which fill about three of the article's seven columns, may have forced the trimming. Cave decided to omit the concluding matter rather than cut notes already set in type or run on to the following page.[44] Thus an essay that is as carefully developed as any *Rambler* must be thought complete without its conclusion. And although the excisions did not obscure the piece's merit, we cannot help but lament all such radical surgery.

The essay on the Crousaz-Warburton controversy was more roughly handled still. When the two magazine installments of the essay are joined together, they make an odd, poorly constructed whole. The first begins with the assertion that a moderator would be useful in such controversies "who might in some Degree superintend the Debate, restrain all needless Excursions, repress all personal Reflections, and at last recapitulate the Arguments on each side, and who though he should not assume the Province of deciding the Question, might at least exhibit it in its true State."[45] The anonymous Johnson had clearly decided to undertake this role. But, he suggests, before considering the controversy itself, he must redeem the character of Crousaz from the aspersions of Warburton, and to this purpose he offers a short quotation from his own translation of the *Commentaire*. The second installment excerpts three more quotations from the same source, all showing the right-headedness and moral probity of the Swiss theologian. Johnson then makes a feeble exit with the suggestion that if Cave and his readers should be interested, he would "descend to particular Passages, show how Mr. *Pope* gave sometimes Occasion to Mistakes, and how M. *Crousaz* was misled by his Suspicion of the System of Fatality."[46] The clearly stated intentions of the beginning are thus rehearsed as possibilities at the end, while the bulk of the piece comprises quotations demonstrating Crousaz's piety. Johnson abandons his grand design of mediating the dispute and does not mention a single area of contention between the two scholars. Crousaz has been restored to the well-intentioned part of the human race, and that is all.

The fault for this failure in structure is hardly Johnson's, for what appeared in the magazine is merely the *disiecta membra* of a larger essay. The first installment occupies one column in the magazine for March 1743. The second was delayed not for the usual month or two, but for eight months, not appearing until the November issue, long after the magazine's readers would have forgotten the promises of the work's beginning. Indeed, the excerpts from the *Commentary,* bringing to the public's attention once again that pile of books sitting in some warehouse, may have been Cave's only reason for soliciting the article or for printing the second installment after so long a delay. Thus, in the November continuation Johnson ignored his initial intentions, slapping on a makeshift ending. And why should he not have? Coherence had been destroyed by the passage of time, and Johnson certainly had no thought of how the piece would look when the two disparate segments would finally be joined in his collected works. He was writing to the moment, and November called for a different tack than the one he had set out on in February. The circumstances, not the nodding of the author, caused the anomalous structure in which a work that began as a formal essay ended as if it were merely another casual letter to Mr. Urban.

The third piece worthy of special attention, the "Life of Dr. Sydenham," presented Johnson with a challenge different from that of any of his earlier biographies, for of Sydenham little was known. No lengthy account existed that Johnson could paraphrase or abridge to a suitable compass. R. G. Latham's comment a century later sums up the problem admirably:

> The dearth of facts connected with the life of Sydenham has been the complaint of each and all his biographers; and when Dr. Lettsom remarks that Sydenham's biography 'scarcely enlarges beyond the information that he was a soldier; that he told Sir Richard Blackmore, who inquired of him the best books to study in order to acquire medical knowledge, to peruse Don Quixote; that he pursued some short studies; and that he died a martyr to the gout,' we have, contained in a single sentence, not only the expression of regret on the part of the writer, but wellnigh the whole biography itself.[47]

Thus when Cave desired a short life to preface to Swan's translation of Sydenham's work, Johnson was put on his mettle. The result is the most personal, and perhaps the least reliable, of Johnson's early lives.

Johnson's primary source appears to have been Birch's one-page life in the *General Dictionary*.[48] Johnson supplemented this work's sparse facts by dipping into Sydenham's writings themselves, especially the dedication of the *Observationes Medicae* to Dr. Mapletoft. He also referred to Pierre Desault's "Dissertation on Consumptions" for the fact that Sydenham travelled to Montpellier to further his studies. Yet Johnson need not have read Desault, for his close acquaintance with Robert James, who was then compiling the *Medicinal Dictionary*, and his likely contact with Swan gave him other minds to draw on, minds filled with reading in the medical literature of the day. From them he may have imbibed much of the lore of Sydenham, especially the doctor's supposed disdain for formal education.

The "Life of Dr. Sydenham" is a contentious biography. The great physician, a proponent of the empirical method, was noted for being "an exact observer of diseases and their symptoms."[49] Preferring clinical experience to the speculations of his predecessors, he was reputed to have despised all medical texts as inaccurate. But the suggestion that Sydenham practiced medicine without deep study and achieved eminence without owing a profound debt to the experiences and accounts of earlier practitioners was abhorrent to Johnson, and its propagation both odious and pernicious. The life is Johnson's attempt to redeem Sydenham from what he perceived as a slanderous misrepresentation of his character, and then to inculcate the necessity of study and to mortify the vanity of those who would rely on their natural sagacity.

Johnson even had a villain before him when writing this justification of cultural tradition. Sir Richard Blackmore, physician as well as epic poet, had reported several conversations with Sydenham in his *Treatise on the Small-Pox,* where he left the distinct impression that Sydenham not only distrusted conventional treatments but deliberately flouted them. He represents Sydenham as having developed his "cool regimen" for treating the small-pox merely because current practice called for a "train of warm Alexipharmic remedies." Sydenham, he says, had "taken a resolution at his first entering upon the practice of Physick . . . to act directly contrary in all cases to the common method then in fashion among the most eminent Physicians."[50] Johnson was unwilling to believe "that a Man, eminent for Integrity, practised Medicine by chance, and grew wise only by Murder,"[51] a conclusion that Blackmore's statements might readily prompt. Thus he included none of Blackmore's reports in the biography, even though they represented the only authentic source of Sydenham's conversation available to him; he nevertheless thought it necessary to discredit their propagator.

The most famous proof of Sydenham's supposed distrust of medical texts was his recommendation to Blackmore of *Don Quixote* as the book that would best prepare him to practice medicine. Johnson ignored, or missed, the wonderful irony that Sydenham's quip displayed for any true empiric: *Don Quixote* teaches the danger of preferring a world of fanciful formulations to that of the senses. Instead, he turned Blackmore's anecdote against him:

That he recommended *Don Quixote* to *Blackmore,* we are not allowed to doubt; but the Relater is hindered by that Self-love which dazzles all Mankind from discovering, that he might intend a Satire very different from a general Censure of all the antient and modern Writers on Medicine, since he might perhaps mean either seriously, or in jest, to insinuate, that *Blackmore* was not adapted by Nature to the Study of Physic, and that, whether he should read *Cervantes* or *Hippocrates,* he would be equally unqualified for Practice, and equally unsuccessful in it.[52]

With Blackmore thus downed, Johnson proceeded to vindicate Sydenham from aspersions that, although they probably represented quite well Sydenham's real opinions, were unacceptable to his biographer.

Johnson's "defense" of Sydenham is all argument and inference; the only substantive testimony was Blackmore's, and that had been rejected. Sydenham, he argues, could not have despaired of the efficacy of books, for he himself had written several, "and it is not probable that he carried his Vanity so far, as to imagine that no Man had ever acquired the same Qualifications besides himself."[53] He could not have despised schools, for he spent several years at Oxford: "Nor was he satisfied with the Opportunities of Knowledge which *Oxford* afforded, but travelled to Montpellier . . . in quest of further Information . . .. So far was *Sydenham* from any Contempt of Academical Institutions, and so far from thinking it reasonable to learn Physick by Experiments alone, which must necessarily be made at the Hazard of Life."[54] Johnson's points are well-taken insofar as they go: Sydenham could not have despised all that was to be learned from books and schools. (He was certainly influenced by Hippocrates, another careful observer of diseases.) But Johnson either could not see or would not accept the principle underlying Sydenham's comments to Blackmore—that all authority untested by experiment is suspect, making bedside practice the only effective way to learn medicine. Books, then, are useless without experience, and where books and experience conflict, experience is to be trusted.[55]

In his final attempt to establish Sydenham in the ranks of the learned, Johnson disputed the commonly held belief that the physician wrote his works in English and relied on friends to render them into Latin. He attributes this "false report" to the enemies of formal education, "who were determined, at whatever

Price, to retain him in their own Party, and represent him equally ignorant and daring with themselves." Johnson offered no proof; he merely trusted in the apparent rightness of his cause. He even dismissed John Ward's identification of the translators in his *Lives of the Professors of Gresham College* because "Mr. Ward, like others, neglects to bring any Proof of his Assertion." But Ward had proof; after a ten-month delay, he wrote the magazine with a detailed account of the translation of Sydenham's various works. Unwilling to persist in error, Johnson altered his text on this matter when the life was reprinted in the second edition of Swan's translation; but the alterations have little effect on the overall thrust of Johnson's argument.[56]

The life of Sydenham is perhaps the only example of Johnson turning a biography into a polemic. That he had few facts is no excuse, for the recollections of Blackmore, even if overstated in themselves, should have given Johnson a more complex vision of his subject than that which he conveyed to his readers. One cannot help but be struck by Johnson's hortatory manner, his insistence that "the only Means of arriving at Eminence and Success are Labour and Study."[57] Yet the life is ultimately a failure as biography: Johnson missed his subject totally, substituting a conventional respect for tradition for Sydenham's rigid empirical strain. Outraged by Blackmore's recollections, with their flippant disdain of learning, Johnson abdicated his sympathetic imagination and wrote from his moral principles; and willy-nilly, Sydenham was made to defend those principles.

This survey of Johnson's contributions to the magazine cannot be complete without some consideration of his editorial relationship to the numerous translations that appear in its pages for 1742 and 1743. The lives of Sarpi and Boerhaave were, of course, Johnson's first abridged translations for the magazine. But in 1741 he began translating nonbiographical works: the "Dissertation on the Amazons," the "Jests of Hierocles," and the "Art of Deciphering." By the next year Cave was employing other hands to carry out similar tasks, producing the mixture of the interesting, the odd, and the useful so typical of his periodical. In 1742 we find an essay on "the Vanity of Fame" by Voltaire (January), two papers on Dutch political matters (March), and the radical abridgment of a "Description of a House of Ice, erected at St. Petersburgh" (November); the next year Cave published excerpts from a history of Morocco (April and May 1743), from a pamphlet detailing a new method of estimating Holland's population (April and June), and from a treatise on fortifications, this last comprising almost as much illustration as text (May, July, and November). There is no reason to suspect a single author for all these, certainly not Johnson; but the specter of his influence remains.

These translations form a logical extension of "Foreign Books," making select works immediately available to Cave's readership. Whether Johnson governed the choice of works cannot be determined, but in a few cases he appears to have provided headnotes or introductions. The translation of Willem Kersseboom's disquisition on Holland's population, for example, is prefaced with a paragraph that expounds the characteristically Johnsonian sentiment that works deserve "the Attention and Gratitude of the Publick, as they are calculated for its Benefit."[58] Although we cannot assert from the evidence that Johnson's editorial duties included some form of direct supervision of the abridged translations, he seems to have had considerable influence in this area. And it is not impossible to believe that he might actually have translated one or two of the works mentioned above.[59]

The translations make it clear that Cave was now paying other writers for copy, but of Johnson's co-workers only one can be conclusively identified, Samuel Boyse. Remembered for his antic distress—pawning the books he was to translate, writing in bed covered only by a blanket for want of clothes, wearing paper collars and cuffs—Boyse the writer has been almost totally obscured. But unlike Savage, who trusted solely to luck and to charm, Boyse worked regularly in Grub Street. What a friend called his "awkward sheepish air" (termed by a less sympathetic biographer a "strong propension to groveling")[60] debarred him from acquiring such patrons as Savage regularly impressed and imposed on, then disgusted and abused. Boyse's primary failing was not an unwillingness to write but an impatience to spend; in his career as a Grub-Street hack, he translated an undiscoverable number of titles, prepared an index, compiled a history, and composed enough poetry to fill six moderate volumes. Unfortunately, whatever profits he reaped from these tasks had generally been spent before they had been earned. His constant distress depressed the value of his work, forcing him to part with it for whatever was offered, in many cases much less than it deserved.[61]

Although considered something of a grotesque even in his own day, Boyse was a man of no small talent. Johnson asserted that he could translate well from the French, and his poem *The Deity* was approved of by both Pope and Fielding. From 1740 to 1743, a significant portion of his income arose from his composing poetry specifically for the *Gentleman's Magazine*. His contributions extended from a tribute to Miss Carter to a long celebration (almost five hundred lines) of Lord Cobham's gardens at Stowe.

Boyse was not the first poet Cave had paid; Savage had apparently been remunerated for some of his work. But Savage wrote few pieces especially for the magazine, and his name was perhaps of more interest to Cave than his poetry. Boyse's contributions, though, were regular and extensive: it was with Boyse that Cave contracted for verse by the hundred lines, expecting "the long hundred."[62] In the three months from June through August, 1742, Cave printed almost six hundred lines of Boyse's poetry. But Boyse's name, unlike Savage's, was little known and so of no import; his works appeared in the magazine under two pseudonyms, giving the appearance of greater diversity to Cave's "correspondents."[63]

Nor does it appear that Cave made use of Boyse's poetical talents alone. In a letter of July 1741, Boyse wrote, "I have all last summer been employed by Mr. Cave in French translation, a province highly agreeable to me, and the most profitable business stirring," a statement that suggests more extensive translating than any of the poetical pieces that can be attributed to him at the time.[64] As we have seen with Johnson, it was a short leap from being a regular translator for Cave to becoming an abridger for the magazine. In all likelihood some of the abridged translations that appeared in the magazine during the early 1740s were Boyse's work.

Boyse's extensive involvement in the magazine makes clear the source of Johnson's direct knowledge of so much of his affairs. It is generally accepted that Johnson provided Robert Shiels with many anecdotes for the life of Boyse in Cibber's *Lives of the Poets,* and John Nichols directly acknowledged his indebtedness to Johnson in his own discussion of Boyse. Although Johnson always seems to have been charitable to his fellow laborer (he once collected money from friends shilling by shilling in order to redeem Boyse's pawned clothes), the recollections that he passed on to Shiels and Nichols seem void of any affection. There is none of the good fellowship of the times with Savage, none of the compassion felt for "poor dear Collins," and none of the limited esteem expressed for Cave. Boyse's faults, which apparently went beyond extravagance, seem to have disgusted Johnson and weakened any sympathy. It is in fact through Johnson's anecdotes that the grotesqueness of Boyse's life has been passed down to us, and it is perhaps ironic that it took Nichols the antiquarian, in his reprinting of some of Boyse's letters, to humanize the character.[65]

There remains one more figure worthy of mention, John Hawkesworth, the primary beneficiary of Johnson's departure from the magazine. Only twenty-one and articled to an attorney in Grocers' Alley when his short fables began to appear in the magazine,[66] Hawkesworth was a young man of little learning and no university degree, but possessed of a fine literary sense. His early work was enthusiastically welcomed by the magazine's poetry editor. When his first poem appeared in the issue for June 1741, it was prefaced with a short editorial note apologizing for the lengthy delay in its publication and suggesting that "we shall be glad to hear from the Author." Over the course of the next eleven months, Hawkesworth contributed nine more poems.[67]

Mid-1741 to mid-1742 was, of course, the period of Johnson's most intense editorial activity. There can be little doubt that the magazine's invitation brought the young poet to the Gate, where he was to make the formative friendship of his literary career. The clear moral purpose of Hawkesworth's easy if uninspired couplets would have drawn Johnson to him much as he had been drawn to Elizabeth Carter several years earlier. In his early thirties, living by his pen, highly respected by the printers and booksellers, Johnson provided a useful model for an aspiring writer without connections. That he exerted a profound influence over Hawkesworth is to be read in every page of the younger man's prose.

But the extent to which Hawkesworth was actively involved in the *Gentleman's Magazine* during the early 1740s is not clear. A lengthy hiatus followed the great rush of his poems in 1741 and 1742, the next not appearing until January 1746. The main source of our information about his early affiliation with the periodical is a letter he wrote to David Henry after Cave's death, which gives few specifics and no dates.[68] Cave, as we have seen, had made use of translators other than Johnson during 1742 and 1743, and although Hawkesworth was no Latinist, he could translate from the French. He may have begun his magazine apprenticeship by rendering into English one of the foreign works that dot the magazine during these years.[69]

For the most part, the talents of Hawkesworth and Johnson were so similar that Cave seems to have had little need of the one so long as the other maintained his station. But as Johnson relinquished his various duties, Hawkesworth gradually assumed them. Not only does he appear to have taken up the debates when Johnson laid them down around the beginning of 1744, he also assisted Cave during the second half of the decade much as Johnson had in the first: he edited the magazine's poetry section, rewrote the work of other contributors, and so forth.[70] Although Hawkesworth complained that Cave paid him "less than £30 a year", his editorial role established him as a man of letters. Through this apprenticeship he earned the confidence of the booksellers and the right to attempt the *Adventurer,* a work modeled on the *Rambler* and the next step in his Johnsonian *cursus honorum.*

There are no accounts of the early friendship between the two men, but they formed a sociable, if not a deeply affectionate, connection. After Hawkesworth's move to Bromley in the mid-1740s, Johnson spent a good deal of time in those rural surroundings. It was Hawkesworth to whom Johnson turned when seeking a burial place for his wife, and it was also he, Johnson told Mrs. Thrale, to whom Johnson's biographers would have to go for anecdotes of his early years in London.[71] But Hawkesworth died eleven years before Johnson, and with him was lost a wealth of detail that can never be recovered.

The end of 1743 appears to have put a period to Johnson's extensive involvement in the magazine. Virtually all trace of his style disappeared from its pages with the conclusion of his debates early in 1744.[72] Johnson had not severed all of his ties with Cave—early in 1744 a greatly revised version of the *Life of Barretier* was issued under James Roberts's imprint, but certainly with

Cave's backing; a year later the *Miscellaneous Observations on the Tragedy of Macbeth* emanated from St. John's Gate; and it was Cave who provided the financial backing for Johnson's proposed edition of Shakespeare in 1745. But Johnson had disappeared into the background of the magazine. The debates aside, we can attribute with confidence no more than a few scattered pages of prose throughout the entire year in 1743. By 1744 "Foreign Books" was languishing and "Foreign History" was being carried on by others. But there is a formidable piece of evidence to suggest that Johnson, though providing no more lives, essays, or translations, continued to assist Cave with some aspect of the magazine well into 1745. The Rev. John Hussey wrote Boswell that Johnson "was the actual editor of the *Gentleman's Magazine* from 1738 to 1745 part of both years inclusive; when he told me this, he could not recollect what month he resigned his employ, but I think he took the management of the Magazine upon him at Midsummer."[73] Hussey on the whole seems a reliable source, and the precision of his *terminus a quo,* which agrees exactly with the stylistic evidence in the magazine, gives the *ad quem* added force. Johnson probably continued to help Cave select or trim materials and may have held some regular post, such as editor of the poetry section, which would have left no trace of his style. A day or two each month stolen from other projects would have sufficed for him to fulfill this commitment to Cave, and the extra monthly guinea or two would certainly have been welcome in what appear to have been several lean years for Johnson.

The matter of Johnson's salary must now be confronted, a problem of great importance but of no easy solution. The only testimony we have issues from Dr. Richard Farmer, a friend of Johnson's old age rather than of his youth, and this we have third hand. In the article on Johnson in the *General Biographical Dictionary,* Alexander Chalmers gives the following account:

> By some manuscript memorandums concerning Dr. Johnson, written by the late Dr. Farmer, and obligingly given to the writer of this life by Mr. Nichols, it appears that he was considered as the conductor or editor of the Magazine for some time, and received an hundred pounds per annum from Cave.[74]

Farmer's "memorandums" themselves are lost to us; Nichols, usually so eager to print anything Johnsonian, left no indication of what they might contain.[75] Thus we have no way of knowing their exact nature or ultimate provenance.

Chalmers's assertion, because of its general character, is fraught with problems. A steady salary suggests regular responsibilities; yet Johnson's role in the magazine shifted greatly and frequently. As we have seen, in 1738 and 1739, he was more vigorously employed on two translations than on the magazine itself; during 1740 he contributed little besides the lives of Blake and Drake before the December issue. For the next year and a half his activity increased markedly—translations, abridgments, debates, essays, economic commentary, various compilations in the "Historical Chronicle"—only to be reduced to little more than the debates after midsummer 1742. It is inconceivable that Cave would have parted with a hundred pounds for Johnson's labors of 1740, but whether Johnson's expanded duties might merit such a substantial wage invites deeper probing.

Some hard facts about the number of pages Johnson contributed between 1740 and the end of 1743 help bring the problem into focus. Excluding any editorial services, in the period from May through November, 1740, Johnson wrote approximately twenty-five double-columned pages for the magazine (consisting almost solely of the lives of Blake and Drake), an average of about three and a half pages per issue. From December 1740 through April 1741 his miscellaneous articles, including the two early debates, filled ten pages per issue, a significant increase.[76] But for the next two months he contributed nothing at all. With his assumption of the debates, Johnson's output takes a startling leap: from July through the Supplement, 1741, Johnson wrote approximately one hundred and sixty pages of fresh copy for the magazine, all but four pages constituting debates. This total, which includes none of the "Foreign Histories" or other material from the "Historical Chronicle," represents an increase to over twenty pages per issue. Thus upon taking up the debates Johnson began to contribute five times the copy he had the previous summer, and more than twice what he had done during his most intensive period of fresh composition up to that point. But the next two volumes of the magazine provide the most surprising figures. In the thirteen issues of 1742 (Supplement included), Johnson wrote two hundred and twenty pages of debates and forty pages of miscellaneous articles; the next year, when Johnson's miscellaneous articles dwindled to the page-and-a-half essay on the Crousaz-Warburton controversy, and a single-page preface to the collected volume, the *Gentleman's Magazine* carried two hundred and fifty-eight pages of Johnson's debates.[77] In each of the two consecutive volumes of the magazine, we find nearly identical totals, and surprisingly round ones: in each year Johnson wrote approximately two hundred and sixty pages over the course of thirteen issues, or twenty pages an issue. Mere coincidence is, of course, a possibility, but Cave appears to have been too hard-headed a businessman to have allowed coincidence to govern the payment of his author. A man who contracts for poetry by the hundred lines is just as likely to contract for prose by the hundred pages. The most reasonable conclusion would seem to be that during 1742 and 1743 Johnson was expected to produce a set amount of copy each year for a set fee. His contributions might vary in nature and in amount from issue to issue, but he owed a definite total for each yearly volume. What he failed to produce in the way of miscellaneous writings for 1743 could be made up for by additional debates.

In order to determine whether Cave might possibly have been willing to pay Johnson £100 for these services, it seems useful to compare Johnson's contributions with those of other authors whose salaries are known. Edward Kimber, as we noted in an earlier chapter, was paid a mere £2 per month to edit the *London Magazine,* and Hawkesworth did not fare much better from all his contributions to the *Gentleman's.* He complained of Cave's parsimony in his 1756 letter to David Henry:

> You will be astonished, and I very think not without some degree of indignation, when I tell you that the whole accumulated profit which I derived from my Connection with the late Mr. Cave was less than £30 a year, and that except a set of his Magazines, I never received from him in gratuities of any kind the value of forty shillings.[78]

Hawkesworth's assistance, though perhaps not as extensive as Johnson's, was by no means inconsiderable. That he wrote at least some debates seems very likely. By 1747 he was editing the magazine's poetry section, regularly filling it out with his own contributions. He had revised the work of one of Cave's other hands and provided translations and reviews, as well as miscellaneous editorial services. In his own words, "I had afforded [Cave] such assistance as he knew he could not procure from another, during ten years." Thirty pounds was paltry compensation, but Hawkesworth had never been given a contract; when paying by the job, Cave apparently would only part with trifling sums.[79]

Nevertheless, Cave was not averse to laying out a significant salary for full-time assistance. Hawkesworth had been sorely disappointed when Cave hired a Mr. Daniel "at the yearly salary of sixty pounds, and all the necessaries of Board & Lodging."[80] Daniel, it seems, was to live as well as work at the Gate, like Cave, to eat, drink, and sleep the *Gentleman's Magazine*. When all of the perquisites are counted, Daniel's salary probably approached £80 per year, four-fifths of the amount supposedly paid Johnson; yet we may feel confident that Daniel was not turning out two hundred and sixty pages of fresh copy each year.

The last case is by far the most suggestive. In 1746 Mark Akenside signed a contract with Dodsley to provide a sheet and a half of copy every fortnight for the *Museum* for £100 per year.[81] Akenside was also to "supervise the whole, and to correct the press of his own part." Initially it would seem that Akenside's output of thirty-nine sheets per year would far surpass Johnson's contributions to the *Gentleman's Magazine*, which averaged one and a quarter sheets per issue, or about sixteen sheets per year; but the printing format of the *Gentleman's Magazine*, with its double columns of long primer, makes any simple counting of sheets misleading. A sheet of the magazine could carry twice the copy of a more standard octavo sheet and up to one and a half times the text of a sheet of the *Museum*. The "Life of Blake" provides an illustration: when it first appeared in the magazine, the Blake filled seven pages, just short of a half sheet; but when reset in pica type and printed as a pamphlet, the same text filled fourteen pages, virtually an entire sheet.[82] Thus the quantity of Johnson's prose, though not equaling that of Akenside's, approximates it much more nearly than the brief comparison of sheets suggests. Bargaining for his services, Johnson would rightfully have expected an inordinately high payment per sheet for his original compositions; if one considers that he may have already been due a guinea or two each issue for his editorial contributions, a total of £100 per year is not an impossible figure to accept. But this sum would be valid only during the period from July 1741 through December 1743, when Johnson not only edited portions of the magazine but filled over a third of its pages with his debates and miscellaneous essays.[83] Thus Chalmers's general statement, based on Dr. Farmer's unspecified "memo-

randums," can provide a guideline for estimating Johnson's income during his periods of full commitment to the magazine, but
it seems more reasonable to gauge his suspected earnings during
other periods by the example of Hawkesworth. Regular editorial
help and a modicum of fresh prose might earn a Johnson or a
Hawkesworth £30 a year from Cave. Their earnings might de-
viate up or down from this figure, depending on Cave's needs
and their willingness to provide original copy. But extraordinary
pay certainly required extraordinary efforts, and these Johnson
appears to have been willing to give for no more than two and
a half years.[84]

One cannot end without attempting to estimate Johnson's
overall contribution to the magazine. Of primary importance was
his general upgrading of the magazine's content. From his first
letter to Cave, Johnson's constant concern seems to have been
raising the intellectual level of the periodical. Before his advent,
Cave relied on correspondents to fill his columns. The magazine
at this time certainly reflected the passions of many of Johnson's
contemporaries, but it bore no resemblance to a literary monthly.
In the magazine for 1737, mathematical problems abound, some
extending to three or four pages. Once Johnson appeared, these
were drastically reduced, surviving primarily in problems of as-
tronomy, which may have been maintained by Cave because they
often called for illustrations. Before Johnson, the primary topics
for "original dissertations" were theological. In the first half of
1737 alone one finds a country curate's scruples with the liturgy,
a country parson's answer, and the country curate's defense; an
argument against "dipping" in Baptism; a Quaker's attack on tithes
and the Quaker answered; "Prescience and Liberty inconsistent"
and "Prescience and Liberty not inconsistent." Such controversies
continued to swell out the magazine through the first half of the
next year. But Johnson's arrival gradually changed all this. The
"Pamphilus" letters provided an interesting diversion from such
wrangling, and the "Life of Sarpi" represented a major step for-
ward in both variety and quality. Johnson's subsequent lives, essays, and debates brought a consistent flow of correct, thoughtful
prose to the magazine's mixed audience. And with the introduction of "Foreign Books" and the increased number of translations, Cave's readers were brought into intellectual contact with

their European neighbors, many for the first time. Under Johnson's influence the magazine broke the insular and narrowly humanistic bonds in which Cave's limited vision had constrained it.

Johnson's efforts at improving quality, though, were often subverted by the unrewarding nature of the tasks put before him. The debates under his charge were perhaps more readable and more trenchant than those of his predecessors or competitors, but in this area he merely did well what Guthrie had already done competently. His contributions to "Foreign History," although adding a new discursive voice, blend so greatly into the work of others that it is impossible to tell their exact nature and extent. And his other various contributions—notes, advertisements, etc.—could have been done by anyone, though perhaps not as interestingly.

Johnson's overall contribution is best summed up in this manner: he found the magazine amateur and left it professional. By 1743 the *Gentleman's Magazine* was no longer Cave and a few nameless assistants trimming essays and gathering material for the "Historical Chronicle," but Johnson and Boyse and Hawkesworth and others. As Cave accustomed himself to the aid of such men, he relied less on the inanities of his correspondents. Competition from the *London Magazine* had prodded him in this direction, and pressure from that quarter had not abated. Johnson's exceptional abilities had elevated the quality and expanded the scope of both periodicals as each strove to outdo the other. Cave could never return to religious disputes and mathematical problems and still hope to maintain his circulation. Johnson had been an expedient when hired in 1738; by 1743 he, or someone like him, was a necessity.

CHAPTER IX

IN SEARCH OF REPUTATION

Mere unassisted merit advances slowly, if, what is not very common, it advances at all.

Johnson, *Life of Morin*

The summer and fall of 1741, as I have suggested above, appear to represent a period of both disappointment and commitment for Johnson: he had abandoned his hopes for *Irene* and given himself over totally to the business of filling the *Gentleman's Magazine*, first through the debates, then through his careful attention to various other departments of the magazine. But as we have also seen, this complete commitment was short-lived. For a year he labored diligently and resolutely under Cave, but by the summer of 1742 his effort began to decline. His various works for the magazine must have seemed like so much marching in place: so long as he devoted himself to debates and anonymous articles, his reputation failed to advance. Not content to remain Cave's anonymous author, in the autumn of 1742 Johnson began a series of projects that at first supplemented and then replaced his efforts for the magazine.

The first of these extramural activities, though, was undertaken not for ambition's sake but friendship's. In June 1741 Johnson had lent a hand to an old Lichfield friend, Robert James, who had decided to establish his own reputation as a physician by publishing a massive medical dictionary.[1] James, six years Johnson's elder, had often made one of the party that had met at Gilbert Walmesley's residence during the late 1720s and early 1730s. He had only arrived in London in 1740, after having practiced in Lichfield, Sheffield, and Birmingham, yet by the end of the year he had completed his first book, *A New Method of Preventing and Curing the Madness Caused by the Bite of a Mad Dog.* Its publisher, Thomas Osborne, was sufficiently convinced of

James's abilities to agree to publish the mammoth *Medicinal Dictionary*, projected to fill three large folio volumes. Whether James sought or Johnson offered help is unknown, but the proposals for the *Dictionary*, dated June 24, 1741, bear many signs of Johnson's style, especially in their first eight paragraphs.[2]

As Johnson plunged headlong into the debates, James began to compile his *Medicinal Dictionary*. "Compile," rather than "compose," is certainly the proper term, for the *Medicinal Dictionary* consists largely of translations, abridgments, and extracts from the best-known medical texts of the day. Scientific information was often lifted directly from the works of such noted medical men as Boerhaave and Friedrich Hoffmann; and the history of medicine, manifested in a series of biographies, was gleaned from Daniel Le Clerc's *Histoire de la Médecine,* James Douglas's *Bibliographiae Anatomicae Specimen,* and John Freind's *History of Physick.* Such work, we may be sure, offered no great lure to Johnson; it differed little from his duties for Cave. Nevertheless, the *Medicinal Dictionary* contains a few scattered signs of Johnson's style, bearing out his statement to Boswell that he helped James not only with the proposals but "also a little in the Dictionary itself."[3] That help, which if extensive has largely escaped detection, seems to have been limited to several minor tasks: he revised his own "Life of Boerhaave," which is reprinted in its entirety, though with some un-Johnsonian additions; he contributed a life of Alexander Trallianus, epitomized from Freind's *History;* he edited the lives of Actuarius and Aegineta, which do not for the most part bear the marks of his style but which begin with passages that seem typically his; and he capped James's first volume with a short but elegant dedication to Dr. Richard Mead.[4] This last constitutes his only acknowledged contribution, for he owned it to Mrs. Thrale and apparently also to the Rev. John Hussey, who reported that Johnson received five guineas for it.[5] Other small editorial tasks or well-disguised bits of translation may still lurk undetected in the *Dictionary*'s three huge volumes, but there is no reason to believe that such pieces would be numerous, significant, or lengthy.

In the summer of 1742, after a year of the magazine's editorial and compositional rigors, Johnson again found the will to write drama. For reasons that we can only guess at, he had shunned any serious pursuit of poetry in the four years that followed the success of *London;* perhaps the bleak prospect of a lifetime of writing debates determined him to re-tread old paths in his search for the solace of reputation. In a letter to John Taylor, post-marked August 10, 1742, he laid out his plan: "I propose to get Charles of Sweden ready for this winter, and shall therefore, as I imagine be much engaged for some Months with the Dramatic Writers into whom I have scarcely looked for many years."[6] The subject may have been suggested to Johnson by Voltaire's an-nouncement that he was collecting materials towards augmenting his extremely successful *Histoire de Charles XII.*[7] Although antag-onistic to much of Voltarie's thought and contemptuous of his character, learning, and criticism, Johnson nevertheless per-ceived the acuteness of Voltaire's mind and admired his narrative abilities, calling the *Histoire de Charles XII,* if William Seward is to be believed, "one of the finest pieces of historical writing in any language."[8]

But Johnson's choice of subject was probably not suggested by Voltaire's notice alone, for Charles's character still amazed Eu-rope, and his intrigues in favor of the Pretender endeared him to Jacobites. For the tragic poet, his life presented the chance to explore the ambiguity of human action: Charles's courage, res-olution, and physical endurance—he lived as a veritable person-ification of the martial virtues—contributed equally to his nine years of victory, to his disastrous defeat at Pultowa, and to his untimely death before Frederikshald. A man above the common vices of royalty, his virtues at one time glorified his nation and at another threatened it with disaster.

That Johnson ever committed a single line to paper seems doubtful, for his natural indolence and his perusal of sources would only have had to dissipate the spare hours of six weeks before another project presented itself. Before September was out, Thomas Osborne would offer Johnson a position that re-quired more regular labor than the projected drama and that lacked any possibility of artistic acclaim, but one that promised more certain profits while offering the chance of scholarly notice.

On June 16, 1741, Edward Harley, the second Earl of Ox-ford, died in his house in Dover Street, London, his death brought about in part by years of anxiety over this straitened finances.

His passions had been building and collecting, neither of which he indulged judiciously. At Wimpole, his Cambridgeshire estate, he had erected an elegant chapel (decorated by Sir James Thornhill) and added an entire wing for his magnificent library, including "a grand room after the designs of James Gibbs." Nearer London, he laid out plans for the development of Cavendish Square on the site of Tyburn manor, which his wife had inherited from her father. There, on the southern limits of St. Marylebone parish, he had erected another fine house, an elegant structure including twelve rooms and two galleries built especially for his printed books.[9]

The library itself was a remarkable collection. The printed books alone are generally estimated to have numbered around 50,000, including particularly fine holdings in incunabula (especially Caxtons) and books printed on vellum. The prints and pamphlets were virtually innumerable.[10] The manuscripts, filling over seven thousand volumes, were housed in one hundred and fifty presses at Dover Street. Harley's passions extended far beyond the library to include coins, Greek and Roman antiquities, engravings, and between five hundred and six hundred "paintings, pictures, [and] portraits."[11] For all of these, it seems, he was likely to pay a premium price.[12] An income of £40,000 a year was insufficient to maintain such habits. The year before his death he was forced to sell Wimpole to Lord Chancellor Hardwicke for £86,740, but even this could not extricate him totally from his difficulties.[13]

Although Oxford had hoped to establish his great collection as a public library,[14] at his death his wife, who apparently shared his extravagance but not his taste or his vision, determined to dispose of the bulk of his collections. The coins, curiosities, antiquities, and paintings (at least those by Italian, French, and Flemish masters) were to be auctioned off immediately by Mr. Cock of Covent Garden, who estimated that the disposal of all the collections, books included, would take four years.[15] Perhaps to rid herself of her husband's clutter more quickly, the Dowager Countess of Oxford decided to sell the library whole. Thomas Osborne, the bookseller from Gray's Inn, first offered £20,000 for it, including the manuscripts, but no deal was struck immediately.[16] Then, in mid-September, 1742, word got abroad that he had indeed purchased the library.[17] The agreement, though, was neither for the entire collection nor for the sum originally offered. The manuscripts at Dover Street were to remain in the family's possession while Osborne acquired the printed books, which had been transferred to the new house in Cavendish Square upon the sale of Wimpole.[18] He paid a mere £13,000, in George Vertue's estimation "the tenth part of what the Cost probably was." William Oldys noted that "the binding only of the least part of them, by his lordship, cost him £18,000."[19] Osborne, it would seem, had made quite a deal. But a bookseller buys libraries not to preserve but to disperse books; thus one of the greatest collections ever gathered on English soil, in the accumulation of which a great part of a great fortune had been expended, was to be sold piecemeal.

The break-up of the library was particularly distressing to scholars, for Oxford had generously opened its doors to them.[20] Well before the sale to Osborne had sealed the library's fate, antiquarians and bibliophiles had already begun to lament its inevitable dispersal. Roger Gale expressed the hope that Oxford University might purchase the manuscripts,[21] but no one was sanguine about the books. The government had not yet fully realized its role as the preserver of the nation's cultural and intellectual heritage and so was not prepared to expend public funds to purchase books.[22] The universities were relatively impoverished; the Bodleian, dependent largely on benefactions for the funds used to expand its collections and sustained by an endowment hardly sufficient to maintain it, was in no position to bid against Osborne.[23] In 1710 Oxford University had managed to offer £3000 for Isaac Vossius's library, whose sale to the University of Leyden was lamented as a national tragedy; but this sum was trifling in comparison to what would have been needed to purchase and display Harley's treasures.[24] A number of private collectors could have surpassed Osborne's paltry offer, but in providing a suitable setting for his newly acquired prize, the purchaser could easily have doubled or tripled his initial outlay. Only Osborne, who had no intention of keeping the books, was free from the predicament of ostentatiously displaying them. His agreement with Oxford's widow apparently permitted him at least nine months' use of the Marylebone library, and the first sale was conducted on its premises.[25] Afterwards, Osborne could display without pomp as many volumes as his Gray's Inn shop would hold, warehousing the rest. Edward Harley had amused and impoverished himself not only by buying books but also by building places to keep them; his contemporaries, some perhaps chastened by his experience, others addicted to less dignified pleasures, chose not to squander their wealth in his particular manner. Before Oxford's death, the library appeared a monument to his foresight, afterwards, only to his extravagance.

Osborne's task in disposing of his new property was not an easy one. Selling a library volume by volume could be expected to take years. The library of Henry Vander Marck, at least a part of which was catalogued and set to scale at The Hague in 1712, was still sufficiently in the hands of the proprietors in 1727 to warrant a fresh catalogue of the remaining stock.[26] Working in Osborne's favor was the reputation of the Harleian Library itself. The rarity of the books, the quality of Oxford's copies (he always demanded the finest specimens available and often traded inferior copies for superior ones with his booksellers), and the elegance of his bindings would have attracted any bargain-hunting collector. In addition, a good many sightseers might be drawn to Marylebone simply for a chance to tour the late Earl's elegant rooms and perhaps to purchase a souvenir bound in the splendid Harleian manner. Nevertheless, Osborne was hardly the man to please a learned or sophisticated clientele. He was devoid of taste or learning, boasting in his advertisements of having "all the pompous editions of the Classicks and Lexicons."[27] He was abusive to authors and ungracious to customers. In the *Life of Pope* Johnson described him as "a man entirely destitute of shame, without sense of any disgrace but that of poverty."[28] Not Pope himself was safe from Osborne's shenanigans. The bookseller had dared to advertise the elegant subscription quartos of Pope's *Iliad* for sale at half price when in fact he possessed no such copies at all; he had merely trimmed the margins of the inexpensive folios. For this Pope would enter him in the 1743 *Dunciad,* pitting him against Curll in a urinating contest and leaving him to walk home defeated with a chamber pot atop his head.[29] Yet his impassive dullness, as Johnson phrased it, was proof against all such attacks, and in his graceless, impudent, ignorant manner he accumulated a fortune of over £40,000.

In September 1742, though, Osborne was uncharacteristically politic. Apparently convinced that the good will of men of learning was needed if his sale was to succeed, he eschewed the simple expedient of having a few copyists compile a catalogue and turned instead to Samuel Johnson. Johnson's first task was to draw up

a scheme for a catalogue. On October 4, Osborne wrote to Thomas
Birch, enclosing Johnson's scheme and soliciting Birch's advice
and his good will. Five days later Johnson dined on the premises
of the library in Marylebone with Birch, Martin Folkes, and William Jones.[30] All three men were members of the Royal Society,
Folkes its president, and all were collectors with substantial libraries of their own. Osborne may have been seeking the Society's informal *imprimatur* for his catalogue, hoping that their approval would quell the common lament over the library's dispersal.

The good will of such men was especially necessary to Osborne, for he intended to sell the first part of his catalogue for
ten shillings. He had to convince the public that the two volumes
he was about to produce constituted not a simple sale catalogue,
which all would have expected for free, but a significant piece
of scholarship.[31] It was largely to this end that Johnson composed
his "Account of the Harleian Library," issued as part of the "Proposals for Printing . . . *Bibliotheca Harleiana*." The "Account" begins with an appropriate defense:

> To solicit a Subscription for a Catalogue of Books exposed to
> Sale, is an Attempt for which some Apology cannot but be nec-
> essary, for Few would willingly contribute to the Expence of Vol-
> umes, by which neither Instruction nor Entertainment could be
> afforded, from which only the Bookseller could expect Advan-
> tage, and of which the only Use must cease, at the Dispersion of
> the Library.
>
> Nor could the Reasonableness of an universal Rejection of
> our Proposal be denied, if this Catalogue were to be compiled
> with no other View, than that of promoting the Sale of the Books
> which it enumerates, and drawn up with that Inaccuracy and
> Confusion which may be found in those that are daily published.
>
> But our Design, like our Proposal, is uncommon, and to be
> prosecuted at a very uncommon Expence, it being intended, that
> the Books shall be distributed into their distinct Classes, and every
> Class ranged with some Regard to the Age of the Writers; that
> every Book shall be accurately described; that the Peculiarities of
> Editions shall be remarked, and Observations from the Authors
> of Literary History occasionally interspersed, that, by this Cata-
> logue, we may inform Posterity, of the Excellence and Value of
> this great Collection, and promote the Knowledge of scarce Books,
> and elegant Editions. For this Purpose, Men of Letters are en-
> gaged, who cannot even be supplied with Amanuenses, but at an
> Expence above that of a common Catalogue.[32]

Such a catalogue would certainly have been worth Osborne's price, and such a one we may be sure Johnson intended to compile. But as Johnson often reminds us, one's highest expectations are seldom realized even when all circumstances appear to favor success. And although the resources needed to create a major contribution to bibliography were certainly to be found in the late Earl's elegant library, an atmosphere conducive to study was not. From the start Johnson was prodded by hurry and watched over by dullness.

The project was doomed to mediocrity before the hopeful proposals issued from the press. The first part of the library, due to be sold the coming April, comprised almost sixteen thousand titles. But the first fascicle of the catalogue, which was to be published serially, was scheduled to appear on December 4, 1742, only two months after work had begun; and the entire first two volumes were to be available in February.[33] Johnson's goal of accurately describing every book, remarking the peculiarities of editions, and interspersing additional commentary could hardly be accomplished by an army of scholars in so little time. And although Johnson did not labor alone in this great effort, the help was by no means equal to the task.

Johnson's co-worker in the project was William Oldys, an antiquarian and bibliographer thirteen years his senior who had achieved some favorable reputation with a *Life of Sir Walter Ralegh* in 1736. Oldys lived by writing for the booksellers, among them Osborne, who in 1737 published Oldys's short-lived periodical the *British Librarian,* "a Compendious Review or Abstract of our most Scarce, Useful, and Valuable Books in all Sciences, as well in Manuscript as in Print." Oldys had apparently begun using the Harleian Library for his antiquarian researches as early as 1731 and was eventually rescued from his dependence on the booksellers when Lord Oxford made him his literary secretary in 1739, at the comfortable salary of £200 per annum.[34] But at the Earl's death Oldys was again thrown upon the mercy of the booksellers and again found his way to Osborne.

An indefatigable researcher and a compulsive annotator, Oldys complemented Johnson well. Though lacking Johnson's expansive intellect, he was perhaps better suited to the task of annotating a book catalogue than his temperamentally restless colleague. As a grubber after facts he had few equals, and his *Ralegh* and his later contributions to the *Biographia Britannica* establish him with Birch among the fathers of modern biography. Unfortunately he collected gossip and hearsay as well as facts, and the limits of his judgment are probably best revealed in the reminiscence of one John Taylor that Oldys's proposed life of Shakespeare was to contain "ten years of the life of Shakespeare unknown to the biographers and commentators."[35] Nevertheless, for the job of library cataloguer Oldys was well suited.

As 1742 drew to a close, the late Earl's placid, elegant library on the perimeter of greater London was transformed into a cataloguer's workshop where transcribers listed titles as a degreeless scholar and a compulsive antiquary pored over exquisite texts and bibliographical handbooks. By February the first part of the *Catalogus Bibliothecae Harleianae* was completed, the two volumes appearing on February 28, 1743.[36] These volumes reveal a series of compromises between the demands of scholarship and those of retailing. In the five months that were given over to compiling this part of the catalogue, only a small percentage of the 16,000 entries could be supplied with any significant commentary.[37] The vast majority list nothing more than author, title, and place and date of publication. Many entries, though, include a series of cryptic annotations. Some, like those noting that a book is printed in black letter or ruled in red, would have been of interest to bibliographers as well as collectors; others, indicating the type of leather used in the binding or the presence of gilt on the leaves or spine, of interest only to Osborne's customers. But the catalogue bore definite signs that the scholarly intentions announced in the proposals had been at least in part fulfilled. Latin was used in all annotations and commentaries on books written in the learned languages. French works received French notes. English appears only with English titles, and these are few in the first two volumes of the catalogue. Thus, at least in appearance, Osborne was bringing out a work not for the English tradesman, who might stroll into the sale in search of a few volumes to fill out a shelf, but for the scholars of all nations.

Nevertheless, the public was not convinced of the value of Osborne's catalogue, and a hue and cry was raised against his selling what other booksellers normally gave away. Since the amount of commentary fell so far short of what Johnson had promised in the proposals, Osborne was forced to back down on one point: although he would not yield on his initial price for the two volumes of the catalogue, he permitted them to be exchanged for any book of equal value.[38] Regardless of this accommodation, the sale went poorly, with many of the rare and ancient volumes still on the library's shelves when the first sale closed.

Johnson and Oldys were soon back at work producing two more volumes detailing the portion of the library to be sold in February 1744. The scene of activity shifted as the library was transferred from Marylebone to Osborne's shop at Gray's Inn. Apparently stung by the public resistance to his initial offering, Osborne had his compilers drop much of the academic pretense that characterized part one. The commentaries of the second part, though often longer and more detailed than those in the earlier volumes, were now all done in English to broaden the catalogue's appeal. In addition, many books that remained in the library after the first sale were listed for a second time in the catalogue's third and fourth volumes, with any Latin or French commentary from the first part made English. This practice perhaps more than anything else undermined the catalogue's claim to scholarly notice. It could no longer be considered an exact account of Oxford's collections, for a reader could no longer be sure if the Earl possessed two copies of a work or a single copy listed twice. As a result of these new policies, the character of the work as a sale catalogue gained prominence in the second part.

With the completion of the third and fourth volumes, published on January 7, 1744, Johnson's work on the catalogue appears to have ended. After the second sale, which began in mid-February, a fifth volume was still to be compiled, but apparently without Johnson or Oldys. When this last appeared over a year later (April 1745), it proved to be an unworthy successor to the preceding volumes. The numerous subdivisions of the earlier parts were abandoned, with all books marshalled simply by language and format. Commentary all but disappeared; the little that remained was for the most part gleaned from earlier volumes. The compilers of this volume did little more than transcribe titles and haphazardly alphabetize several sections. Osborne was hardly likely to pay Johnson to do such work. Oldys, on the other hand, had already been given new responsibilities. As the second part of the catalogue neared completion, Osborne made him editor of the *Harleian Miscellany*, the projected reprinting of numerous scarce pamphlets found in Oxford's collections. Although Johnson wrote both the proposals and introduction for the *Miscellany* and was later to add about ten short prefaces to individual pamphlets, he

does not seem to have had a major hand in this work. Thus we
may assume his departure from Osborne's regular service with
the completion of the second part of the catalogue in January
1744. If he remained after this date, Osborne had nothing to
show for it.[39]

The sale on the whole was a great disappointment to Osborne; Johnson assured Boswell that there was not much gained
by it.[40] The English market for old books, even rare ones in excellent condition, was apparently both small and close to being
saturated. Oxford's own extensive purchases had created an artificial demand that dissipated at his death. Although for Johnson the catalogue allowed a chance to work as a scholar and to
pore over books that would normally have been beyond his reach,
the drudgery of the task and the hurry demanded by Osborne
must have soured the experience. By the fall of 1743, Johnson
was already involved in a new project for Cave even though still
employed on the catalogue.[41] From this atmosphere of shared
discontent, one may assume, arose the famous altercation in which
Johnson felled the bookseller with a folio.[42] Unfortunately, this
event has received most of the attention given to Johnson's association with Osborne while the catalogue that he labored on
for at least fifteen months is virtually ignored.

The *Catalogus Bibliothecae Harleianae* suffered from its association with Osborne and cannot be looked on as a successful
scholarly venture; besides the weaknesses already mentioned, it
has other faults, especially of organization. Many of these would
have been rendered tolerable if the compilers had added the index of authors promised in a Johnsonian note in volume II, but
Osborne apparently had spent enough money on scholars, transcribers, and printers and was not about to pay an index-maker
too. Perhaps the greatest failure of the catalogue is that the commentaries follow no fixed order or pattern. This randomness de-
feats any value the catalogue might have as a reference work.
Although a bibliophile can never browse in its pages without adding to his store of literary history, he cannot turn to it with the
expectation of finding any specific fact. A tour through the volumes discovers a great deal of learning, but to very little practical
purpose. Nevertheless, the inclusion of scholarly notes raises the
Harleian catalogue above its predecessors. The catalogues of the
Thuanian, Heinsian, and Barberinian libraries, noted by Johnson in the proposals for their usefulness to men of letters, con-

tain nothing more than lists of works;[43] only the catalogue designed by Johnson and prosecuted with the help of Oldys carries its own informative commentary.

The commentaries that Johnson and Oldys scattered throughout the first four volumes of the catalogue also deserve some brief comment. For the most part these are the product of the library itself. In some cases the editors appear merely to have copied annotations left in the volumes by previous owners. It is no coincidence that one of the most heavily annotated sections of the catalogue is the listing of English Bibles in volume I, a subject on which Humphrey Wanley, Lord Oxford's librarian from 1705 until 1726, was particularly knowledgeable.[44] The books themselves were examined for interesting colophons, which might then be reprinted, or for informative prefaces, which could be epitomized in a note. A great many other commentaries were merely gleaned without acknowledgement from such standard reference works as Johann Albert Fabricius's *Bibliotheca Graeca* and *Bibliotheca Latina* or Michael Maittaire's *Annales Typographici*. In a few cases the cataloguers challenged the precision or the completeness of Fabricius and Maittaire, but not always correctly.[45] In keeping with his commercialization of volumes III and IV, Osborne had his compilers stress the physical appearance of many books, especially those printed on vellum; a number of commentaries in these volumes are swelled out by descriptions of the elegance of the typography, the luster of the ink, or the splendor of the ornaments, initials, or illuminations.[46] On the whole the commentaries tend to add little to the eighteenth century's stock of bibliographical scholarship, but they do provide an interesting series of observations touching randomly on the history of Western culture as manifested in a single great library.

If the dispersal of the library was indeed a tragedy, the production of a catalogue, even one with all the faults of the *Catalogus Bibliothecae Harleianae,* must have provided some mitigation of the loss. The scholars who were so graciously admitted to Lord Oxford's library could not have made effective use of its treasures, for they would have found no exhaustive inventory of the library's holdings. During the lifetimes of the two Earls of Oxford, their library was only partially catalogued; at his death, Edward Harley himself would not have known the full extent of the treasures ranged along his walls.[47] Orderly though a library may appear, it is uncharted territory until it is catalogued. Only a portion of Oxford's domain had been mapped for him. He could make random incursions into the rest, but he could hardly be said to govern it. The Harleian catalogue, on the other hand, made at least a small contribution to historical bibliography, a study then in its infancy. During the first half of the eighteenth century, no authoritative history of printing could be written because of the general dispersal of the artifacts on which any such history must be based and the paucity of catalogues detailing the holdings of the great private collections.[48] At the least the catalogue represented an irregularly compiled supplement to Maittaire's *Annales Typographici;* that Johnson found it a useful undertaking for other reasons as well, the "Account of the Harleian Library" makes clear.

Johnson certainly entered the project hopeful of gaining some scholarly reputation: the meeting with the members of the Royal Society, the inclusion of learned commentary, and the reliance on Latin in the early volumes all point to a seriousness of purpose not to be associated with a mere hack project. Before he had been long at it, though, the public resistance to Osborne's scheme and the compromises that vitiated the scholarly quality of the work must have disabused him of all such hopes. It was for this work that Johnson gradually curtailed his efforts for the *Gentleman's Magazine,* keeping up only the debates on a regular basis; yet the catalogue was to do no more than all his previous works to help Johnson escape anonymity.

In late summer 1743, as the promise of the Harleian catalogue dissipated, Johnson took upon himself another substantial project, a "Historical Design" about which nothing is known beyond the reference to it found in three of Johnson's letters. Writing to Cave, who was to publish the work, he notes his intention of giving "the most complete account of Parliamentary proceedings that [can] be contrived."[49] The project appears to have included the extensive use of some specific documents, referred to as "the Naked Papers," which are to be set in their historical context by Johnson. The finished product is supposed to strike

> the proper medium between a Journal which has regard only to time, and a history which ranges facts according to their dependence on each other, and postpones or anticipates according

to the convenience of narration. I think our work ought to partake of the Spirit of History which is contrary to minute exactness, and of the regularity of a Journal which is inconsistent with spirit.

The subject was at least in part quite modern. A second letter to Cave and one to Thomas Birch show Johnson investigating the events of the early 1720s: the trials of Christopher Layer and Bishop Atterbury arising from the abortive Jacobite plot of 1722; Lord Chancellor Macclesfield's trial for corruption in 1725; and the South Sea Bubble.[50]

In spite of the paucity of facts available to us, some contemporary events make possible a few reasonable speculations about the project. On May 31, 1742, the House of Commons decided to print one thousand copies of its manuscript Journals for the use of its members.[51] Although the Commons Journals were a secret document protected from the eyes of "strangers" by Parliamentary privilege, the decision to print appears to have raised the hopes of publishers. In 1744 Caesar Ward and William Sandby announced their plans for printing a *Parliamentary History of England* to run from "the first Institutions of those August Assemblies . . . to the Restoration of Charles II" and to be collected from, among other sources, "the Parliament Rolls and Journals."[52] William Guthrie, whose *General History of England* began to appear in February 1744, was given access to the Commons Journals, which are cited frequently in the last volume of his three-volume work.[53] The House, it appears intended to maintain its right to privacy while still allowing judicious use of the Journals by historians; it could choose to exercise its privilege according to the individual case.[54]

The Commons Journals seem precisely the type of source described by Johnson in his letter to Cave: they detail the business of the House, yet with few references to individual members and no notice of the matter or extent of debate.[55] They present actions without the motivations, conflicts, or personalities that lay behind them. Johnson's narrative would provide all this. In addition, Cave would have needed some such authoritative source to make the venture attractive to the public, for two extensive Parliamentary histories covering the period after the Restoration were already appearing in print—Richard Chandler's *History and Proceedings of the House of Commons* and Ebenezer Timberland's

similarly titled work for the Lords. These, though, were compiled from public sources and primarily comprised debates, the
most recent of which were simply reprinted from the *Gentleman's*
and *London Magazines*. Cave and Johnson apparently intended to
supersede these works, and the Commons Journals would have
provided the most obvious means of accomplishing that goal.[56]

Like the Sarpi project of five years earlier, the "Historical Design" was never to reach print. A few sheets at least were probably run off, for Johnson assures Cave in one of the letters that
he "need not be in care about something to print";[57] but there
is no indication of how long either Johnson or Cave persisted in
their hopes for this work. If indeed Cave had intended to make
extensive use of the Journals, the demise of the project may have
been inevitable. In the initial report to the Commons concerning
the printing of the Journals, Nicholas Hardinge, the Clerk of the
House, noted, "It is not doubted but that the House will effec-
tually restrain the printing or selling of any Edition of the Journals, or any Abridgment thereof, or any Collections therefrom,
which shall not be warranted by their own Order."[58] Johnson and
Cave may have been guilty of too great a trespass in the Commons' private preserve.

The extent to which Johnson considered this project as a means
to reputation cannot be known. Whether he would put his name
to it would have depended on the work's exact nature: compilations like the *History and Proceedings* were generally anonymous,
but men like Birch and Guthrie were acknowledging their histories. Perhaps the best indication of the value that Cave placed
upon this work is the amount he was willing to pay: over two
guineas per sheet of copy.[59] This rate of payment did not extend
to other works. For the *Life of Savage,* carried on simultaneously
with the "Historical Design," Johnson received only fifteen guineas, probably less than half the pay per-sheet of the larger project.[60] Cave must have been particularly sanguine about the profits to be made from a Parliamentary history. There was another
factor, though, to push up Johnson's price: he was still engaged
on the Harleian catalogue. Indeed, never before had there been
such a demand for his services. The fall of the year found him
composing the Parliamentary debates, compiling the catalogue
for Osborne at Gray's Inn, writing Savage's life, and beginning
this Parliamentary history. The obvious failure of the catalogue
to garner him any recognition may have encouraged him to un-

dertake this added burden, but Cave, it seems, was compelled to bid high in a labor market that offered no other worker of Johnson's ability.[61] Unfortunately he was to find once again that Johnson's genius was no guarantee of profit, or even that a project would reach print.

On August 1, 1743, Richard Savage died in a Bristol jail. Four years had passed since he had parted from Johnson with tears in his eyes, but exile did not keep him totally out of public notice. The *Gentleman's* and *London Magazines* rushed his poetry into print as it trickled in from Wales or Bristol, and Orator Henley, the quack preacher from Lincoln's Inn Fields, revenged himself on Pope by fulminating against the great man's supposed ill-usage of Savage.[62] When the unexpected news of Savage's death reached St. John's Gate, Cave and Johnson lost little time determining to publish a life. To forestall any rivals they announced on August 25 in the *General Evening Post* that an account of Savage's life, drawn up by a personal acquaintance and based in part on original letters, was in the press and speedily to be published.[63] Johnson also composed a letter for the August issue of the *Gentleman's Magazine,* asserting the uniqueness of his materials and contemning as fiction any life that might be written without them.[64] Nevertheless, months passed and the promised life failed to appear. The press of Johnson's many duties, for Osborne as well as for Cave, certainly delayed his progress, and the anguish of thinking of his friend's death must have aggravated the chore. It was not until December that he finally brought the work to completion. Cave, who published the life under James Roberts's imprint, paid Johnson fifteen guineas for it on the fourteenth of that month; on February 11, 1744, it finally appeared in print.[65]

The two-month delay between payment and publication was apparently brought on by the need for extensive revision. As J. D. Fleeman has demonstrated, the last six half-sheets of the work (excepting the misnumbered final pages) were printed separately from the rest and probably represent the forty-eight pages that Johnson said he composed in one night.[66] The re-set pages narrate the story of Savage's retirement, from Pope's initial suggestion of it to Savage's death. In all likelihood, more information had come to light and Johnson felt compelled to perfect his account. Luckily, though, the long delay was of little consequence, for no rival appeared to challenge the sale of Johnson's little book. Although the *Life of Savage* appeared to critical acclaim from the *Champion*,[67] it achieved only a moderate sale, a second edition not being called for until 1748.

The *Life of Savage*, although generally acknowledged as one of the great achievements in biography in our language, embodies many of the same weaknesses of Johnson's other early lives. For the early part of Savage's life, Johnson made use of several printed sources, but especially an anonymous biography of Savage written at the time of his trial for murder.[68] As in his earlier biographies, Johnson made no attempt to verify the information he found in his sources. Shortly before retiring to Wales, Savage had sent a copy of the early life to Elizabeth Carter, noting several of its inaccuracies in an accompanying letter.[69] None of his corrections found their way into Johnson's work. For the period between the trial and Savage's departure for Wales, Johnson relied upon his remembered conversations with Savage, adding perhaps a few details gleaned from the memories of Savage's acquaintances. Yet Johnson may have limited himself to those old friends of Savage that chance threw in his way. Although one is not surprised that he refrained from pestering Lord Tyrconnel, who might treat with suspicion anyone intending to make a public display of his kindnesses to and quarrels with Savage, there is no indication that Johnson sought out Savage's more accessible benefactors such as Solomon Mendes and James Thomson. This laxity led to blunders. By placing the publication of *The Bastard* in the wrong year, Johnson misrepresented Tyrconnel's reasons for admitting Savage to his house and attributed to Savage greater restraint than he actually evidenced.[70] Such an error could easily have been prevented by hunting down any of the poem's first five editions, all of which appeared in 1728, or by chatting with Aaron Hill, who knew Savage long before the poem's publication. If Johnson did talk to Hill, which seems unlikely, he made no attempt to establish the chronology of Savage's activities during the years of their association.[71]

For the last part of Savage's life, his exile in Bristol and Wales, Johnson's account was more authoritative, for he was forced to rely on Savage's own letters and whatever other testimony Cave could gather from his contacts in the Post Office and in Bristol.[72] In addition, Johnson made extensive use of material that could only have come from Pope, including what appear to be extracts from his correspondence with Savage.[73] Yet this final section, though based on better materials, has significant gaps, especially concerning Savage's stay at Swansea.

Thus the *Life of Savage* is often sparse in detail and sometimes inaccurate. Johnson was happy to rely on early printed sources and on memory, unreliable though both might prove, and only sought documentary evidence when these could no longer be tapped. Throughout the work he shows a disdain for dates that leaves his reader adrift: one can follow a sequence of events as Savage's sufferings are aggravated or remitted, but the duration of those vicissitudes is lost in the flow of narrative. In all this, Johnson's method contrasts sharply with the antiquarian trend in biography fathered by Bayle and pursued by Birch and his document-hunting contemporaries.

Nevertheless, the *Life of Savage* remains one of the outstanding achievements in English biography, for insofar as biography is a humanistic rather than an antiquarian pursuit, this work has few rivals. Johnson wrote of Savage with a deep sympathetic understanding tempered by a clearheaded appraisal of his subject's follies. His concern was human action and its consequences. If Johnson extenuated Savage's faults, as some of his contemporaries suggested,[74] he nevertheless displayed them copiously. Johnson's Savage is both attractive and reprehensible—charming, generous, possessed of genius; ungrateful, proud, pathologically irresponsible. He is an uncommon man in his talents and his vanities. Above all, he is a picture drawn from life. This, without doubt, was Johnson's intent. One cannot simply dismiss the lapses in research, for in biography actions must be established before motives can be explained. Yet such faults, although sufficient to damn the work of an inferior writer whose merit resides in his diligence rather than his genius, cannot obscure Johnson's achievements. He sought to portray Savage's adaptations to good and ill fortune, and having done that, he neglected to pursue the details that might alter the distribution of light and shadow in his portrait but that could not affect the figure itself. To relapse into an eighteenth-century distinction—had Johnson taken more care of his facts, he might have increased our esteem for the *Life of Savage*, but not our love.

1743 represents an *annus mirabilis* for Johnson. The autumn found him shouldering four major projects simultaneously—the debates, the Harleian catalogue, the parliamentary history, and

the life of Savage. It is no wonder that with the end of the year
he dropped his load and rested, resigning as debate writer if not
as editor, and ceasing to compile the rest of Osborne's catalogue.
That Johnson continued to compile the "Historical Design" long
into the new year also seems unlikely, for the project never reached
the stage of issuing proposals. All of Johnson's major efforts appear to have ceased together.

Despite the many projects that occupied Johnson during the
late months of 1743, at the end of the year he was in financial
difficulties. In December he was forced to ask for a two-month
delay in paying £12 in overdue interest on his mother's mortgaged house in Lichfield, and even then he apparently had to
rely on the help of Henry Hervey Aston to make the payment.[75]
Why Johnson, whose income certainly surpassed one hundred
pounds in 1743,[76] should have been unable to scrape together
this relatively small amount is difficult to understand. It is tempting to speculate that Tetty's habits were behind his impecunity,
but likely as this may seem, we have no direct evidence of it. Yet
poverty seems no longer to have been able to goad Johnson into
sustained labor. The new year, much of which he appears to have
passed without any regular employment, continued him in his
distress. The famous story of Johnson so shabbily dressed that
he chose to dine behind a screen while Walter Harte extolled
to Cave the virtues of the *Life of Savage* gives melancholy confir-
mation of his poverty.[77] The few literary efforts that we can find,
at least through the first three quarters of 1744, are such as would
have offered little pay.

At various times throughout the year he contributed to Osborne's latest project, the *Harleian Miscellany*, but his help in that
was far from regular. Preliminary work on the *Miscellany* had begun while Johnson was still employed on the catalogue, but
whether he took part in this is unknown.[78] For the proposals,
which appeared on December 30, 1743,[79] he wrote a short, elegant essay on the ravages of time upon fugitive pieces. In spite
of Johnson's contribution to the proposals, during the early months
of 1744 Oldys emerged as the primary compiler. It is his style
rather than Johnson's that appears in the prefaces to the various
pamphlets. Nor is this surprising, for Oldys had long had an antiquarian's interest in fugitive pieces. In 1731 he had written a
"Dissertation upon Pamphlets" as a means of boosting interest in
Phoenix Britannicus, a collection that stands as one of the primary

forebears of the *Harleian Miscellany*.[80] Oldys may in fact have convinced Osborne to undertake the *Miscellany*.

Although Oldys was editing the compilation, Johnson was called on to provide an introduction. When the first fascicle of the work appeared on March 24, 1744, it included what is now commonly known as Johnson's "Essay on the Origin and Importance of Small Tracts and Fugitive Pieces." A glance at the turgid, often impenetrable prose of Oldys's "Dissertation" explains why Johnson was enlisted to introduce the collection. Such a difficult, pedantic performance as Oldys's, which could easily have been adapted to fit this new collection, would only have discouraged subscribers. Johnson, on the other hand, speaks to the gentleman collector; his work, which includes a succinct history of pamphlet literature in England and a discussion of the effect that political freedom has on the proliferation of small tracts, is learned yet lucid. Nevertheless, it shows signs of hurry. After noting that the *Harleian Miscellany*'s predecessors "have ranged the Pamphlets . . . without any Regard either to the Subject on which they treated, or the Time in which they were written; a Practice, in no wise, to be imitated by us," he proceeds to explain why the current collection will indeed also be miscellaneous, that is, arranged by neither subject nor date.[81] Several small grammatical errors made their way into the published copy, indicating that the work may have been dashed off as the first number was about to be issued and neither re-read by the author, which of course was typical of Johnson, nor carefully proofread by a printer's lackey.[82]

The early numbers of the *Miscellany* show no sign of Johnson beyond the Introduction. The prefaces to individual pamphlets, quite numerous in the first volume, lack both the balanced phrasing and the trenchant observations typical of his style. As the weekly numbers of the second volume appeared over the summer, prefaces and editorial footnotes grew scarce as Oldys also tried to produce "A Copious and Exact Catalogue of Pamphlets in the Harleian Library," to be published as a series of appendixes to the regular text of the *Miscellany*. When Oldys's double duties finally caused delays in publication,[83] Osborne turned to Johnson for help.

In late September 1744, the fascicles of the third volume of the *Miscellany* began to appear, with an increase in the number of editorial prefaces. Donald Greene has identified ten of these as Johnson's.[84] But once again Johnson did not persist in his duties: by the end of October, all traces of his style disappeared from the prefaces. If Johnson continued to aid Osborne in any capacity at all, it was merely to choose what should be printed; yet even this task seems more likely to have fallen to Oldys, who was regularly perusing the pamphlets in the course of making his catalogue and who continued, at least for a short while, to contribute sporadic prefaces.[85]

Besides his work for Osborne, Johnson probably continued some minor editorial duties for the *Gentleman's Magazine,* but his other publications appear limited to the revised *Account of the Life of John Phillip Barretier,* brought out by James Roberts in April, and the proposals for James Crokatt's ill-starred periodical *The Publisher.*[86] In preparing the *Barretier* for separate publication, Johnson did not merely conflate his earlier magazine accounts. He rearranged his material extensively, excised speculative or superfluous paragraphs, provided smooth transitions, and made numerous small changes in expression as was his wont when revising. In addition he returned to Formey's *Vie de Baratier,* the source of the supplemental "notes" he published in the *Gentleman's Magazine* for 1742, extracting material for six new paragraphs. Johnson improved upon his original performance in every way. Nevertheless, Cave, who certainly held the copyright on this publication, had already paid Johnson for the earlier installments and could not have been expected to contribute more than a guinea or so for revisions; after all, the profits from a sixpenny pamphlet would be small at best, and Roberts had to be paid for publishing the work.[87] As for the *Publisher* proposals, perhaps the most interesting fact is that they were dated in late September, about the same time that Johnson had assisted Osborne with the *Miscellany.* Although we find traces of Johnson's activities in the spring and fall of 1744, the summer appears a barren time; some temporary debility may have left him unable to work. But as he regained energy in the autumn, the next large project on which he was about to embark must have been taking shape in his mind.

When Johnson's *Miscellaneous Observations on the Tragedy of Macbeth* was published in April 1745, the text was accompanied by "Proposals for Printing a New Edition of the Plays of William Shakespear, with Notes Critical and Explanatory." Cave was to publish the new edition in ten small volumes of unstated format. In hopes of stimulating interest, he offered the complete works to his subscribers for only one pound five shillings, a fraction of the cost of the Pope, Theobald, and Hanmer editions.[88] The "observations" themselves comprise nothing more than a series of editorial comments elucidating specific passages of the play: they provide not an independent analysis of *Macbeth,* but a specimen of an editor's abilities. The pamphlet, then, was written for the sake of the edition. To contrast his abilities with those of Shakespeare's most recent editor, Johnson added to this work some remarks on Sir Thomas Hanmer's Oxford edition, pointing out numerous flaws in that editor's judgment and procedure. Johnson was obviously hoping to convince prospective buyers that they would receive a better text at less cost by subscribing to his edition. His *Observations* and Proposals provide clear indications of the extent and intensions of Johnson's new enterprise for establishing himself as a man of letters: he would combine in his edition of Shakespeare the taste of Pope, the learning of Theobald, and judgment superior to both.

In all likelihood, Johnson had been engaged on his edition for a considerable time before the publication of the *Miscellaneous Observations.* If we can trust the analogy of numerous other projects by Johnson as well as by others, the issuing of proposals did not precede composition; rather, it may have corresponded to a readiness to print. Thus the Sarpi translation was begun on August 2, 1738, but the proposals were not issued until October 21. Similarly, the Harleian catalogue, prosecuted at breakneck speed, was probably begun in late September or early October 1742; yet its proposals did not appear before the middle of November. Even the little we know of the "Historical Design," for which proposals were never issued, accords with this practice: after Johnson had already been paid more than twelve guineas for copy, he and Cave were discussing the possibility of serial publication, a step that would have required issuing proposals sometime in the future.[89] In a case unrelated to Johnson, Thomas Birch appears to have been enlisted to compile the *General Dictionary* in 1731; its proposals, though, did not appear until January 19, 1733, only two months before the first number was published.[90] In each of these cases the publisher had issued proposals as an attempt to gauge and to attract public interest, but only after a significant amount of copy had accumulated. The proprietor's hurry to publish or the size of the project seems to have affected the interval between the commencement of the work and the appearance of the proposals. Since Johnson's *Shakespeare* was neither to be prosecuted with the haste of the Harleian catalogue nor to amount to the size of the *General Dictionary,* Cave in all likelihood waited something more than the month and a half of the one, and less than the year-and-more of the other. Cave must have allowed Johnson at least three or four months, perhaps considerably longer, before bringing out a specimen of his editor's abilities. Since the *Miscellaneous Observations* was first announced as "speedily" to be published in the *Gentleman's Magazine* for February 1745,[91] Johnson's labor on his edition probably commenced as early as October or November, 1744.

Arthur Sherbo has suggested that Johnson's sanguine expectations in 1756 of completing his proposed *Shakespeare* in eighteen months may in fact have been the result of far more extensive progress in 1745 than anyone has ever suspected.[92] He points to nineteen passages in Johnson's notes to the 1765 edition (from fourteen different plays) in which Johnson says of certain rejected emendations, "I had once put it in the text," or "I had once read thus." Although one might demur from Sherbo's unflinching assertion that "Johnson would not be calling attention to conjectures made and discarded in the course of his editorial labors between 1756 and 1765" (for indeed he might have inserted a reading in a text in 1756 or 1757 that several years' delay made him think better of), the one case in which Johnson calls attention in his 1765 *Shakespeare* to a change of opinion from the *Miscellaneous Observations* argues strongly in Sherbo's favor. Rejecting "Note XXXI" of his early work, in which he suggested an emendation of the phrase "all to all," Johnson writes, "I once thought it should be 'hail' to all, but I now think that the present reading is right."[93] "Once" here indicates the work of 1744–45, and it may do so in the other cases as well. There is no reason to conclude that Johnson began with *Macbeth* in 1745 and went no further. Cave agreed to publish Johnson's edition of Shakespeare, not his scattered reflections on a single play; and all indications are that Johnson prosecuted his task with vigor, annotating and emending texts and dissecting the work of his predecessors. Indeed, it is not beyond belief that Johnson began this project even earlier than I have suggested, and that what has been interpreted as a period of despair and inaction over the summer of 1744 may have been passed collating texts and examining the commentaries of previous scholars.

Within a week of the publication of the *Miscellaneous Obser-*

vations, the entire project came crashing down. Jacob Tonson, who asserted a dubious claim to the copyright of Shakespeare's plays, threatened Cave with a suit in Chancery for violation of his property. Although the copyright statute of 1709 appeared to abolish perpetual copyright, Tonson and his fellow booksellers maintained their spurious rights by seeking interim injunctions from the Court while avoiding an actual legal test of their position.[94] Cave was apparently unwilling to enter the morass of Chancery Court; indeed, he could always use the good will of members of the trade, and Tonson may have made other threats or offered other incentives for Cave to drop his project. What immediate effect Tonson's action would have had on Johnson remains unknown: he may have desisted immediately, or he may have continued editing plays for several months under the provisions of a contract. By midsummer, though, work must certainly have come to a halt, with Johnson again in need of employment.

The remainder of 1745 stands forth as another of those troubling gaps in Johnson's career during which few traces of literary work can be found. While employed on the *Shakespeare,* Johnson had provided Cave with other assistance—in a game of rapid composition, he competed with Stephen Barrett in revising a poorly done piece of Latin poetry;[95] and he may have contributed the debate on Hanoverian troops printed in the *Gentleman's Magazine* for December and the Supplement, 1744.[96] In addition he provided Cave with "Proposals for Publishing the Debates of the House of Commons, from the Year 1667 to the Year 1694, Collected by the Honourable Anchitell Grey, Esq.," which were inserted in the magazine for March 1745.[97] Yet all such signs of Johnson disappear from the magazine after the Shakespeare fiasco. His only other known activities for the year include his composing a charity sermon for his friend Henry Hervey Aston, preached at St. Paul's on May 2, and his blotting a great many lines from Samuel Madden's interminable panegyric, *Boulter's Monument.* The first of these may have netted Johnson two guineas, his regular fee for pulpit eloquence; the second brought him a more sizeable and, perhaps, a more desperately needed present of ten guineas, which came in late summer when Johnson appears to have had no other support, and which he told the Rev. Thomas Campbell, "was to me at that time a great sum."[98]

Johnson's recent biographers have suggested that this was the

period in which he asked Dr. Adams to find out if he might practice as an advocate in Doctors' Commons without a degree in
Civil Law.[99] If so, Johnson was again trying to escape the repeated failures and intolerable frustrations that had marked his
career as a writer-for-hire. Project after project had come to
naught. On his first arrival he had endured the petty tyranny of
Fleetwood and the arresting coincidence of the rival Sarpi translation. In recent years he had experienced the public's disregard
of his work on the Harleian catalogue, the abandonment of his
Parliamentary history, and the quashing of his *Shakespeare* by the
dubious claims of a powerful bookseller. While he labored on
these works and toiled for the magazine, he earned at least a
competence—in all probability, a better wage than most of his
fellow authors. But these periods of exertion appear to have al-
ternated with others of exhaustion. For an entire year following
the abandonment of the Sarpi translation, during much of 1744,
and throughout the last half of 1745, Johnson had little certain
income, and the few glimpses we have of the accompanying poverty sober us and shock us. During one of these periods of distress, Tetty was forced to sell the silver keepsake cup that Johnson's mother had bought when she carried her son to London
to be touched by the Queen for his scrofula. Richard Cumberland heard him tell that he subsisted "for a considerable space
of time upon the scanty pittance of fourpence halfpenny per day,"
and Hervey Aston not only had to advance Johnson money on
the Lichfield mortgage, but to relieve him from an arrest.[100] And
even during his periods of relative prosperity, Johnson's condition was hardly eased by the need of providing Tetty with the
trivial luxuries that she certainly craved. One is perhaps surprised with nothing so much as his resilience. Repeated disappointment is borne only with difficulty, even by a sanguine temperament; it crushes a melancholic one. Yet Johnson continued
to pass from one unsatisfying project to another.

By the end of 1745, Johnson began to cast about for another
enterprise. This time he was to settle on a dictionary of the English language. One is tempted to attribute this choice to deep
policy—a desire to undertake such a work that no Tonson could
veto and that no rival could frustrate—but circumstance had much
to do with the decision. Although Johnson had apparently long
considered the idea, it was Robert Dodsley who had first broached
it as a practical undertaking, attractive to both booksellers and

the public.[101] The need for a dictionary to "fix" the language had become the common sentiment of all learned Englishmen. Nevertheless, it was a daunting venture. Pope and Addison had considered it; Ambrose Philips had issued proposals. But no one had persevered beyond the initial stage of gathering quotations.[102]

The magnitude of the task was staggering, and the pitfalls were many. Johnson's bravado in contrasting his projected three years' labor with the forty years taken by forty French Academicians makes for brilliant repartee but sobering reality. Illness, exhaustion, depression, unforeseen costs, and unforeseen difficulties could all protract the undertaking beyond the patience of the proprietors. Should the work come to completion, there were other uncertainties. The checks that a multitude of minds provide would be lacking from a single man's work, and there was no certainty that the product of one mind, necessarily replete with prejudices, obliquities, and lapses, would be accepted by the public as the standard to which all should defer. And finally, persistence rather than genius would seem the requisite quality of a lexicographer; one could not be sure that the public would not admit the compiler the first while denying him the second. Although the man who would provide a dictionary would certainly deserve the thanks of his nation, he could hardly be certain of their praise. All of Johnson's lesser projects had foundered on coasts with fewer shoals than that he was now setting out for. The great accomplishment of the *Dictionary* deceives us into believing that its success was inevitable and Johnson's reputation assured from the moment he conceived of attempting it, but this is to judge from effects, a privilege allowed only to posterity.

On April 30, 1746, Johnson completed a "Short Scheme for Compiling a New Dictionary of the English Language." A month and a half later he breakfasted with the booksellers who were to back his effort and signed a contract for fifteen hundred guineas, a salary that would have provided considerable profit for three years' labor.[103] In his hopes of gain, Johnson was again to be disappointed, but in all other aspects—the temporary triumph over indolence and melancholy, the vindication of his genius, and the establishment of his reputation—he was finally to succeed.

APPENDIX A. THE AUTHORSHIP OF THE "CHARACTER OF THE *MEMOIRS OF A MAN OF QUALITY*"

An unsigned letter inserted in the *Gentleman's Magazine* for May 1740 takes notice of proposals recently issued for printing a translation of the Abbé Prévost's *Mémoires et avantures d'un homme de qualité,* apparently the version done by a Mr. Erksine and published in three volumes by T. Cooper in 1743. The letter includes a "character" of the work, said to be excerpted from the proposals, that sounds strikingly Johnsonian:

> In our Author's own Adventures, the Reader will see a brave Man struggling with the Storms of Fate, Virtue oppressed but never over-power'd; and Villany prosperous, but never happy. He will observe that the principal Ingredient of Happiness does not lie in exterior Circumstances, but in the inward Composure of Mind. As this is the great Maxim which our Author lays down, there is scarce a Page of his Book, but what proves this important Truth, and, at the same Time, that the best and the most virtuous Passion may border upon Vice, when carried too far, and when not directed by Reason and Religion. It will be easily discerned that "the Marquis de Bretagne" has been a Man of Passions so strong, that he has been sometimes transported beyond the strict Bounds of both; but still it must be admired, how, amidst such a Multitude of Events, and such Variety of Pressures, he should always have found Resources in his own Courage and superior Capacity, which have extricated him out of Difficulties, under which a Man of less Virtue and Patience would have sunk, or, by yielding to the Torrent, have exchang'd the solid Pleasures of Virtue for the gay Trappings of Vice. The Moral that is convey'd us by every Incident of his Life, is such as may be expected from a Philosopher and a Christian. We every where find the

Satisfaction arising from Villany transitory and delusive, and the virtuous Man rising in the Home-felt Joy of Mind and Conscience, in Proportion as he sinks in the Eyes of the Vulgar and the Mean. In short, the Translator may venture to affirm, that, of all the numerous Productions of this Kind, no Author has equally found the Secret of reconciling the Marvellous with the Probable, the Pathetick with the Noble, and Variety with Use. The Great may here view how transitory their State may prove; the Oppressed may learn, that there is no Condition of Life so abject, but that Virtue and Patience may soften and retrieve. The Lover may perceive, that nothing but Merit can lay a solid Foundation for Happiness, and every Man, be his State and Condition of Life ever so low or high, may observe, that nothing is so valuable as Sincerity and Truth.[1]

But the magazine's correspondent goes on to note that this "character" of the work was in fact plagiarized from the preface to an extant translation issued by J. Wilford two years earlier. The Johnsonian sentiments and cadences are indeed taken from the preface to the Wilford edition, which appeared on April 25, 1738,[2] and is listed in the *Gentleman's Magazine* register of books for that month (p. 224). The question that remains is whether Johnson can somehow be linked to a 1738 work published by Wilford. In fact, there is such a connection.

Only the first volume of the *Memoirs of a Man of Quality* appeared under Wilford's imprint in 1738. The letter on the "character" of the work, quoted in part above, concludes with an announcement that the remainder is to be issued in a second volume. This second volume appeared late in 1741 under Cave's imprint.[3] A year later a second edition of volume one was issued, also by Cave.[4] By 1742, then, Cave would appear to have held copy on both volumes.

As we have seen in the case of the Crousaz *Commentary*, Cave was not averse to issuing a work under the imprint of a trade publisher, then later reissuing it under his own name. The publication on the *Memoirs* may represent just such a practice. Cave's pointing out in the magazine that the proposals for a forthcoming edition were plagiarized from the preface of the extant one confirms the suspicion that Cave was involved in the project from the start: it was not his habit to note disinterestedly that one bookseller was stealing from another. The letter to the magazine for May 1740 was apparently an attempt to protect his property against competition while advertising the remaining stock of the first volume. Wilford may have shared in the copy of the first volume; if so, he certainly sold out to Cave before the publication of the second, for there could be no reason for Wilford, a bookseller with a shop, to be left off the title page of his own property. In all likelihood, though, Cave was the lone backer of the book from the start, with Wilford being paid a fee for publishing the work, as well as a percentage of his sales.[5]

Some speculations can now be offered about Johnson's role in the *Memoirs*. The preface to the 1738 edition does not seem entirely Johnsonian. The first three sentences have no sign of his style:

> The following *Memoirs* have already been so well receiv'd in the World, that there is no occasion to make any Apology for introducing them to the Reader in an *English* Dress. A great many People who are now living have seen their Author, and they all own that, as to his Person, he was one of the handsomest Men of his Age. The Reader will find the other Part of his Character described in the following Pages; where he will see. . .

The first passage quoted above begins at this point, continuing through the phrase "the Vulgar and the Mean" (about two-thirds of its length).[6] A second paragraph then begins, returning to the nondescript style of the opening sentences. The preface concludes with the remainder of the passage quoted above.

Johnson, as we have seen, made his first contribution to the *Gentleman's Magazine* in March 1738, a month before the appearance of the first volume of the *Memoirs*. Something like the following probably occurred: Johnson visited St. John's Gate, perhaps to discuss *London,* which Cave was enthusiastic to publish. Finding completed sheets of the *Memoirs,* Johnson began to read as much as had been printed off. Either he offered or Cave requested improvements to the preface, resulting in its patchy style. Two years later, a subsequent would-be publisher pirated the more elegant parts of the 1738 preface for his own proposals, perhaps thinking the entire thing to have been merely translated from Prévost.[7]

If these speculations are correct, they present one of the earliest instances of a Johnsonian preface and perhaps the first case in which Johnson's work was plagiarized.

APPENDIX B. THE DURATION
OF JOHNSON'S DEBATES

Johnson wrote the debates for three years, 1741 through 1743—
at least so he told Boswell.[1] That he assumed the full-time duties
of debate writer in July 1741 is beyond dispute.[2] Hawkins marked
the end of Johnson's contributions at the debate on the Spiritous
Liquors Bill, which began to appear in November 1743 and continued until the next February; but on what evidence Hawkins
made this assertion, which agrees closely with Johnson's own report, we do not know.[3] The debate on "pay for Hanoverian
troops," which actually took place before that on spiritous liquors
but which was not printed until after (*Gentleman's Magazine*, February and March, 1744), is also generally included in the canon,
although no sound argument from either internal or external
evidence has ever been offered in its favor. The debate on the
Corporation Bill (*GM*, March and April, 1744), which took place
in the same Parliamentary session as the two debates already
mentioned, has traditionally been excluded.[4] The probable reason for the exclusion of the Corporation Bill debate is that it
appears in the magazine without the Lilliputian disguise and thus
seems to mark a natural break in the sequence. It is on such a
tenuous basis as this that the terminus of Johnson's debates has
generally been decided.[5]

Style is of little aid in resolving the difficulties, for although
Johnson's early contributions seem to stand out in bold relief
against Guthrie's work and the lightly retouched plagiarisms from
the *London Magazine*, by the end of 1743 a new candidate for the
authorship of the debates had appeared on the scene, one who
formed his own style on a close imitation of Johnson's—John
Hawkesworth. Hawkins stated quite matter-of-factly that
Hawkesworth took over the debates after Johnson, an assertion

that is given some credibility by Benjamin Hoover's comparative analysis of the style of the May 1744 debates with earlier debates known to be by Johnson.[6]

Despite Johnson's statement that he wrote the debates only through 1743 and the likelihood that Hawkesworth continued them in a Johnsonian style, all of the Parliamentary debates that appeared in the *Gentleman's Magazine* for 1744 have recently been attributed to Johnson. F. V. Bernard suggests, on very slender evidence, that Johnson wrote the debate on the Corporation Bill, and Donald Greene attributes to him all of the debates from May through the Supplement, 1744.[7] Neither of these attributions is convincing. Greene himself dismisses the Corporation Bill debate as un-Johnsonian, and Bernard's explanation of why Johnson would have been interested in the topic does not compel a reader to search again for proofs of Johnson's style.[8] As to the series of debates attributed by Greene, the style does not, on the whole, seem convincingly Johnsonian, nor, as I mentioned above, have they passed a statistical test based on Wimsatt's analysis of Johnson's style. Using a sample from the first of these questionable debates, Benjamin Hoover found comparatively low incidences of parallel and antithesis.[9] There are also other problems with Greene's attribution. The five debates between May and the Supplement do not, as Greene suggests, create a set piece concerned with a single topic—dismissing the Hanoverian troops in British pay. The first two (May through September, 1744) focus on the matter of the Hanoverians, but the third (October and November), although beginning as if on the same topic, actually considers a problem of parliamentary procedure. With the conclusion of this debate, the discussion of the Hanoverian troops appears to come to an end. A fourth debate begins (November, p. 582) on addresssing the King concerning the machinations of the French and the Pretender. After this very brief debate is concluded in December, the debates surprisingly return to the matter of the estimates for paying the Hanoverians (December and the Supplement). The intrusion of the short debate on the Pretender, which is out of chronological order, makes it clear that the 1744 series is not a set piece: the last of the Hanoverian debates is clearly an afterthought. This is an important matter, for if we see the 1744 debates as a unified account, we must assume a single author; but if we merely see five debates, the last a vigorous re-examination of a topic considered earlier, we are forced to consider each one individually. Thus, neither Hawkesworth nor Johnson need be the author of the entire series. I happen to find, in an impressionistic rather than scientific response, certain passages from the last of these debates (December and Supplement, 1744) denser, more "nervous," than anything in the earlier considerations of the same topic. Might Johnson have volunteered to cap off the question of maintaining the Hanoverians with an energetic reworking of the issues (for a badly needed fee, of course)? I do not offer this suggestion with unflinching confidence, for I am not totally convinced that Johnson wrote the last of the 1744 debates; I merely wish to suggest that those with particular expertise in stylistic analysis treat each debate separately. Perhaps a statistical analysis of all of the 1744 debates in the manner of Wimsatt and Hoover could help solve some of these problems.

Until more detailed and more convincing analyses can be done, we must rely on external evidence to determine the end of Johnson's contributions to the Parliamentary debates. Since Hawkins's assertions agree so well with Johnson's statements to Boswell, it is perhaps safest to fix the debate on spiritous liquors as Johnson's last, even if it means consigning that on "pay for Hanoverian troops" (February and March, 1744), long accepted as Johnson's, to the limbo of questionable attributions.

ABBREVIATIONS USED
IN NOTES

"Autobiography"
: [John Gough Nichols], "The Autobiography of Sylvanus Urban," in the *Gentleman's Magazine*, July–September, November, December, 1856; January–April, 1857.

Barker
: A. D. Barker, "Edward Cave, Samuel Johnson, and the *Gentleman's Magazine*," D.Phil. thesis, Oxford University, 1981.

Carlson
: C. Lennart Carlson, *The First Magazine* (Providence: Brown University Press, 1938).

Clifford
: James Clifford, *Young Sam Johnson* (New York: McGraw Hill, 1955).

DA
: *Daily Advertiser*

DNB
: *Dictionary of National Biography*

GD
: Pierre Bayle, *General Dictionary, Historical and Critical*, translated and augmented by Thomas Birch, John Peter Bernard, and John Lockman, 10 vols. (London, 1734–41).

Gleanings
: Aleyn Lyell Reade, *Johnsonian Gleanings*, 11 pts. in 10 vols. (Privately printed, 1909).

GM
: *Gentleman's Magazine*

Greene, *Politics*
: Donald Greene, *The Politics of Samuel Johnson* (New Haven: Yale University Press, 1960).

Greene, "Some Notes"
: Donald Greene, "Some Notes on Johnson and the *Gentleman's Magazine*," *PMLA* 74 (1959): 75–84.

Hawkins
: Sir John Hawkins, *Life of Samuel Johnson, LL.D.* in Samuel Johnson's *Works* (London, 1787), vol. 1.

Hazen
: Allen T. Hazen, *Samuel Johnson's Prefaces and Dedications* (New Haven: Yale University Press, 1937).

Hoover
: Benjamin Hoover, *Samuel Johnson's Parliamentary Reporting* (Berkeley: U. of California Press, 1953).

J. Misc.	*Johnsonian Miscellanies,* ed. G. B. Hill, 2 vols. (Oxford: Clarendon Press, 1897).
Letters	*Letters of Samuel Johnson,* ed. R. W. Chapman, 3 vols. (Oxford: Clarendon Press, 1952).
Life	James Boswell, *Life of Samuel Johnson,* ed. G. B. Hill, rev. L. F. Powell, 6 vols. (Oxford: Clarendon Press, 1934–64).
Literary Anecdotes	John Nichols, *Literary Anecdotes,* 9 vols. (London, 1812–16).
Lives of the Poets	Samuel Johnson, *Lives of the Poets,* ed. G. B. Hill, 3 vols. (Oxford: Clarendon Press, 1905).
LM	*London Magazine*
Osborn, "Birch and the *GD*"	James M. Osborn, "Thomas Birch and the *General Dictionary,*" *Modern Philology,* 36 (1938–39): 25–46.
Political Writings	*Yale Edition of the Works of Samuel Johnson,* vol. 10, ed. Donald Greene (New Haven: Yale University Press, 1977).
Poems	*Poems of Samuel Johnson,* ed. David Nichol Smith and Edward L. McAdam, 2nd. ed. (Oxford: Clarendon Press, 1974).
"Rise and Progress"	John Nichols, "Rise and Progress of the *Gentleman's Magazine,*" *Index to the Gentleman's Magazine, 1787–1818,* pp. i–lxxx.
Waingrow	*Yale Edition of the Private Papers of James Boswell,* Research Edition, *Correspondence,* vol. 2, *Relating to the Making of the Life of Johnson,* ed. Marshall Waingrow (New York: McGraw Hill, n.d.).
Wiles, *Serial Publication*	R. M. Wiles, *Serial Publication in England before 1750* (Cambridge: Cambridge University Press, 1957).

NOTES

CHAPTER I

1. *Life*, I, 102.
2. Johnson either held or applied for at least six teaching positions (including Edial) between 1731 and 1737: *Gleanings*, V, 64–67, 75–87, 108–113; VI, 29–49. See also Waingrow, pp. 87, 90.
3. *Gleanings*, V, 100–101.
4. *Letters*, I, 3–4.
5. The matter of Tetty's fortune is of great importance to a study of Johnson's early career, for there is no indication that Johnson earned any money from his literature until he sold *London* to Dodsley in April 1738. A. L. Reade has established that Tetty received approximately £600 from her husband's estate (*Gleanings*, VI, 34–35). That the Johnsons would have spent such a sum in fitting out Edial school seems highly unlikely. A deed to the property of Edial dated "28th Oct. 1721" sets the rent at ten guineas for a half year (*Gleanings*, VI, 39). It is unlikely that the rent varied at all by 1736. The school itself was probably quite Spartan, and the expenses of living in the country were considerably less than those of the city. In the *Life of Savage* Johnson was to say that £50 constituted "a salary which, though by no means equal to the demands of vanity and luxury, is yet found sufficient to support families above want, and was undoubtedly more than the necessities of life require" (*Lives of the Poets*, II, 398). If we allow Johnson and his wife the extravagance of spending £150 per year and another £100 for setting up the school, approximately £200 would still have remained from Tetty's fortune. We must assume that it was some such amount that sustained the Johnsons until the middle of 1738.
6. *Life*, I, 101 n.
7. *Life*, I, 103.
8. Hawkins, p. 43.
9. *Life*, I, 102 n.
10. Johnson received a mere five guineas for the Lobo translation (*Life*, I, 87). In order to have earned half of the sum borrowed from Wilcox, Johnson in all likelihood would have had to perform a considerable amount of hack labor. Had he undertaken any project of significance, some trace would most likely have been found.
11. *Life*, I, 103–05.
12. For estimates of the wages of laborers in the eighteenth century, see John Burnett, *History of the Cost of Living* (Harmondsworth: Penguin, 1969), pp.

164–66. Burnett notes that the years 1730 to 1750 formed a Golden Age for English labor, yet even of such a favored period he can only say that meat appeared "on the laborer's table 2 or 3 times a week" (p. 133). The diet of the country people consisted largely of bread, butter, and cheese, with meat perhaps once or twice a week: see J. C. Drummond and Anne Wilbraham, rev. Dorothy Hollingsworth, *The Englishman's Food* (London: Jonathan Cape, 1958), p. 206.

13. A stark contrast to the sort of tavern Johnson frequented and the sort of company he kept is given by Smollett in *Roderick Random,* where he describes chairmen, draymen, and out-of-place footmen dining in a steamy cookshop. A meal of shin of beef, small beer, and bread could be had there for twopence half-penny: see Drummond and Wilbraham, p. 218.

14. I am indebted for this observation to Mr. George DeVoe. For the distinctions between a commoner, a batteller, and a servitor, see *Gleanings,* V, 155.

15. Johnson's background was not quite so obscure as he suggested. His mother was a Ford, described by Boswell as "descended of an ancient race of substantial yeomanry in Warwickshire" (*Life,* I, 34–35).

16. *Life,* I, 106.

17. *Letters,* I, 8.

18. Clifford (p. 183) suggests that Johnson and Cave met at this time and that Cave made the young author "a vague promise of work"; but the diffidence of Johnson's subsequent approaches to Cave makes this unlikely.

19. Johnson told Boswell that he had only three acts completed before retiring to Greenwich, where he proceeded "somewhat further" but did not complete the play (*Life,* I, 106).

20. See Dorothy Marshall, *Dr. Johnson's London* (New York: John Wiley & Sons, 1968), pp. 23–26; and Sir John Summerson, *Georgian London* (New York: Scribners, 1946), pp. 81–94.

21. *Life,* I, 110–11; *Letters,* I, 9.

22. *Life,* I, 111.

23. This discussion of eighteenth-century theater is primarily dependent on two sources: *The London Stage, 1660–1800,* pt. 3, 1729–1747, ed. Arthur H. Scouten (Carbondale: Southern Illinois U. Press, 1961); and Allardyce Nicoll, *A History of English Drama, 1660–1900,* 6 vols. (Cambridge: Cambridge U. Press, 1952). The figures that I adduce below on the number of main pieces produced at each of the London theaters during the seasons of 1735–36 through 1737–38 are gathered from the entries in *The London Stage.*

24. See Scouten's Introduction to *The London Stage,* pt. 3, pp. l–li.

25. G. B. Hill's note (*Life,* I, 111 n. 2) that Johnson "could scarcely have solicited a worse manager" than Fleetwood is easily discounted. Rich at Covent Garden was the only alternative, and he had virtually given up producing new dramas, favoring opera instead. By the season of 1736–37, Rich was leasing his theater to Handel as often as twice a week (Scouten, *London Stage,* pt. 3, p. 597). He did, though, produce two new dramas in August 1738, after the normal theater season had come to an end. Rich is described by John Loftis as a man "grossly unfit for the responsibility" of holding one of the only two theater patents: *The Politics of Drama in Augustan England* (Oxford: Oxford U. Press, 1963), p. 152.

26. Nicoll, II, 59.

27. James J. Lynch, *Box, Pit, and Gallery* (Berkeley: U. of California, 1953), pp. 32–33. In addition, Johnson appeared on the scene with *Irene* seven years after Lillo's *London Merchant* had ushered in bourgeois domestic tragedy.

28. Loftis, p. 151.

29. For a discussion of the politics of *Irene*, see Greene, *Politics*, pp. 72–80.

30. The accusations of plagiarism arose from the questionable nature of Cave's original design. He reprinted material from various periodicals without permission. The popularity of the magazine, which offered numerous abridged essays, hurt the sales of many of the journals themselves. The publishers of the *LM*, some of whom had interests in periodicals excerpted by Cave, felt justified in stealing Cave's entire format because he had stolen their articles first. See the introduction by Donald F. McKenzie and J. C. Ross to *A Ledger of Charles Ackers* (Oxford: The Bibliographical Society, 1968), pp. 4–8, where the early disputes between the magazines are discussed from the point of view of *LM*.

31. *GM*, 1738, pp. 59–61.

32. *J. Misc.*, I, 377.

33. See p. 4.

34. *GM*, 1738, p. 156.

35. For an example of the speed with which Johnson could compose Latin verses, see James M. Osborn, "Dr. Johnson's 'Intimate Friend,'" *TLS*, October 9, 1953, p. 652.

36. The Oxford editors of Johnson's *Poems* assert that "Ad Urbanum" appeared unsigned, although "in some reprints [of the March 1738 issue of the *GM*] it is signed 'S. J.'" I have not seen any copies where the poem is unsigned.

37. *Letters*, I, 9; *Life*, IV, 409.

38. *J. Misc.*, I, 318; letter from H. Greswold to Walmesley: *Gleanings*, VI, 30.

39. *Letters*, I, 10–12 (numbers 6–8).

40. *Life*, I, 124.

41. The draft manuscript of poem is dated "12 May" (*Poems*, p. 60), but the work was not advertised as published in the *Daily Advertiser* until the next day. See also, *Life*, I, 127, n. 1.

42. Hawkins, p. 60; Waingrow, p. 105.

43. The Reverend Nicholas Carter, in a letter to his daughter Elizabeth dated June 25, 1738, says of Johnson, "I a little suspect his judgment, if he is very fond of Martial": Montagu Pennington, *Memoirs of the Life of Mrs. Elizabeth Carter* (London, 1807), p. 26.

44. *GM*, 1738, p. 210. Although some have doubted whether Johnson wrote this poem, its appearance in the *LM* for November 1741, p. 565, where it is attributed to "Sam. Johnson," would seem to confirm his authorship; for Savage was at that time submitting some of his own poetry to the *LM* and was probably himself responsible for both submitting the poem and attributing it.

45. *Letters*, I, 12.

46. *GM*, 1738, pp. 210–11.

47. *J. Misc.*, I, 255.

48. The poem's source in the *Greek Anthology* is noted in the Yale Edition of the Works of Samuel Johnson, *Poems*, ed. E. L. McAdam Jr. and George

Milne (New Haven: Yale U. Press, 1964), p. 365. See also *Life,* I, 70; IV, 384. Whether Johnson also wrote the English translation that accompanies this poem is uncertain, but it was not unlike him to render a Greek original into both Latin and English.

49. There was yet another Latin poem included in the April issue, some lines "Ex Cantico Solomonis." Although this poem has no clear claim to John-son's authorship, it was attributed to him by John Gough Nichols in the *GM* for September 1856, p. 272. Perhaps the best argument that can be made in its favor is its proximity to the five other Latin or Greek poems, all apparently by Johnson. Since unsigned Latin verse was a rarity in the magazine, a number of such poems suggest a single source.

J. G. Nichols, the grandson of John Nichols and the editor of the *GM* from 1851 to 1856, was the author of a history of the early years of the magazine entitled "The Autobiography of Sylvanus Urban," which appeared in the *GM* in nine monthly installments (July 1856 to April 1857). The accuracy of many of Nichols's statements about this period is doubtful; he is especially speculative in his treatment of Johnson and Savage: see my article "Was Savage 'Thales'?: Johnson's *London* and Biographical Speculation," *Bulletin of Research in the Humanities* 85 (1982): 329–30. Nevertheless, he had certainly been brought up on the stories of Johnson told by his grandfather and passed on through his father. Some of his assertions about the magazine may represent the ideas of three generations of Nicholses.

50. J. G. Nichols (*GM,* September 1856, p. 272) attributed a poem in the May issue to Johnson, but this one, entitled "The Logical Warehouse" and signed "Philologus," has less claim to being Johnson's than those of the month before. The others have the strength of their appearance together in one issue and their anonymity. There is no evidence to corroborate the word of Nichols in this case. He also suggested that two long Latin epitaphs, one on Dr. Radcliffe by Noll Broxholm in the April issue and the other on Prince George of Den-mark by Henry Aldrich in the May, were supplied by Johnson. Nichols's con-jecture on this point was probably based on Johnson's offer of 1734 (see p. 4) to provide Cave with "poems that deserve revival." It is highly doubtful.

CHAPTER II

1. *Life,* I, 192.

2. Johnson's *Life of Cave* first appeared in the *GM,* 1754, pp. 55–58. He revised it for inclusion in the second edition of *Biographia Britannica* (1784). J. D. Fleeman prints this revised version in his edition of *Early Biographical Writings of Dr. Johnson* (Westmead: Gregg, 1973), pp. 407–10. See also Hawkins, p. 46 ff. Carlson (*The First Magazine*) provides a useful, more detailed look at Cave, but his work has been superseded by the diligent investigations of A. D. Barker, whose D.Phil. thesis "Edward Cave, Samuel Johnson, and the *Gentleman's Magazine*" (Oxford, 1981) greatly expands our knowledge of Cave and his man-agement of the *GM.* My portrait of Cave draws variously from all these sources.

3. Hawkins, p. 46.

4. Hawkins, pp. 46–47 n. Hawkins erred slightly in his account. It was not

Browne's title, but the spelling of his name that apparently caused offense: the name appeared without the final *e,* which was inserted with a caret. The engraving depicts "two uncommon ways of catching fish," and thus its dedication to Browne, identified as the "Author of Piscatery Eclogues," is particularly appropriate. The engraving is supposed to be bound into the first volume of Cave's Du Halde, facing page 330; in the Newberry Library copy, it faces page 325.

5. Carlson, p. 76.

6. In 1742 Cave went so far as to purchase a corn mill in Northampton, diverting its water power to drive Lewis Paul's experimental (and ultimately unworkable) cotton-spinning machines. For a complete account of Cave's venture into cotton spinning, see Barker, pp. 147–80.

7. *Life,* IV, 409.

8. *Life,* IV, 187.

9. See the letter dated October 14, 1731, printed on the verso of the title page of *GM,* April 1732. A portion of this letter is reprinted in Carlson, p. 59.

10. Carlson, pp. 60–61.

11. Ibid.

12. *GM,* 1731, Introduction. Some London papers were designed for country distribution, but on the whole the country was beginning to depend on provincial newspapers. In 1731, twenty-two of these were extant: see the chronological chart in R. M. Wiles, *Freshest Advices: Early Provincial Newspapers in England* (Columbus: The Ohio State U. Press, 1965), inserted after p. 372. None of these provincial newspapers, though, could provide the complete spectrum of London information that the *GM* afforded.

13. Wiles, p. 136. See also Carlson, p. 60 n. Barker (pp. 118–40) gives a detailed explanation of how Cave used his position in the Post Office to send his magazines in bulk throughout the kingdom.

14. *Life,* I, 111.

15. *GM,* June and July, 1736, pp. 360, 428. The Edial school was at least six months old when the advertisements appeared, and they may have represented a last ditch attempt to attract enough pupils to keep the school going (*Gleanings,* VI, 43–44). Hawkins refers to the advertisements as the "usual method of raising a school" (p. 36), and J. H. Plumb, in *Sir Robert Walpole,* 2 vols. (London: Cresset, 1956–60), I, 31 n. 1, states that over 100 were advertised in the Northampton Mercury between 1720 and 1760. But I have found no other such advertisements in the *GM* at this time. Johnson must have had special confidence that the magazine would reach a wide and varied audience.

16. Carlson, pp. 10–11.

17. Benjamin Hoover, *Samuel Johnson's Parliamentary Reporting* (Berkeley: U. of California Press, 1953), pp. 11–13. Mr. Hoover gives a useful, brief history of Parliamentary reporting.

18. Hoover, pp. 12–13.

19. The two letters, dated July 15 and July 21, 1737, are printed by Boswell, *Life,* I, 151. Boswell misdated one of the letters as 1735.

20. *GM,* April 1734, p. 197. Floyer was the physician who recommended to Michael and Sarah Johnson that they take their scrofulous child to London to be touched by Queen Anne (*Gleanings,* III, 61). In his letter to Cave from Birmingham, Johnson mentions Floyer's article as an example of the type of ne-

glected piece that he would seek out and supply to the magazine.

21. Carlson, pp. 198, 210. There were apparently a few original pieces in the magazine before 1733, but on the whole Cave was not open to submissions from his readers.

22. Only the May issue was without an excerpt, and they continued through the first several months of 1735. For the most part Cave trod gingerly around the rules of copyright; periodicals, it seems, could be pillaged mercilessly, but not books. Anonymous pamphlets were apparently also fair game for the periodical publisher. In 1739, though, Cave was to be taken to Chancery for a copyright violation: see below, Chapter 3.

23. For a complete history of Cave's poetry contests, see Carlson, pp. 210–23.

24. *Early Biographical Writings*, ed. Fleeman, p. 409.

25. *GM*, 1735, p. 726; 1736, p. 59. As A. D. Barker has remarked to me in a personal letter, Cave's attempts to obtain respectable judges were not always futile: "Pope and Spence may have turned Cave down, but he managed to get William Broome, Pope's collaborator on the *Odyssey* translation, Dr. Isaac Watts, and the antiquary Cromwell Mortimer to help with the judging of his competitions."

26. Cave had published several poems by Savage before 1736, but all had appeared previously in other periodicals. For Savage's unique agreement with the competing periodicals, see Clarence Tracy, *The Artificial Bastard* (Cambridge: Harvard U. Press, 1953), pp. 121–22.

27. Hawkins, p. 49.

28. Hawkins had reason to depreciate Browne, for both men had brought out editions of Walton's *Compleat Angler,* and a controversy arose between the two over which was superior (*DNB*). So far, in fact, was Johnson from despising Browne that it was he who suggested to Browne that he edit this work. Browne refers to Johnson in the Preface (1750) as "an ingenious and learned Friend, whose Judgment of Men and Books is sufficiently established, by his own Writings, in the Opinion of the World" (quoted in *Life*, II, 520).

29. *DNB.* The letter by which he offered his services to the new government is given in *Life*, I, 117 n. 2, along with an example of his outrageous behavior.

30. *Life*, II, 52.

31. This work, which appeared in five installments (*GM*, May, September, and October, 1738, pp. 232, 469, 521; and January and February, 1739, pp. 20, 73), was never completed. Hawkins mistook it for Johnson's and printed it in his 1787 edition of the complete works.

32. Montagu Pennington, *Memoirs of the Life of Mrs. Elizabeth Carter* (London, 1807), pp. 3, 25.

33. Pennington, p. 26.

34. See Elizabeth Carter's *Poems Upon Particular Occasions.* This slender volume was printed by Cave for the Carters in 1738 for private distribution: Barker, p. 277.

35. *GM*, 1738, p. 272. "Fortune" is followed by a Greek epigram by Eliza to the epigrammatist of the previous month, that is, Johnson. Eliza's Greek is then anonymously turned into Latin; Johnson is a likely candidate for the authorship of this translation, but there is no solid evidence to support this supposition.

36. *Poems,* pp. 115–16.

37. *J. Misc.,* II, 11.

38. Tracy, *Artificial Bastard,* p. 121; Clifford, p. 186.

39. *GM,* September 1856, p. 274.

40. Had Savage simply wished to submit the poem, it would have been much more direct to send it to Cave; a submission through Birch may have been a means of expediting payment. See Tracy, p. 122, for one of Savage's brief letters to Birch.

41. *GM,* 1736, 156. Besides announcing the winner of one of Cave's poetry contests, Birch may also have written the headnote to the reprinting of the first "Volunteer Laureat," which was signed "T. B.," *GM,* 1738, p. 210. (Savage himself may have written this.) There is also a letter to the magazine (1737, pp. 199–202) defending the practice of tithing against the objections of a Quaker that is signed "T. B.," but we cannot be positive that this is Birch's work.

42. See Hoover, p. 157, for an exchange of letters between Cave, Birch, and Philip Yorke on the matter of getting an original copy of Yorke's speech in Parliament. So far was Birch from having an intimate knowledge of the workings of the *GM* that Cave must explain to him that some speakers had in the past conveyed their original speeches to him.

43. Birch appears to have been something of a snob. His diary (B. M. Add. MS. 4478c) reads like an eighteenth century "Who's Who," his acquaintances including Warburton, Savage, Thomson, Hogarth, Walter Harte, Dr. Richard Mead, and many more. But the entries are selective, and a person's qualifications are often listed along with his name. Cave was too insignificant to merit mention; his name does not appear in the diary during this period. Cave's letters to Birch are generally quite formal, with the exception of several that relate to social occasions on which Cave was apparently acting as chaperone for Elizabeth Carter (see below, note 49).

44. James M. Osborn, "Birch and the *GD,*" pp. 26, 33.

45. *Letters of Horace Walpole,* ed. P. Cunningham, 9 vols. (London: 1857–59), VII, 326.

46. Hawkins, p. 209.

47. *Life,* V, 255.

48. P. 654. A translation of this into Latin, perhaps by Johnson, appeared the next month (*GM,* 1739, p. 4).

49. The Birch-Carter relationship is detailed by Edward Ruhe in "Birch, Johnson, and Elizabeth Carter: An Episode of 1738–39," *PMLA,* 73 (December 1958): 491–500. Mr. Ruhe errs slightly, though, by accepting the entries in Birch's diary as complete (see note 43). As a result he asserts that Birch and Miss Carter had at least forty-seven unchaperoned meetings, including a seven day trip to Oxford. Such meetings would have been scandalous and the Oxford trip unthinkable. Birch simply omitted the rest of the company from his diary. One example is readily documentable: the diary entry for August 8, 1738, suggests that Birch and Miss Carter went alone to see Cannons, the seat of the Duke of Chandos; but a letter from Cave to Birch makes it clear that Cave had been along (see *James Thomson: Letters and Documents,* ed. A. D. McKillop [Lawrence: U. of Kansas Press, 1958], p. 123). The chaperone was there, he was just too insignificant to mention.

50. Ruhe, p. 498.

51. In 1743, when working on a "Historical Design" for Cave, Johnson sought information from Birch (*Letters*, I, 24–25). Birch may also have contributed towards the *Life of Savage*.

52. See, for example, Clifford, pp. 186–87.

53. Barker, p. 216. Barker has identified at least five such assistants, and Carlson (pp. 13, 75) two more. Many were Cave's relatives.

CHAPTER III

1. The earliest debate recorded in Cave's original series took place on February 3, 1738 (Hoover, p. 215).

2. The entire incident, including, ironically, excerpts from speeches, is narrated in "Autobiography," November 1856, pp. 538–41.

3. *LM*, 1738, p. 238. Magazines appeared at the beginning of the month following that on the masthead; thus, the May issue, in which the debates of the Political Club first appeared, reached the public in the first week of June. Since the magazines purported to be chronicles of the writings and occurrences of a given month, they were dated according to their content rather than their month of publication.

4. P. 285.

5. Each of the magazines' ruses had its difficulties. As a record of the debates in Parliament, the *London Magazine*'s version had a major drawback: the reader could not easily identify who the actual speaker was supposed to be. That Walpole was "Cicero" and Pulteney "Cato" was nowhere indicated in the magazine. Cave's plan obviated this difficulty, for the speakers were readily identifiable. But if the anagrammatical names eliminated one problem, the entire Lilliputian machinery created an equally great one. The debates become trivialized by the constant intrusion of absurd names and places. Even a reader familiar with the fact that "Mildendo" is London cannot always pass over the term without it breaking his concentration.

6. *Life*, I, 502. Greene (*Politics*, p. 92) sees the piece as "evidently by Johnson," and Clifford agrees. But J. G. Nichols attributed it to Guthrie ("Autobiography," *GM*, December 1856, p. 668). Although the beginning of the piece sounds Johnsonian, the fifth through eleventh paragraphs have few indisputable signs of his style. The remainder may contain the work of both men.

7. P. 285. See Johnson's treatment of the "savage" races in the "Life of Drake" in Chapter 6, below.

8. Waingrow, p. 234. This statement is excerpted from a list of "Memorandums on reading Hawkins's *Life of Johnson*" that Hussey sent Boswell to aid him in preparing the *Life*.

9. Hawkins, p. 123. Hawkins is a major source of information about Cave's duties; unfortunately, his evidence is often suspect. Editing the poetry section would seem an obvious task for Johnson; in the late 1740s, John Hawkesworth, Johnson's successor in many of his editorial tasks with the magazine, had this duty. But whether Cave relinquished it to Johnson at a later date and then to Hawkesworth, or to Hawkesworth alone after Johnson's departure, is unknown. For Hawkesworth, see Chapter 8, below; for Hawkins's early contributions to

the *GM*, see Bertram H. Davis, *A Proof of Eminence: The Life of Sir John Hawkins* (Bloomington: Indiana U. Press, 1973), p. 11ff.

10. Barker notes the extensive coincidence between the publication dates of the abridged essays and the days of Cave's attendance at the post office (p. 33). Once Johnson takes on expanded duties for the magazine in 1741, his contributions to the "Historical Chronicle" often become discernible. The lack of any signs of his style in this department at this time suggests that he had no influence over it.

11. *Letters*, I, 12–13.

12. Guthrie's writing does not seem burdened with "Scotticisms" to a modern reader, but several of his contemporaries commented on the lack of purity of his English. Charles Churchill suggested that he wrote a "rude unnat'ral jargon, . . . half *Scotch*, half *English*"; and Johnson himself reported Guthrie's dispute with his fellow translator of the Du Halde: "Green said of Guthrie that he knew no English, and Guthrie of Green that he knew no French" (*Life*, I, 118 n.; IV, 30).

13. Hawkins, p. 95.

14. "Autobiography," *GM*, September 1856, p. 273 n.

15. *GM*, 1738, p. 366. If the letter to Cave noting that the "Chinese Stories" were finally selected was written, as appears, in September, Cave may have been justified in any censure of Johnson's dilatoriness, for the excerpts were promised for the August issue.

16. *GM*, 1738, p. 365.

17. For the political background, see Donald Greene's introduction to the piece in *Political Writings*, p. 14.

18. This last possibility is plausibly suggested by Greene, ibid.

19. *GM*, July 1738, pp. 347-49; October 1738, pp. 536–537. These two pieces have been attributed to Johnson convincingly by Jacob Leed, "Two New Pieces by Johnson in the *Gentleman's Magazine?*", *Modern Philology*, 54 (1957): 221-29.

The names "Eubulus" and "Pamphilus" were both used by Erasmus in his *Colloquia*: see the translation by Craig R. Thompson (Chicago: U. of Chicago Press, 1965), pp. 88, 103, 112, and elsewhere. A copy of the *Colloquia* (edition unknown) was among the books that Johnson took to Oxford (*Gleanings*, V, 217). For further information about the name "Eubulus," see E. A. Bloom, "Symbolic Names in Johnson's Periodical Essays," *Modern Language Quarterly*, 13 (1952): 351 n.

20. Only one response to the queries besides that done by Johnson ever appeared in the magazine, that in September, p. 465.

21. *GM*, 1738, p. 349. This reading of the final sentence is noted by F. V. Bernard in "New Evidence on the Pamphilus Letters," *Modern Philology*, 62 (1964): 42–44. Madame von Wallmoden landed in England in June 1738.

22. *GM*, 1738, p. 537.

23. *GM*, 1736, p. 170.

24. Duick was a relation of Browne's and the winner of several lesser prizes in Cave's contests. He would probably have been among the "luminaries" that Cave escorted Johnson to see at the tavern in Clerkenwell.

25. *GM*, 1739, p. 166.

26. There is yet another epigram on Miss Carter, beginning "Quid mihi

cum cultu," which was first published by Pennington in *Memoirs*, p. 271 n.; it probably also dates from this early period.

27. *GM*, 1738, p. 372. Although Croker first attributed the Latin version to Johnson solely on the basis of style, G. Hampshire has found corroborating evidence in one of Elizabeth Carter's letters. See "Johnson, Elizabeth Carter, and Pope's Garden," *Notes and Queries*, June 1972, pp. 221-22.

28. Elizabeth Carter's description of the garden is given by Hampshire, p. 221. See also *Poems*, p. 82.

29. *GM*, 1738, p. 429. By signing the poem "Urbanus," Johnson was identifying himself as the editor of the magazine.

30. The probable amount of Johnson's earnings is discussed below in Chapter 5, p. 84, and Chapter 8, p. 166ff.

31. An announcement that proposals had been issued, naming Johnson as translator, precedes the "Life": see *GM*, 1738, pp. 581–83.

32. For a detailed analysis of Johnson's handling of his source, see John L. Abbott, "Dr. Johnson and the Making of the 'Life of Father Paul Sarpi,' " *Bulletin of the John Rylands Library* 48 (1966): 255–67; and E. L. McAdam, Jr., "Johnson's Lives of Sarpi, Blake, and Drake," *PMLA* 58 (1943): 466–70.

33. *GM*, 1738, pp. 491, 578–79. The death notice shows no sign of Johnson's hand.

34. The *Oratio Academica in Memoriam Hermanni Boerhaavii* (Leiden, 1738) was the sole source of Johnson's life. A reprint of the *Oratio* was published by A. Dodd in January 1739, probably with Cave's backing.

35. *GM*, 1739, pp. 37–38, 72–73, 114–116, 172–76. Unlike the "Sarpi," the "Boerhaave" appeared anonymously.

36. Johnson's handling of Schultens's *Oratio* is analyzed by Richard R. Reynolds, "Johnson's *Life of Boerhaave* in Perspective," *The Yearbook of English Studies* 5 (1975): 115–29.

37. *GM*, 1738, pp. 638–41. As an extra benefit, this piece gives a view of the abridging technique used by Cave. All excess words were removed, leaving the style very spare, but containing the entire argument of the piece. The *LM* tended to preserve the exact language, but as a result was often forced either to omit more paragraphs of a given essay or else to print fewer essays than the *GM*.

38. P. 641.

39. See F. V. Bernard, "Common and Superior Sense: A New Attribution to Samuel Johnson," *Notes and Queries*, May 1967, pp. 176–80, where this piece is first attributed to Johnson.

40. This piece, with the heading "To the Reader," was attributed to Johnson by Boswell on the basis of style alone, but all subsequent students of Johnson have accepted it as his. The preface for 1738, like all the magazine's prefaces, was published with the yearly supplement. Thus it reached the public in mid-January, 1739.

41. Johnson noted that the *GM*'s unhappy competitors had "Seventy Thousand *London Magazines* mouldering in their Warehouses, returned from all Parts of the Kingdom, unsold, unread, and disregarded," a fact that he repeated several months later in the March 1739 issue (p. 111). Considering Johnson's

extreme veracity, this must be taken as a sign of the *GM*'s predominance over its rival.

42. *GM*, 1739, pp. 3, 111, 223. A letter comparing the *GM* and *LM* to the advantage of the first, printed in the *Daily Advertiser* for April 18, 1739, and reprinted in the *GM* (1739, p. 202), was attributed to Johnson by John Nichols: see "Rise and Progress," p. xxvii. The attribution of the letter is highly questionable.

43. *GM*, 1739, p. 4.

44. *GM*, 1739, pp. 54, 79, 80, 82, 148.

45. Ibid., pp. 24–25, 29, 78–84, 129.

46. Ibid., p. 83.

47. Ibid., p. 29.

48. Ibid., p. 129.

49. Several single-paragraph summaries of essays and intruded editorial notes appeared in the *GM* during the early months of 1735: see, for example, pp. 66–67, 132, 136, 140; but none has the disdainful tone of those of 1739.

50. Greene, *Politics*, p. 91.

51. *LM*, 1739, pp. 244–45. The material was not taken directly from *Marmor* but from the periodical *Old Common Sense* (not to be confused with *Common Sense*) for May 19, 1739, and appears among the Weekly Essays.

52. Carlson, p. 163. Astronomical problems continue to appear, but pure mathematics disappears soon after Johnson's arrival. The index to the collected volume of the *GM* for 1737 lists at least twenty articles under "Mathematics"; that for 1738 lists thirteen, only four of which appeared after July. The 1739 index does not even include a heading "Mathematics."

53. The excerpts from Maupertuis (*GM*, 1738, pp. 577, 635; 1739, p. 14) are an abridgment of the English translation published in July 1738 by T. Cox et al. The excerpts from Bougeant's work are widely spread out over an entire year of the magazine, beginning in April 1739 (p. 194) and not concluding until the next April, although there were only a total of five installments. The delay may have been brought about by Cave's subsequent legal troubles with abridgments.

54. The extracts appeared in the *GM* for June 1739, pp. 288–92. Although they were supposed to be continued in July, they never were. In October Cave noted in the magazine that he was being sued (p. 543), complaining about the injustice of the matter and arguing that the extracts promoted, rather than hindered, the sale of the work. In April 1740, he asked his readers to inform him if anyone had been led to purchase a book by reading an abridgment in the magazine (p. 183), and in June he printed a letter by a reader who had in fact bought Trapp's sermons after reading the *GM* extracts (p. 297).

Johnson's place in all this is uncertain. The exact date of his defense of abridgment is unknown. Since the case dragged on well into 1740, Johnson could have written it after his return to Cave's service early that year. The legality of abridging copyrighted materials was a topic of major importance at the time, and Cave was apparently saved by a precedent-setting decision that was handed down after suit had already been brought against him. In *Gyles vs. Wilcox* (argued March 6, 1740) Lord Chancellor Hardwicke ruled that an abridgment does not infringe upon copyright: see R. M. Wiles, *Serial Publication in England before 1750* (Cambridge: Cambridge U. Press, 1957), pp. 160–62.

CHAPTER IV

1. *Life*, I, 131–34; *Gleanings*, VI, 101–102.

2. *Life*, I, 84.

3. *Life*, I, 133. A variant of this text appears in the account of Johnson's life published shortly after his death in the *European Magazine*: "than be starved to death in _____ translating for Booksellers." See Donald Greene's discussion of this in *Philological Quarterly* 54 (1975): 967–68.

4. For a further discussion of this matter, see below, Chapter 5.

5. For more detailed explanations of the divisions within the trade, see William M. Sale, Jr., *Samuel Richardson, Master Printer* (Ithaca: Cornell U. Press, 1950), p. 86ff; Michael Treadwell, "London Trade Publishers, 1675–1750," *The Library*, Ser. 6, 4 (1982): 99–134; and Donald F. McKenzie, *The London Book Trade in the Later Seventeenth Century*, the Sandars Lectures for 1976 (privately published), pp. 25–28.

6. A complete analysis of the role of trade publishers is given by Treadwell. Mercuries were wholesale distributors as well as retailers of newspapers and pamphlets; hawkers were street sellers (McKenzie, p. 25; Treadwell, pp. 123–24).

7. Treadwell, p. 107. The distinctions in the lower branches of the trade were not quite so rigid as this description might suggest. Some of the more important mercuries, like Anne Dodd, acted on occasion as trade publishers (see Treadwell, pp. 123–24; McKenzie, p. 28). Several works for which Cave held copy were issued under Dodd's imprint.

8. The sale of Samuel Boyse's poem *The Deity* is said by the author of Boyse's life to have been blighted initially because it issued from the shop of a publisher whose stock consisted of "an abundance of trifles": Cibber's *Lives of the Poets* (London, 1753), V, 172. The publisher was James Roberts, the most important trade publisher of the day. Eighty-five percent of the books that appeared with his imprint between 1743 and 1746 sold for a shilling or less (Treadwell, pp. 121-22).

9. Thomas Osborne wrote to the Society for the Encouragement of Learning that "it is in the booksellers' power to hinder the sale of any book by giving their Correspondents a bad acc[ount] of it, and consequently preventing them sending commissions for it": quoted in Clayton Atto, "The Society for the Encouragement of Learning," *The Library*, Ser. 4, 19 (1938–39): 282.

10. *GM*, 1739, p. 111.

11. Treadwell, p. 120.

12. Terry Belanger, "Booksellers' Sales of Copyright" (Ph.D. dissertation, Columbia University, 1970), pp. 143, 146–47, 153.

13. The proprietors of the *London Magazine*—Thomas Cox, John Wilford, John Clarke, and Thomas Astley, booksellers, and Charles Ackers, a printer— pleaded their right to appropriate the plan of Cave's monthly on the basis of

Cave's plagiarisms from *Fog's Weekly Journal* and *The Weekly Register*, properties of Wilford, Clarke, and Ackers: see the introduction by D. F. McKenzie and J. C. Ross to *A Ledger of Charles Ackers* (Oxford: The Bibliographical Society, 1968), p. 5. Some of the weekly papers were driven out of business by the magazines.

14. *GM*, 1732, p. 684; see also *GM*, 1731, p. 408. Some of his titles were in questionable taste: *The Benefit of Farting*, 14th edition; *Lives and Amours of Queens and Royal Mistresses, with Some Intrigues of Popes*; *A General History of Executions for the Year 1730*. Most of the works offered for sale by Cave were mere ephemera and have disappeared without a trace. From some hints left by Johnson it seems likely that at least some of these, if not printed by Cave, were underwritten by him: "He wrote an Account of the Criminals [perhaps the *General History of Executions* already mentioned], which had for some time a considerable sale; and published many little pamphlets that accident brought into his hands, of which it would be very difficult to recover the memory" (see "Life of Cave," in Fleeman, ed., *Early Biographical Writings*, p. 408).

15. The members of Prevost's syndicate are listed in the advertisement for the first number in the *Daily Advertiser* for March 29, 1733: see R. M. Wiles, *Serial Publication*, p. 287; and Osborn, "Birch and the *General Dictionary*," pp. 27–31. Birch's copy of the contract has been preserved in the British Library. Of the sixteen proprietors, thirteen were booksellers; one is simply listed as Henry Vander Esch of the Tower of London, Esquire; and two were printers—Cave and James Bettenham, the latter of whom actually printed the work.

16. The fourth volume was completed in June 1736. Bettenham was also omitted from the imprints of the first three volumes. The omission was almost certainly based on the snobbery of the trade hierarchy, for Cave is mentioned in the *GM* advertisements, but only as a vendor of the work, not among the proprietors: see *GM*, 1734, p. 395, and subsequent issues.

Cave must have been annoyed at this treatment, for in July 1735 he accepted an advertisement for the rival edition of Bayle, the *Dictionary Historical and Critical*, translated by M. Des Maizeaux (see *GM*, 1735, p. 392). Two months later the advertisement for the rival appeared for the last time; on the same page, the *General Dictionary* is advertised with Cave listed, for the first time, as one of the proprietors (p. 564). When the fourth volume appeared, Cave flaunted his position as proprietor, noting the work as "Printed for E. Cave at St. John's Gate; and others" (*GM*, 1736, p. 360).

17. For Voltaire's opinion of this work, see *Life*, II, 483. The first volume contains thirty-six "maps, plans, and cuts"; the second volume, over twenty.

18. See G. R. Crone, "John Green: Notes on a Neglected Eighteenth-Century Geographer and Cartographer," *Imago Mundi* 6 (1949): 85–91; and idem, "A Note on Bradock Mead, alias John Green," *The Library*, Ser. 5, 6 (1951): 42–43. Green made a number of additions and corrections to the maps that appeared in the original French version.

19. Cave may have taken this step in order to distance himself from his actual place in the trade, that of printer, and to solidify his position as bookseller. Cave is noted in the imprint of the second volume as its printer.

20. He sought one thousand subscribers but certainly settled for fewer.

21. See Wiles, *Serial Publication*, pp. 184–85, 307. Once begun, the project continued to encounter delays: the first volume was not completed until No-

vember 1738, the second not until 1742 (*GM*, 1742, p. 168).

22. For a copy of the proposals, see J. A. V. Chapple, "Samuel Johnson's *Proposals for Printing the History of the Council of Trent*," *Bulletin of the John Rylands Library* 45 (1962–63): 340–69.

23. In a letter to Cave written in late November, 1738, Johnson promises Cave that he will provide "copy to spare" the next morning if Cave would send a messenger to him (*Letters*, I, 14). Johnson, then, must not have kept his materials at St. John's Gate but at home, and could have labored there or at a convenient tavern.

24. Frances A. Yates, "Paolo Sarpi's *History of the Council of Trent*," *Journal of the Warburg and Courtauld Institutes* 7 (1944): 125. A portrait of Sarpi in the Bodleian, reproduced in Yates (facing, p. 140), denominates him "Concilii Tridentini Eviscerator." The subsequent discussion of Sarpi and the English Church is gleaned from Yates's comprehensive article, especially pp. 125–29, 137–40.

25. *Letters*, I, 13.

26. Nichols, "Rise and Progress," p. xx; he gives no indication of his source for this figure, which may be inflated.

27. Edward Ruhe has ferreted out the details behind the conflicting translations: see "The Two Samuel Johnsons," *Notes and Queries*, October 1954, pp. 432–35.

28. Both John Johnson's letter and Cave's response (given in part below) are quoted in Ruhe, pp. 433–34.

29. Cave's note, addressed to "John," has generally been thought to be directed to Johnson, but Barker (pp. 313–14) has cogently argued that the directive was for the supervisor of the presses rather than for the author of the work. For the specifics of the letter to Cave and of his endorsement, see Chapple, pp. 353–54, 366–67.

30. *Letters*, I, 14.

31. A. T. Hazen and E. L. McAdam, Jr., believed that the reference was to the Crousaz translation (discussed below), which is the primary subject of Johnson's letter; they thought it unlikely that the Sarpi would have been in the press so early: "First Editions of Samuel Johnson," *Yale University Library Gazette* 10 (1936): 50. But as Cave's note to John Chaney shows, sheets of the Sarpi were in fact in the press at this time. And it is unlikely that Johnson would be sending copy for the Crousaz when in the same letter he counsels Cave against continuing the work.

32. Nichols, "Rise and Progress," p. xv n.; Hawkins, p. 65. See also, Chapple, pp. 367-69.

33. Ruhe, p. 435.

34. *Life*, I, 135–36. The exact wording of the "Account" at first appears ambiguous, for the phrase "in relation to a version of Father Paul, &c." seems to imply that the receipt may be for more than just the Sarpi. This, though, is unlikely. As Chapple suggests (p. 363), the "&c." indicates the additional aspects of the work beyond the translation itself—"with the Author's Life, and Notes . . . from the French Edition of Dr. *Le Courayer*; to which are added Observations . . . by S. Johnson." The same convention is found in a receipt signed by John Bernard, one of the contributors to the *General Dictionary*, where that work is described as "the General Dictionary Historical & Critical &C" (see Os-

born, "Birch and the *General Dictionary*," p. 31 n.). All of those who saw the actual account appear to have understood it to refer to the Sarpi alone.

35. Johnson generally gauged his work by the sheet: *Life*, IV, 127, 494; *Letters*, I, 15, 20, 21. John Feather notes that John Nourse, the bookseller, "paid by the sheet when the length of the book was in doubt"—see "John Nourse and his Authors," *Studies in Bibliography* 34 (1981): 206-207.

36. BM Add. MS 4254, f. 116.

37. Pay varied with different types of publications. In the 1730s, John Nourse was willing to pay two guineas per sheet to one Thomas Barlow for a "Treatise concerning the Duty and office of a Justice of peace," and the same rate to a Joseph Shaw for "a new treatise Intitled Parish Law." But John Landen was only to receive a single guinea per sheet for his *Mathematical Lucubrations* in 1755, as was Marie Le Prince de Beaumont for her *Magasin des Adolescentes* in 1764 (see Feather, p. 207). In a letter to Cave of unknown date, Johnson states that Alexander Macbean was willing to compile a "Military Dictionary" for twelve shillings a sheet (*Letters*, I, 15). But as we shall see, translators were often paid considerably less than even Macbean's paltry demands.

38. *The English Book Trade* (London: Allen & Unwin, 1939), p. 75.

39. *The Correspondence of Alexander Pope*, ed. George Sherburn, 5 vols. (Oxford: Oxford U. Pr., 1956), I, 373.

40. Excerpts from Lintot's account book given by John Nichols in *Literary Anecdotes* (VIII, 293–304) include the following:

To "Mr. Digby"
1713, June 10. For translating Quintus Curtius £10 15s. 0d.
To "Mr. Morehead"
1712, Dec. 16. For Part of Quintus Curtius £1 0s. 0d.
To "Dr. Sewel"
1714–15, Mar. 10. Paid Dr. Sewel, for translating Part of Quintus Curtius, and Part of Lucretius £6 19s. 9d.

For Quintus Curtius, then, Lintot paid £11 15s. 0d. (to Morehead and Digby) plus a portion of his payment to Sewel. At ten shillings per sheet, £11 15s. 0d. would recompense the translators for twenty three and one-half sheets. A collation of Lintot's 1714 edition of Quintus Curtius, printed in the *National Union Catalogue* (130:190) indicates that the work comprised twenty five and one-half sheets duodecimo. The difference of two sheets may represent the work of Sewel. If Sewel contributed more than two sheets, the rate of pay for all three authors was higher than 10s. per sheet, rising to 12s. if half of Sewel's total wages were for the Quintus Curtius.

Other entries from Lintot's accounts confirm the range of 10s. to 12s. as fairly standard. He paid "Mr. Shoree" £5 for a translation of Cornelius Nepos that comprises eight sheets, a total of 12s. 6d. per sheet. And "Mr. Morehead" and "Captain Stephens" were paid a total of £29 7s. for translating Louis Ellies Dupin's *Compendious History of the Church* at a rate of about 10s. 6d. per sheet. (See *Literary Anecdotes*, ibid.)

41. *Literary Anecdotes*, VIII, 295; Ralph Straus, *Robert Dodsley* (London: John Lane, 1910), pp. 87, 323. Digby may have agreed to translate the work for a lump sum rather than at a per-sheet rate.

Although Dodsley paid Mrs. Jarvis only £21 ready money (about 4s. 6d. per sheet), the fifteen copies of *Don Quixote* may have provided a substantial income if she was able to dispose of them all. The work sold for either 2 guineas (*GM*, 1742, p. 224) or 50 shillings (Straus, p. 323). In all likelihood the widow would have been forced to dispose of her copies through a trade publisher. If she received £25 from the sale of her copies, her total profit would have amounted to £46, or about ten shillings per sheet of translation.

42. *Literary Anecdotes*, VIII, 298, 301. Theobald's translation is entitled *Plato's Dialogue of the Immortality of the Soul*; Lewis's work appeared in 1715 under the title *Letters of Love and Gallantry*.

43. The payment for the Lobo translation was far below this rate: five guineas for almost twenty-five sheets of text, a rate of about four shillings per sheet. Johnson may simply have agreed to translate the book for the stated sum. But it seems unlikely that once he had arrived in London he would have settled for anything below the going rate.

44. Several receipts for payment in the Birch papers in the British Library confirm this rate of payment. James Osborn, making use of one of these receipts, concluded that Bernard may have been paid only ten shillings per sheet for his contributions ("Birch and the *GD*," p. 31 n.). Unfortunately Osborn misidentified the portion of the *GD* (fascicle xiv) referred to in the receipt he quotes. Number xiv consists of the eighty-first through the hundredth sheets (pp. 321–400) of the second volume. Bernard was paid £1 15s. for his contributions to this installment, in which he has four signed articles totalling five and a half pages, or slightly less than one and a half folio sheets. Thirty-five shillings would be the proper payment for such a contribution at twenty-five shillings per sheet. Whether Bernard was responsible for any of the unsigned articles is unknown. Other contributors were apparently also paid at that same rate as the contract authors: William Oldys received twenty-five shillings for his four-and-a-half-page article on Sir John Fastolff in the fifth volume of the *GD*, a payment basically in keeping with the contract rate (Osborn, p. 46).

45. Although all three of the authors of the *GD* were little known at the start of the project, its success had brought them at least a minimum of reputation. Birch, as we have noted above, was admitted to the Royal Society for his contributions. Nor should the figure of 25s. per sheet be thought in any way penurious. The authors were required to provide twenty sheets of copy per month; they would thus share a total of £25 each month—no small sum. Birch in fact appears to have done most of the work and thus received most of the pay.

46. In the autumn of 1743, Johnson was paid something more than two guineas per sheet by Cave for a "Historical Design" that was never published, but the circumstances under which that work was undertaken differed so greatly from those under which the Sarpi translation was begun that no comparison of rates seems valid. See Chapter 9.

47. A. L. Reade was so taken by the size of Johnson's payment—"an average of over twenty-five shillings a week"—that he remarked, "No doubt this represented the completion of the translation" (*Gleanings*, X, 143). Although I suspect that Reade has overstated the case, it is not beyond the realm of possibility that Johnson was paid so poorly and accomplished so much.

48. Straus, *Dodsley*, pp. 257–58. In this later case, either party could suspend work on three months' notice.

49. That Johnson was instrumental in Cave's decision to publish the Crousaz translations may be inferred from their unique place in all of Cave's publishing ventures. Never before or after did he stray into the area of literary or moral controversy, yet these topics would have had considerable appeal for Johnson.

50. *Lives of the Poets*, III, 164.

51. *GM*, 1738, p. 496.

52. This advertisement provides insight into the extent that various booksellers sold works in which they held no part of the copy. Although Curll's advertisement lists eleven sellers of the *Commentary* (including Dodsley and A. Dodd) the work was "printed only for E. Curll." Dodd's appearance among Curll's retailers of the book is particularly interesting, for she was soon to "publish" Elizabeth Carter's translation of the *Examen* (*DA*, November 23, 1738) and, apparently, also Johnson's version of the *Commentary*.

53. *Letters*, I, 13.

54. Hazen and McAdam, pp. 48–49.

55. See *GM*, 1741, p. 614. Cave apparently had a great deal of trouble ridding himself of this work. On November 10, 1742, both the *Commentary* and the *Examination* were advertised in the *Daily Advertiser* as "just publish'd." Cave called attention to these works in 1743 by having Johnson write an essay on the controversy between Crousaz and Warburton that arose from Crousaz's criticisms of the *Essay on Man*. Johnson's essay is discussed in Chapter 8.

56. *A Commentary on Mr. Pope's Principles of Morality, or Essay on Man*, by Mons. Crousaz (London, 1742), p. 123.

57. *Commentary*, p. 40.

58. *Commentary*, p. 109.

59. In the essay on the Crousaz-Warburton dispute and again in the *Life of Pope*, Johnson treated Crousaz as a pious man with solid opinions and good intentions.

60. *Life*, IV, 127, 494. Either Johnson's memory failed him slightly or Boswell erred in his journal, for he recorded Johnson as saying that he did "Six sheets in one day: 48 Quarto pages of a translation of Crousaz on Pope." The *Commentary* was published in duodecimo, and six sheets constituted one hundred and forty-four pages, not forty-eight.

CHAPTER V

1. This figure is based on the discussion of pay for translation in the previous chapter.

2. The Boerhaave filled about twenty columns of the magazine—ten pages, or slightly more than half a sheet. Since the work was merely an abridged translation, Johnson's pay for it may in fact have been very slight. Johnson was probably paid nothing extra for the "Life of Sarpi," which was an abridgment of the life to be prefaced to the on-going translation. It seems unlikely that Cave would have paid Johnson once to translate the life from Le Courayer, then again to abridge it.

3. McKenzie and Ross, *A Ledger of Charles Ackers*, pp. 14–15.

4. Alexander Chalmers suggested that Johnson was paid £100 per year by Cave for editing the *GM* (*General Biographical Dictionary*, 32 vols. [London, 1812–17], XIX, 53), but this figure, if correct, must pertain to Johnson's later, more extensive involvement with the magazine during the early 1740s. For a more detailed consideration of these matters, see Chapter 8, pp. 166–70, below.

5. Johnson's total income for this period would have exceeded what he received from Cave, for he was also paid for the two political pamphlets, *Marmor Norfolciense* and *A Compleat Vindication of the Licensers of the Stage*. How much, though, is unknown.

6. *Life*, I, 440. Richard Cumberland cited Johnson as saying that he once lived on four and one-half pence per day, a total of only about seven pounds per year (see below, Chapter 9, p. 196, and n. 100). See also Chapter 1, Note 5, above, for Johnson's statement on the value of £50.

7. The estimates given both above and below are deduced from Burnett's *History of the Cost of Living*: see especially pp. 135–38, 145–46, 165–68, 175–76, and 186. Lodgings could be rented for under ten pounds a year, and beef and cheese could be had for under three pence per pound.

8. *GM*, 1731, p. 37.

9. M. Dorothy George, *London Life in the Eighteenth Century* (London: K. Paul, 1925), pp. 167–68, 369 n. 38. Figures on clothing for the gentry are difficult to obtain, but Burnett notes that Nicholas Blundell, Squire of Crosby and Ditton near Liverpool, spent almost £7 for a servant's livery in the first quarter of the century, and £177 on the complete wardrobes for two of his daughters about to enter society (p. 152). See also Burnett, pp. 145–46, 151.

10. James E. Thorold Rogers, *A History of Agriculture and Prices in England*, 7 vols. (Oxford: Clarendon, 1866–1902; rpt. Vaduz: Kraus, 1963), VII, 439. The most common prices for fabrics were apparently between four and eight shillings per yard. Information about both fashion and cost during the first half of the century can be gleaned from C. Willett Cunnington and Phyllis Cunnington, *Handbook of English Costume in the Eighteenth Century* (Boston: Plays, Inc., 1972), pp. 106–80, 422–23.

11. *Life*, I, 115.

12. *Life*, I, 163. Johnson closed the November 1738 letter to Cave, in which he promises to send "copy to spare," with the words "Yours, *impransus*," that is, without having dined. Boswell interpreted the phrase as an indication of Johnson's poverty. Johnson probably meant nothing more than that he had not stopped work to dine; he was not one to broadcast his misery: see *Letters*, I, 14 n. 3.

13. Hawkins, p. 52; *Life*, I, 162.

14. To do Hawkins justice, it should be noted that he did not suggest that Savage was driven to the Gate in search of work; this is Boswell's conclusion from Hawkins's more general statement. Poverty, of course, could have driven Savage to the Gate in search of a meal.

15. Clarence Tracy, in *The Artificial Bastard*, pp. 121–122, suggests that Savage made a deal with the editors of both magazines in March 1734 to have his poetry simultaneously published in their competing journals. If Savage had such an agreement, he did not exploit it vigorously for several years. His poem "The

Gentleman" appeared in both magazines for December 1734, but only after appearing in the *Grub-Street Journal* for December 12 of that year. A character of the Rev. James Foster appeared in the *LM* for March 1735 and in the *GM* a month later. Savage's poetry did not begin to appear regularly in directly competing issues of the magazines until the "Volunteer Laureat" of 1736. Six more poems—four new ones and two revisions of earlier works—appeared simultaneously in both magazines during the remainder of the year. In 1737 Savage stopped his double submissions, printing his work primarily in the *GM* until after his retirement to Wales, when he again began to send his work to both. A list of Savage's contributions to the *GM* (omitting "The Gentleman" and the "Verses occasioned by . . . Mrs. Knight" [March 1737]) is given in Carlson, p. 261. Tracy gives the publication history of each poem in his edition of Savage's *Poetical Works* (Cambridge: Cambridge U. Press, 1962).

16. The early date of "Fulvia" is plausibly suggested by Tracy in his edition of the *Poetical Works*, p. 92.

17. *Lives*, II, 406, 408.

18. These traces of Savage's activities are gleaned from Birch's diary and from two letters to Birch preserved in the British Library, one from Cave and the other Savage's letter of September 1. All of these materials, including the two letters and select quotations from the diary, have been collected in A. D. McKillop's edition of James Thomson's *Letters and Documents*, pp. 123–24. A photostat of Savage's letter to Birch is given by Tracy.

19. A concerted effort was mounted in the pages of the *GM* to procure Savage the continuance of his pension. "Volunteer Laureat, No. VII" appeared in the March issue of the *GM* (along with "Ad Urbanum"). The next month the first "Volunteer Laureat" was reprinted with a headnote signed "T.B.," apparently Thomas Birch, that set out the history of Savage's relation to the Queen and her approval of his actions as Volunteer Laureat. (Despite the signature on the headnote, Johnson stated in the *Life of Savage* that it was actually written by Savage himself: *Lives of the Poets*, II, 382.) In the June issue his "Genius of Liberty" was printed. Savage had written this last poem on the occasion of the marriage of the Princess Anne to the Prince of Orange. Cave was allowing his magazine to be used to remind the King of his late wife's regard for Savage and of the poet's faithfulness in his somewhat irregular office. Unfortunately the scheme failed.

20. Many students of Johnson, following Hawkins, have suggested that Johnson met Savage sometime in 1737 and that he modeled the character of "Thales" in *London* on Savage; but this is refuted by Johnson's own testimony. Rev. John Hussey wrote Boswell that "Johnson told me, that when he imitated the third Satire of Juvenal, he did not intend to characterise any one under the name of Thales, and further said, the Poem was written and published before he was acquainted with Savage" (Waingrow, p. 233). The supposed parallels that link "Thales" to Savage are on the whole either commonplaces that could be applied to many eighteenth-century personalities or specious resemblances founded on patent misreadings of the poem. For a full discussion of these matters, see my article "Was Savage 'Thales'?: Johnson's *London* and Biographical Speculation," *Bulletin of Research in the Humanities* 85 (1982): 322–35.

21. *J. Misc.*, I, 371.

22. Johnson was paid by Cave for various works through April 1739 and possibly into May, at which time he probably received some additional income from his political pamphlets. Although Johnson had no certain income for some time afterwards, there is no reason to conclude that he was homeless.

Hawkins (pp. 88–89) asserted that Johnson and Tetty were temporarily separated during Johnson's friendship with Savage, Johnson lodging in Fleet Street while Tetty was "harboured by a friend near the Tower." But this story is most likely an embellishment on the real separation that occurred when Johnson left for the Midlands to seek the post at Appleby School during the summer of 1739, leaving Tetty behind in London. When Johnson wrote Tetty from Lichfield in January 1740, he addressed the letter to her "at Mrs. Crow's in Castle Street near Cavendish Square" (*Letters*, I, 15). Tetty had probably never left their Castle Street quarters. Hawkins, in all likelihood, knew of a separation, but not of its cause, and so he assumed what to him was the most likely one— Savage. This had the added benefit of helping to explain Johnson's all-night rambles.

23. *Life*, II, 406–07. For Mrs. Thrale's lament about Johnson's late hours, see *J. Misc.*, I, 231–32.

24. *Life*, I, 250-51. Although Boswell relates the anecdote under the year 1752, he notes that it took place while Johnson lodged in the Temple. For the period of his stay there, see *Life*, III, 535.

25. Hawkins, p. 53.

26. *Life*, I, 164.

27. The first of these is the common attitude towards the political writings of 1739, the second the attitude of Joseph Wood Krutch in his *Samuel Johnson* (New York: Holt, 1945), p. 66.

28. At the time of Walpole's fall, "Tories" made up only a quarter of the Commons, 136 out of 558 seats: see John B. Owen, *The Rise of the Pelhams* (London: Methuen, 1957), pp. 66–67. For general discussions of the nature of Toryism and the place of Tories in the opposition to Walpole, see Owen, pp. 66–75, and Archibald S. Foord, *His Majesty's Opposition, 1714–1830* (Oxford: Clarendon, 1964), pp. 136–42.

29. John Brooke, "Party in the Eighteenth Century," in *Silver Renaissance: Essays in Eighteenth-Century History*, ed. Alex Natan (London: Macmillan, 1961), pp. 22, 24.

30. Foord, pp. 78–79.

31. Brooke, p. 25.

32. For a "Whiggish" speech by Hanmer, see Foord, pp. 79–80.

33. The dread of the "moneyed corporations" as the seat of corruption is discussed at length by Isaac Kramnick in *Bolingbroke and His Circle* (Cambridge, Mass.: Harvard, 1968), pp. 56–76. The extent to which many Tory attacks on the power of the Crown were sincere is problematic. As Foord points out, Hanmer's attack on the danger posed by a standing army was "a standard debating point for any grumbletonian" (p. 80). But to assume that all members of the opposition ignored principle and treated politics merely as a game played for power is to ignore the complexity of human motivations. Many politicians, we may be sure, were mere opportunists; but others had reason to dislike the di-

rection the country was taking. As Kramnick makes clear, the typical Tory (that is, a man interested in preserving traditional values and the system of subordination in English society) had cause for malaise. In Parliament, Tory rhetoric was often adapted to the repetitive objections of the opposition program, but this may reflect more the limitations imposed by the questions up for debate than the insincerity of the speakers. Although pious moralisms are often the refuge of those who find themselves excluded from power, it is unthinkable that the high moral tone of the opposition was in all cases insincere; and the Tories, for whom the acquisition of power was a moot point, would be less than human if they did not see their exclusion from the government as a sign of the nation's decay. The causes of Tory malaise are discussed below.

34. Kramnick, p. 27.

35. Walpole, who is often cited as the author of this "political axiom," is reported by his eighteenth-century biographer, William Coxe, to have referred only to the Whig "patriots" of the opposition, actually saying, "All those men have their price" (*Memoirs of the Life and Administration of Sir Robert Walpole* [London, 1798], I, 757). Most of them justified Walpole's observation shortly after his fall.

36. J. H. Plumb, *Sir Robert Walpole*, 2 vols. (London: Cresset, 1956–60), II, 91-96.

37. At the time of his fall from power in 1742, Walpole had built up, either through personal connections or patronage, a solid bloc of over one-hundred-fifty dependents in the Commons: Owen, p. 45.

38. Plumb, II, 123.

39. His use of Secret Service funds, which did not require a strict accounting, was staggering. In a ten-year period from 1732 to 1742, he spent almost one and a half million pounds, fifty thousand of which went to support partisan periodicals. The total can be compared to the expenditure of something less than three hundred fifty thousand pounds by various ministers between 1707 and 1717, a period that included a foreign war, the change of dynasty, and the first Jacobite rebellion, all situations that would encourage secret expenditures. See *A Further Report from the Committee of Secrecy, Appointed to Inquire into the Conduct of Robert, Earl of Orford* (London, 1742), pp. 25–26, 29, and Appendix 13.

40. Kramnick, pp. 39–55.

41. See Kramnick, pp. 206, 209.

42. "Epistle to Bathurst," 11. 69–70, *Poems of Alexander Pope*, ed. John Butt (London: Methuen, 1963), p. 574.

43. W. E. H. Lecky stated that Walpole regularly paid his supporters from £500 to £1,000 at the end of each session, and Walpole himself supposedly lamented that "he was obliged to bribe Members not to vote against, but for their conscience." *History of England in the Eighteenth Century*, 8 vols. (New York: Appleton, 1882-90), I, 399, 403.

44. *Poems of Alexander Pope*, p. 766.

45. The merchants and tradesmen of London generally opposed Walpole because of his connections with the great trading companies, but only because the great power of the companies limited their own profits. Their allegiance was to commerce and their attitudes truly Whig.

46. See John H. Middendorf, "Johnson on Wealth and Commerce," in *Johnson, Boswell, and Their Circle, Essays Presented to L. F. Powell* (Oxford: Clarendon, 1965), pp. 50, 61.

47. *Poems*, p. 70.

48. See *London*, ll. 23ff., 99ff., 117ff., and 248ff.; and Kramnick, pp. 25, 180.

49. Ll. 91–151.

50. The emphasis on foreign corruption is not the only instance of Johnson's straining to preserve Juvenal's images or ideas. Johnson himself left a manuscript note in a copy of the fifth edition stating that the passage on Orgilio (ll. 194–209) was "justly remarked to be no picture of modern manners, though it might be true at Rome": see *Poems*, pp. 64, 77.

51. Donald Greene (*Political Writings*, p. 20) notes that *Marmor* was first advertised for sale on May 11 in the *Daily Advertiser*, but it may have appeared earlier, for it is listed in the *GM* register of books for April 1739 (p. 220). It was listed a second time, though, in the May register (p. 276).

52. The terseness of the Latin contrasts sharply with the more flowery English translation. Compare the following passages:

> Nec fremere audebit
> Leo, sed violare timebit,
>
> Omnia consuetus
> Populari pascua laetus.

(The lion will not dare to roar; he will fear to violate all of the pastures that he was both accustomed and happy to plunder.)

> Nor shall the lyon, wont of old to reign
> Despotic o'er the desolated plain,
> Henceforth th' inviolable bloom invade,
> Or dare to murmur in the flow'ry glade.

53. *Political Writings*, p. 23.

54. The advertisement is reprinted in *Political Writings*, pp. 53–54.

55. Brooke's original advertisement called for subscription books "on royal paper at five shillings each copy"; non-subscription books sold for 1s. 6d. (*GM*, 1739, p. 276).

56. *A Project for the Advancement of Religion, and the Reformation of Manners*, in Swift's *Prose Works*, ed. Herbert Davis (Oxford, 1939), II, 56. Noted by L. W. Conolly, *The Censorship of English Drama, 1737–1824* (San Marino: Huntington Library, 1976), p. 165.

57. First advertised for sale on May 25 (*Political Writings*, p. 54).

58. *Political Writings*, pp. 55–56.

59. Greene, *Politics*, p. 103.

60. *Political Writings*, p. 57.

61. See Coxe's *Walpole*, I, 515–17; and Calhoun Winton, "Dramatic Censorship," in *The London Theatre World, 1660–1800*, ed. Robert D. Hume (Carbondale: Southern Illinois University Press, 1980), pp. 303–04.

62. For Johnson's own definition of Whig and Tory, see *Life*, IV, 117.

63. *Marmor* was reprinted in 1775 with the intention of embarrassing Johnson; the *Monthly Review* at that time styled it "a bloody Jacobitical pamphlet": quoted in William Prideaux Courtney, *A Bibliography of Samuel Johnson* (Oxford: Clarendon, 1915), pp. 9–10.

64. *Political Writings*, p. 28.

65. *Lives of the Poets*, III, 446.

66. Hawkins (p. 72) stated that warrants were issued for the arrest of the author of *Marmor* and that Johnson took refuge in obscure lodgings in Lambeth Marsh, but this seems unlikely. John Brett, the publisher whose name appeared on the pamphlet, would have been arrested at the same time and so was in more immediate danger than the anonymous author. But Brett was not harassed for this pamphlet, although he was arraigned before the Court of King's Bench shortly afterwards for publishing a "libel" in *Common Sense* for June 23, 1739: see H. R. Plomer, et al., *Dictionary of Printers and Booksellers, 1726–1775* (Oxford: The Bibliographical Society, 1932), p. 33.

67. The snipe at the Hanoverian intruders, quoted above, seems to acknowledge such an acquiescence—it does not call Hanoverian rule invalid, but it bases it on voluntary grant (which by inference might be withdrawn); the Georges do not rule, though, by hereditary right. Johnson expressed this view more clearly in later life. In a letter to the Duke of Portland dated July 26, 1779, William Burke describes Johnson and Jacobites of his stripe as having "only lent, not sold their principles; . . . they make his Majesty Tenant at will of their Loyalty; but I remember about two years agoe that Leviathan Jacobite, saying in Company 'No Madam, we have not relinquished our principles, we think the right to be, what we always thought it; various circumstances induce us to an acquiescence in what *is*, without abandoning our opinions of *what ought to be.*'" Portland Papers (Nottingham University Library), Pw F 2149, by permission of the Trustees of the Portland Estate.

68. It is possible, but by no means demonstrable, that it was Johnson who made the "extracts" from Joseph Trapp's *Four Sermons*, which appeared in the *GM* for June 1739: see Chapter 3, p. 60, and note 54.

69. There is no evidence indicating just when Johnson left town. Hawkins, who put the Appleby application in 1738, stated that Johnson went to Leicestershire in August that year. Since Gower's letter (see Chapter 4, above) is dated August 1, it seems likely that either late July or early August 1739 was the proper time for Johnson to set about his personal application for the position.

70. See *Gleanings*, VI, 102, 110–11.

71. Reade (*Gleanings*, VI, 120) suggests that Johnson's sojourn in the Midlands may have lasted until the middle of 1740, but it seems unlikely that after the news of Tetty's injury he would long remain away from her.

CHAPTER VI

1. *Gleanings*, IV, 8–9.

2. *Letters*, I, 15–17.

3. Johnson repaid Garrick's kindness by writing a prologue for Garrick's

farce *Lethe*, first performed on April 15, 1740, as part of a benefit for Henry Giffard.

4. Donald Greene ("Some Notes," pp. 75–76) attributes to Johnson a letter on swearing, signed "S. J.", in the April issue (*GM*, 1740, p. 167), as well as two introductory paragraphs to "The Characters of the Lilliputian Senators" appended to the debates in March (*GM*, 1740, p. 99). These do not seem Johnsonian to me, though an insertion into the character of Lyttelton in May (*GM*, 1740, p. 227), also pointed out by Greene, does. Such disagreements best show the difficulty of establishing the canon of Johnson's anonymous contributions to the magazine.

5. *GM*, 1740, p. 191.

6. *GM*, 1740, p. 212.

7. Johnson's style was first noted in this work by F. V. Bernard in "The History of Nadir Shah: A New Attribution to Johnson," *British Museum Quarterly*, 34 (1970): 92–104. The following account is based in part on Bernard's work.

8. See especially *GM*, 1739, pp. 555, 607, and 663.

9. Bernard (p. 93) demonstrates that Cave had at least a share of the copyright, even though his name does not appear in the imprint. Of the four names listed there, three—A. Dodd, E. Nutt, and E. Cook—were insignificant members of the trade who certainly sold the work on commission. (They were among those listed by Curll in the *Daily Advertiser*, November 21, 1738, as publishers of the Forman translation of Crousaz's *Commentary*: see above, Ch. 4, note 52.) Wilcox, whose name appears first in the imprint and who is the only publisher listed for the work in the *GM* register of books for May 1740 (p. 264), may have shared the copyright with Cave. As in the case of the Crousaz translations, for which he initially used Dodd as publisher, Cave left his name off lesser works that he was backing.

10. Cave may have been trying to pre-empt his competition in this work in the same way that Curll had beaten him to publication in the case of the Crousaz *Commentary*—by publishing only a partial account of the work.

11. The cluster of pronouns at the end of the following passage would not, I think, have been written by Johnson in his most careless moments:

> About this Time *Kuli Khan* offered his service to the Prince, with his little Army, and undertook, on the Forfeiture of his Head, to expel the *Aghwans*, and re-establish him upon the Throne of his Ancestors, if he would promise to make him his General. (p. 7)

Nor would he, even when translating, be reduced to the following clause: "which first threw him into a deep Melancholy, and afterwards into downright Madness " (p. 10). In addition the phrase "in the mean time" (or "in the mean while") appears three times between pages 7 and 11. For more examples of both Johnsonian and un-Johnsonian phrasings, as well as for several of Johnson's interpolations, see the introduction to the *Kuli Khan* in *The Shorter Prose Writings of Samuel Johnson*, ed. O M Brack Jr. (New York: AMS Press, forthcoming, 1987).

12. For a brief description of the War of Jenkin's Ear, see Basil Williams, *The Whig Supremacy*, 2nd ed., in the Oxford History of England (Oxford: Clarendon, 1962), pp. 210, 234.

13. E. L. McAdam Jr., in "Johnson's Lives of Sarpi, Blake, and Drake," mistakenly suggests that Johnson worked from the original sources, but Brack (*Shorter Prose*) notes that "although Johnson refers to many sources, all of his quotations are taken from the text or notes . . . in the *General Dictionary*."

14. *GM*, 1740, p. 352.

15. The collected pamphlets were published by Nicholas Bourne at London in 1653.

16. For an excellent analysis of Johnson's use of sources in this work, see the introduction to the "Life of Drake" in Brack, *Shorter Prose*. His discussion of sources supersedes that of McAdam in "Johnson's Lives of Sarpi, Blake, and Drake." Brack has also noted variants in *GM* copies of the lives of Blake and Drake, owing to a complete reprinting of the first work and a reprinting of the January 1741 installment of the second.

17. Cave, apparently possessed of the same instincts as the producers of movie serials, tantalized his audience by breaking off the first installment just as Drake and his men were about to ambush a Spanish treasure train, only to disappoint his readers in September with an account of how the Spanish eluded Drake's plot.

18. *GM*, 1741, p. 44

19. See *GM*, 1740, pp. 511, 512, 600, 603; 1741, p. 41.

20. *GM*, 1740, p. 513.

21. *The World Encompassed*, p. 79, in *Sir Francis Drake Revived* (London: Bourne, 1653). This pamphlet is separately paginated in Bourne's collection.

22. *GM*, 1741, p. 41.

23. See Pennington, pp. 47–65, for the story of the correspondence, including two letters from Baratier to Miss Carter. See also, "Foreign Books" in *GM*, April 1742, p. 223.

24. In 1744, Johnson conflated his two accounts, making numerous changes. Cave then published the life in pamphlet form.

25. Johnson may have been responsible for the advertisement for Cave's "Miscellaneous Correspondence" (*GM*, 1740, p. 250). The epitaph on Phillips was apparently written extemporaneously over a cup of tea and may have been submitted to the magazine by Garrick: see *Poems*, pp. 89–90. A Latin translation of a Welsh epitaph on Prince Madoc (*GM*, 1740, p. 519) has also been attributed to Johnson, but with little foundation. This piece slavishly follows an English version printed in the magazine two months before (p. 409) and thus does not conform to Johnson's usual practice as an epigrammatist. For the authorship of a letter on "the Character of the *Memoirs of a Man of Quality*" (*GM*, 1740, p. 251), see Appendix A.

26. Since the life was brought to a sudden conclusion after the completion of the second voyage, it seems safe to say that Johnson had never fully rendered the last two pamphlets.

27. Hoover, p. 21. Johnson's role in revising these debates is difficult to determine. There are no signs of his style in most, but the editor did little more than condense or rearrange phrases—just enough to disguise the fact that they were being plagiarized.

28. The theater season generally began in September: for Fleetwood's promise to Garrick to produce *Irene* at the beginning of the coming season, see *Letters*, I, 16. A letter from Cave to Birch, dated September 9, 1741, indicates that

Johnson's own diffidence may have prevented the play's performance (*Life*, I, 153).

29. See Chapter 5, p. 84.

30. *GM*, 1740, pp. 593–96

31. *GM*, 1740, p. 579.

32. *GM*, 1740, pp. 585–92. This debate was first attributed to Johnson by F. V. Bernard, "Johnson and the Authorship of Four Debates," *PMLA* 82 (1967), pp. 412–15.

33. The opening sentence accords very closely in both language and sentiment with an observation in the "Eubulus" letter of 1738. The essay on the Acta begins: "As we are apt to look, either with an Eye of Contempt or Surprize on the Customs of other Nations, which differ from our own, so we cannot help being pleased with any, which bear some degree of Resemblance to those of our Country" (*GM*, 1740, p. iii). Over two years earlier he had written as follows: "Any Custom or Law unheard and unthought of before, strikes us with that *surprize* which is the effect of Novelty; but a Practice conformable to our own pleases us . . ." (*GM*, 1738, p. 365).

34. *Praelectiones Academicae* (Oxford, 1692), p. 651ff.

35. This is made clear by a comparison of citations. Dodwell quotes a passage from Cicero's *De Oratore*, Bk. 2, ch. 12 (*Praelectiones*, p. 653). The essay on the Acta is provided with an epigraph from the same chapter of the same work, but a different quotation from Dodwell's. Other curious parallels in the notes suggest that the compiler of the information on the Acta used in the *GM* checked Dodwell's sources and made independent use of them.

36. One of the notes (p. v) refers the reader to an unspecified attack on the authenticity of the Acta by Petrus Wesseling. But Wesseling's discussion of the Acta in his *Probabilium Liber Singularis* (Franaquer, 1731) was not the intermediate source. Since Johnson was unlikely to have known about this work independently, it seems reasonable to conclude that the author of the intermediate source had made some reference to it, placing the date of the source after the publication of Wesseling's work.

37. *LM*, 1740, pp. 221–23; *GM*, 1740, pp. 290–91. The *LM* also received a copy of Lord Gage's speech on the Place Bill, which Cave reprinted. Both speeches were revised slightly in the *GM*.

38. The January issue of the *GM* appeared on February 2, 1741 (see *DA*), only six days after the actual debate took place. Although it might seem difficult to believe that the debate could be composed and the new sheets run off in such a short time, it nevertheless seems too great a coincidence that Cave decided to publish a debate on the impress and that the same topic then came up in the Commons. There are signs in the magazine itself that the debate was a last-minute insertion. The inclusion on page 16 of a letter dated "Bath, Jan. 19, 1741" indicates that the second half-sheet of the magazine, which includes a large part of the debate, was not printed until late in the month. The letter is set in unusually small type to prevent it from running into the next gathering. In addition, a note indicating that the conclusion of the "Life of Barretier" would be postponed until the next issue appears on page 15, an odd place for such an announcement. Cave may have cancelled a *LM* debate and the "Life of Barretier" in favor of Johnson's quick rendering of the debate on registra-

tion, which had a great affinity in both speakers and arguments to the debate then raging in Parliament.

The debate on registration was first attributed to Johnson by G. B. Hill (*Life*, I, 509). Supporting and, I think, conclusive evidence was adduced by F. V. Bernard ("Four Debates," p. 410), who first noticed the extensive parallels between this and Johnson's later "Seamen's debate." Although I find Bernard's use of parallel pages convincing, his discussion of Johnson's anti-Whig bias seems to me dubious (see below, Chapter 7).

39. *GM*, 1740, p. 652.

40. The original pamphlet was printed at London in 1660 by John Redmayne for Philip Chetwind. Johnson apparently used Sir Bulstrode Whitelocke's *Memorials of English Affairs* to supply some of the dates on which meetings took place and may have used other sources to help clarify certain arguments in the piece.

Cave issued a reprint of the original pamphlet, possibly edited by Johnson, in the spring of 1742. For Donald Greene's discussion of both the "Debate" and the reprint, see *Political Writings*, pp. 74–79.

41. *GM*, 1741, p. 93.

42. From a cursory comparison of the original with Johnson's abridgment, it appears that the assignment of speakers is not always accurate.

43. For one possible application, see *Political Writings*, p. 74.

44. For a close look at Johnson's method in this piece, see John Lawrence Abbott, "Dr. Johnson and the Amazons," *Philological Quarterly*, 44 (1965): 484–95.

45. Besides publishing abridgments of works by Maupertuis and Bougeant (see above, p. 60), Cave included in the magazine the abridged translation of the case of Martin Guerre from Gayot de Pitival's *Causes Célèbres et Intéressantes* (a collection of famous trials that Cave considered bringing out in English). Johnson does not appear to have been responsible for this translation, although he may have written a short introductory paragraph for it (*GM*, 1739, p. 167).

46. Guthrie's debates from May through October averaged twenty-two pages per issue. From November through April, the period of the "stolen" debates, the average dropped to under seventeen pages.

47. Although the Lords' Protests had already been printed, Cave was nevertheless taking a chance by inserting them in the magazine. In the spring of 1738, Thomas Cooper was held in custody for over a month by order of the Lords for publishing a collection of protests; a year later, James Watson was committed to Newgate for printing *The Lords Protest against the Convention Treaty* (see the *Journals of the House of Lords*, xxv, 189–92, 231, 314–16). Cave, though, was apparently willing to risk the Lords' anger for the sake of such obviously popular copy. The *LM* did not print the Protests at this time, and Cave waited for the session to end before using them.

48. *A Review of the Late Motion for an Address to his Majesty against a certain Great Minister* (London, 1741). Cave maintained his customary impartiality by inserting a response to this pamphlet in the June issue. Neither work shows any indication of Johnson's editing.

49. F. V. Bernard, "Four Debates," p. 409, suggests on grounds of style that Guthrie was the author.

50. There can be no doubt that Cave would have liked Johnson to assume the debates. The debates of the previous December and January show that Johnson's contributions to the series were welcome. If Johnson did not shy away from the monotony and thanklessness of the task, the matter of pay may have kept him and Cave apart. When Johnson finally assumed the debates, he may have received as much as £100 per year for his labors; see below, Chapter 8, pp. 166–70.

CHAPTER VII

1. Benjamin Hoover's extensive analysis of the debates "as fact" (pp. 55–130) demonstrates the uneven quality of the various debates as records of the actual proceedings.

2. After establishing the probable content of Walpole's speech, Hoover remarks, "we can say that Johnson's version has almost no relation to it if we expect [except?] some possible verbal similarities toward the end" (p. 102).

3. For an example of how Johnson refashioned a speaker's language when it was available to him, see Hoover, pp. 114–19.

4. *Life*, IV, 409.

5. *Life*, I, 118.

6. Hawkins, p. 99.

7. *Life*, IV, 409.

8. G. B. Hill (*Life*, I, 506) asserted that the debates lack dramatic verisimilitude, a position echoed by Benjamin Hoover, who states that "the *Debates* lack the qualities that we expect of imaginatively re-created parliamentary controversy" (p. 140). Donald Greene (*Politics*, p. 114ff) disputes these conclusions in his consideration of the debates, which provides the most enlightening discussion to date of Johnson's practice.

9. Hawkins, p. 100.

10. *Life*, I, 506.

11. Hawkins, p. 96.

12. *GM*, 1742, p. 175.

13. *DNB*. The motives of the two men also differed: Hervey appears to have opposed the bill for political reasons, Secker for moral ones. But for politicians even more than for the rest of us, the appearance of sincerity can be crucial, and so one should not be surprised that motives were blurred in the magazine accounts.

14. *GM*, 1741, p. 569.

15. See Greene, *Politics*, pp. 125–29, for a fine discussion of the most dramatic moment in all Johnson's debates—Walpole's speech to the Commons on the motion to remove him from the King's councils.

16. *J. Misc.*, I, 379. Hawkins (p. 122) says that Johnson never was in either House.

17. Thucydides, *The Peloponnesian War*, trans. Rex Warner (Harmondsworth: Penguin, 1972), p. 47.

18. Whether this was due to faulty materials or conscious choice cannot always be determined. In the Lords debate on Walpole, Carteret's opening speech

is reasonably detailed and accurate, but Abingdon's seconding speech is limited to the debate's most important issue—whether "common fame" of corruption is sufficient reason to oust a minister. According to Bishop Secker's notes of this debate, Abingdon began with this point but proceeded to new indictments. If Johnson had this additional information, he chose to ignore it in favor of the larger thematic concerns of the debate; see Hoover, pp. 68–69, 78.

19. Such a prejudice would appear to be necessary in a democratic society, whose leaders must be chosen on the basis of their demonstrated abilities; but in Johnson's day, when most seats in Parliament were obtained through connections or some form of purchase (bribery being too harsh a term), democracy had not yet made such strides as to make the preservation of a speaker's actual words essential. The modern candidate, though, has managed to evade even this test of ability by hiding behind speech writers and allowing himself to be marketed as if he were a new form of cola.

20. For Thucydides' practice, see F. E. Adcock, *Thucydides and His History* (Cambridge: Cambridge U. Press, 1963), pp. 27–33; for Livy's, see P. G. Walsh, *Livy, His Historical Aims and Methods* (Cambridge: Cambridge U. Press, 1961), pp. 219–20, 228–30. The relationship between the classical historians and the writer of modern debates is even more pronounced in Thomas Gordon, Johnson's counterpart for the *LM*, who published a translation of Tacitus in 1728.

21. Johnson's dismay at finding out that people took the speeches to be authentic, supposedly the primary cause of his quitting the debates (*Life*, I, 152), may be explained by his having a sense of the works as rhetorical exercises on significant topics, with the actual debates providing only a loose structure. But an expanded reading public, not universally trained in the classical tradition, was evolving, and even the more sophisticated readers of the magazine might be misled to a large extent by the non-rhetorical basis of that newly developing industry, journalism. Johnson was again looking over his shoulder while the bulk of his audience was facing front.

22. *J. Misc.*, I, 379.

23. Johnson first portrayed Walpole in the debate on registering seamen, which appeared in the *GM* for January 1741 and was written before he took on the duties of the regular compiler.

24. *GM*, 1741, pp. 471–72.

25. Smith asserted that the foundation of civil government was the maintenance of property: *Wealth of Nations*, ed. R. H. Campbell et al. (Oxford: Clarendon, 1979), p. 715. For Burke's vigorous defense of the rights of property, see his *Reflections on the Revolution in France*, in *Works*, 12 vols. (Boston, 1866), III, 297–98 and passim.

26. *GM*, 1741, pp. 564–65.

27. *GM*, 1741, pp. 472–73.

28. In the seamen's debate, which is really a series of debates relating to a single bill, Walpole has eleven speeches, a number of which are relatively insignificant responses to objections raised by his opponents. But these responses are always informed and often persuasive. His major speeches offer many more examples of clear-headedness than those given above: he compliments his fellow members of the House on the coolness of their deliberations (*GM*, 1741, p. 470), shows sympathy for the plight of sailors (p. 472), demonstrates an

awareness of the potential for abuse of authority by unscrupulous men, and explains the bill's safeguards against such abuses (p. 522). If there is some malignity against Walpole, it is to be found not in the speeches themselves but in his introduction as the "Prime Minister," a detested term at the time, in his first four speeches (pp. 457, 465, 470, and 511).

F. V. Bernard ("Four Debates," pp. 411–12) asserts that Johnson slanted the debate on registering seamen (not to be confused with the seamen's debate discussed above) against Walpole, saying that Walpole "takes aim at eloquence, but strikes only the hollow note of patriotic attitudinizing." Bernard interprets Walpole's hard-headed practicality as a veneer hiding cynicism and brutality. A reading of the entire speech from which Bernard draws his arguments does not, I think, confirm his assertions. He also argues, on very little evidence, that Johnson implanted slovenly diction in the mouths of the Whigs. But Bernard appears to use the term "Whig" for supporters of the ministry and "Tory" for members of the opposition. This oversimplification of the party structure undercuts his attempts to show bias.

29. Greene, *Politics*, pp. 127–29.

30. Greene (*Politics*, p. 122), speaking of the Mutiny Bill debate, describes Sandys and Gybbon as "two perpetual opposition gadflies"; but such a tag would not be appropriate for these speakers in the debate on the removal of Walpole.

31. Greene, *Politics*, pp. 125–26.

32. Hoover (p. 130) implies that vehemence betrays Johnson's beliefs, something that cannot be demonstrated. Vehemence is the mode of any opposition party and should be treated as a rhetorical stance, nothing more. This is especially important because we do not know at what point Johnson parted company with the opposition. In the Commons debate on Walpole's ouster, the opposition is at its most vituperative, yet this is the debate in which Walpole is treated most sympathetically.

33. *GM*, 1741, p. 524.

34. Paul Korshin, in "The Johnson-Chesterfield Relationship: A New Hypothesis," *PMLA* 85 (1970): 247–59, argues that Chesterfield, another opposition Whig, may be the butt of Johnsonian bias, for his speeches against the Spiritous Liquors Bill appear "overzealous and extreme." Korshin sees this as "Johnson's deliberate ironic undermining of Chesterfield" (p. 257). I cannot agree with this interpretation. Johnson puts the conventional sentiments of those opposed to the bill in Chesterfield's mouth, but tinges them with irony. The opponents of the bill, including his Lordship, show an almost obsessive fear of the danger to society from wide-spread drunkenness. Korshin sees this concern as approaching hysteria in Hervey's speech. But Korshin's judgment seems to me to be lacking in historical perspective. The arguments of Hervey, Chesterfield, and the rest of those opposing the bill reflect the same distress that was given pictorial representation by Hogarth in "Gin Lane." That their fears ultimately proved unfounded does not mean that at the time they were ridiculous. The stridency of the speeches is in proper proportion to the perceived moral significance of the issue. Few who saw gin cellars opening all around London would have thought Chesterfield, as reported by Johnson, excessive.

35. It is quite possible that the sympathetic portrait of Walpole in the Commons debate on his ouster was brought about by Johnson's realization of the

duplicity and self-interest of his accusers, for Johnson's account of that debate did not appear in the magazine until February 1743, two years after the debate had actually taken place and one year after Walpole had resigned.

36. Hervey had even supported the much hated Excise Bill: see Robert Halsband, *Lord Hervey* (Oxford: Clarendon Press, 1973), pp. 145–47.

37. *GM*, 1741, pp. 340, 349; 1742, p. 514. Carteret very likely owed his position to Walpole, who guided the King in his choice of ministers. For the details of the change of governments, see Owen, *Rise of the Pelhams*, pp. 91–95.

38. See *GM*, 1742, pp. 367, 511.

39. In all of this, though, Johnson would be doing little more than depicting positions actually taken in the debates. Thus, as a chronicler of the debates he simply brought to public attention the change of principles that the politicians themselves had effected.

A more direct depiction of Carteret as a "Whig Dog" might be found in the debate on spiritous liquors, where, in the midst of universal denunciations of drunkenness, he asserts that "the immediate Consequence of a heavy Duty would be the Ruin of our Distillery," a profitable trade sustaining many laborers (*GM*, 1743, p. 684). This economic argument, reiterated by Pulteney (pp. 687–88), seems to miss the moral thrust of the debate. But Johnson may simply have reported an actual argument and may not have intended to show a lack of principle in these two Whigs. That a government might continue to support an industry whose product is acknowledged as harmful to the populace is evidenced today by the subsidies paid to tobacco growers in the U.S.

40. A good example of such questioning of motives is to be found in the speeches of Pelham (Plemahm), Yonge (Yegon), and Lyttelton (Lettyltno) in the debate on a public enquiry into Walpole's administration (*GM*, 1743, pp. 242, 294, 297).

41. Perhaps the surest sign of Johnson's fairness is the inability of those who allege bias to agree on where it lies. Some see him undermining the opposition. Hawkins's assertion that "when a mere popular orator takes up a debate, his eloquence is . . . represented in a glare of false rhetoric, specious reasoning, an affectation of wit, and a disposition to trifle with subjects the most interesting" (p. 100) can apply to virtually all of the opposition speakers in the Commons. Paul Korshin has added his own arguments about how Chesterfield, a major opposition figure, is subtly undermined by Johnson (see n. 34, above), in spite of the fact that Chesterfield's reputation as an orator in his own day was dependent at least in part on speeches penned by Johnson. Others see Johnson attacking the ministry. F. V. Bernard has argued unconvincingly that Johnson loaded the speeches of Walpole and his supporters with solecisms (see n. 28, above). Although Benjamin Hoover found the debates largely even-handed, his belief that the vehemence of opposition speeches represented the passionate out-pouring of Johnson's own view implies an antiministerial bias in spirit if not in argument. Yet the sympathetic treatment of Walpole in the Commons debate on his removal indicates a possible bias in his favor. After sorting through these conflicting claims one is left with only one conclusion: the bias is in the reader, not in the text.

42. *GM*, 1742, pp. 59–66.

43. *GM,* 1742, pp. 227–40, 283–84.
44. *GM,* 1742, p. 117.
45. *GM,* 1742, p. 622.
46. *GM,* 1741, pp. 618–19.
47. Hoover (p. 125) notes that in this speech Johnson followed "the general contours" of Argyll's original, even reproducing some of its intricate arguments.
48. *Life,* I, 506.

CHAPTER VIII

1. *Life,* I, 153. Cave also offered the play to John Gray, a London bookseller. This letter appears to confirm that Garrick had convinced Fleetwood to produce the play during the 1740–41 season (see above, Chapter 6), for Cave writes that "Fleetwood was to have acted it last season, but Johnson's diffidence or _____ prevented it."

2. Johnson's life of Morin is discussed by John L. Abbott in "Samuel Johnson's 'A Panegyric on Dr. Morin,'" *Romance Notes,* 8 (1966): 55–57. The Morin may have been written for inclusion in an earlier issue of the magazine, being put off in favor of the timely political material of the previous several months.

3. "The Jests of Hierocles" is given brief but solid treatment by Donald Greene in "Some Notes," pp. 80–81.

4. Donald Greene ("Some Notes," pp. 81–83) gives an excellent, detailed account of the "Foreign History" section of the *GM* and of Johnson's role in it.

5. *GM,* 1741, p. 444.

6. Greene ("Some Notes," p. 82) lists only four issues of the magazine between April 1742 and the end of 1743 that contain definite traces of Johnson's style—August, November, and December, 1742, and April 1743. He adds, though: "It is somewhat tempting to see Johnson's hand in the installments for August, September, and October, 1743. . . . But these passages do not entirely convince me; I could believe that they are Hawkesworth trying to sound like Johnson." Greene's determinations in the area of "Foreign History" are extremely convincing. Although other examiners might quibble with his inclusion or exclusion of a particular article, his general outline of Johnson's contributions is undoubtedly correct.

7. See *Life,* I, 284. For more detailed arguments attributing the conduct of "Foreign Books" to Johnson, see Greene, "Some Notes," p. 83, and Jacob Leed, "Two Notes on Johnson and the *GM,*" *Papers of the Bibliographical Society of America,* 54 (1960): 101–05. Both articles include interesting quotations from this department of the magazine.

8. See above, Chapter 6, p. 114.

9. *GM,* 1741, p. 670; 1742, p. 112.

10. There was, though, a serious attempt to get foreign scholars to send word of their undertakings to the magazine. See the Latin note at the end of the articles for March and April 1742 (pp. 167, 223), reprinted in Greene, "Some Notes," p. 83.

11. In 1743, "Foreign Books" appeared in the *GM* for March, May, August, and September; in 1744, for January and September.

12. *GM,* 1741, p. 441; 1742, p. 161; 1743, p. 551. Jacob Leed suggests, on the basis of the introductory sentence, that Johnson contributed the account of Walpole's fall: "Samuel Johnson and the 'Gentleman's Magazine': Studies in the Canon of his Miscellaneous Prose Writings, 1738–1744" (doctoral dissertation, U. of Chicago, 1959), pp. 98–100. It is a questionable attribution, though; the opening is almost certainly Johnson's, but the remainder of the article may have been by another hand.

13. See *GM,* 1741, p. 641; 1742, pp. 136, 152; 1743, pp. 425, 537.

14. Johnson's remarks on economics were first noted by Donald Greene in "Some Notes," pp. 77–80.

15. In *Wealth of Nations,* Adam Smith asserted that this belief was "perfectly false" (p. 651).

16. As early as 1739 Cave began including material on the subject. In February that year he printed "Considerations laid before Parliament relating to the Running of Wool" (pp. 93–94).

17. The controversy dealt largely with the problem of deducing the amount of wool produced in Great Britain from the number of sheep listed in the toll books at Smithfield Market; see *GM,* January through April, 1741 (pp. 2, 86, 107, 154, and 170). A direct reference to the controversy appears in Samuel Webber's *An Account of a Scheme for Preventing the Exportation of Wool* (London, 1740), p. 23. (Although its imprint reads 1740, the book did not appear until March the next year; see *GM,* 1741, p. 168.) The last of the notes in the *GM* (p. 170) appears to be Johnson's. None of the other notes, some of which are admittedly very short, shows signs of his style.

18. See the introductory note to the pamphlet in *GM,* 1741, p. 633. The introduction does not seem Johnsonian but may be his nevertheless. The actual arrests took place on December 2 and 3, 1740; see *Commons Journals,* vol. 23, pp. 545–46.

19. The pamphlet mingles political innuendo with economic speculation, both of which aspects are censured in the remarks. That Johnson was this commentator can be demonstrated by his repetition of one of the "remarks" in the debate on the Corn Bill; see F. V. Bernard, *Notes and Queries,* February 1964, p. 64, and May 1964, pp. 190–91.

20. P. 635.

21. This pamphlet is followed immediately by the "abstract" of another, *The Groans of Ireland,* which continues in the Supplement. Whether Johnson, as editor of material on economics, was responsible for the inclusion or editing of this work is beyond determining.

22. *GM,* 1741, p. 634. Elsewhere, though, Johnson's tone is curiously ambiguous. Although he supported the government's measures in imposing the embargo, he had no illusions about the men in power. When the pamphleteer urges that the method of proclaiming the embargo was intended "to create servile Applications, . . . great Dependence upon Men in Power, and possibly great Corruption," Johnson remarks: "All this is highly probable, but when was it known that Men in Power in prosecuting the publick Good, neglected the Advancement of their own Authority?" (*GM,* 1741, p. 635).

23. P. 635. There is an interesting contrast between this passage, where Johnson is writing for victory, and one that appeared two months later commenting on a cause of the decline in the wool trade. The charge that England had acted unfairly and inconsistently towards Ireland evoked the following response: "This Allegation deserves to be attended to, not only for its Certainty and its Importance upon the present Question, but as an Instance that the Consequences of Oppression seldom fail to fall upon the Authors" (*GM*, 1742, p. 87). In the first case, where the principle of governmental authority is at stake, Johnson holds compassion at arm's length; in the second, less confrontational situation, he embraces justice as the only possible foundation for political stability. Each response is reasonable in its context and each typical of a different side of Johnson's character.

24. *GM*, 1742, pp. 83–89. Although we do not have the benefit of passages echoing known works by Johnson, much of the prose in the notes and observations is sufficiently Johnsonian to attribute the work to him. There are on occasion difficult sentences, but these could have resulted from editorial trimming or from hurried writing. This series of articles was not specifically mentioned by Greene, but he seems to have it in mind when he speaks of Johnson's "observations" following the extracts from pamphlets ("Some Notes," p. 79).

25. One of the moral objections to this scheme is perhaps the best evidence of Johnson's authorship: "It is proper to Observe here, that no Scheme which requires Oaths ought to be admitted. Trade itself is not to be preserved at the Expence of Virtue. Frequent Temptations to Perjury will not always be resisted, the Crime once committed will be repeated, and he that is conscious of habitual Perjury will soon grow consistent with himself, and throw off all the Restraints of Religion. A Custom House Oath is already become a Proverb for a false Oath[;] every Man hardens himself by the Example of his Neighbour, the Guilt of Perjury is incurred, and no Fraud is prevented" (*GM*, 1742, p. 149).

26. *GM*, 1743, pp. 32–34, 42–43. The end of Johnson's commentaries on the wool question had little effect on the magazine's content, for the controversy was picked up by Cave's correspondents; see *GM*, 1743, pp. 75, 150, 259, 318, 537, 541, 657, and 658. Whether Johnson edited this correspondence is unknown. There are several editorial notes (pp. 151, 539, 657–58), but none shows the distinctive marks of his style.

27. The best introduction to mercantilism remains Adam Smith's *Wealth of Nations*.

28. His open-mindedness in this is evident in his attitude towards Webber's scheme. Even though the magazine had clashed with Webber, Johnson defended his scheme against the objections of two of its rivals and left the impression that with proper modifications it would be the most eligible of the proposals.

29. *GM*, 1743, p. 43.

30. *GM*, 1742, p. 89. The suggestion that parish officers enforce the regulations appears on p. 88.

31. P. 89.

32. For glimpses of Johnson's life-long hatred of the excise, see *Life*, I, 37 n., 295 n., and 525.

33. Johnson's untitled essay on the memoirs of the Duchess of Marlbor-

ough, which appeared in the form of a letter to Mr. Urban (*GM*, 1742, pp. 128–31), should not be confused with the "Review of the Account of the Duchess of Marlborough's Conduct," the abridgment of a pamphlet attacking the reliability of the memoirs, which appeared in the magazine from April to June, 1742; see Jacob Leed's discussion of this problem in *Notes and Queries*, May 1957, pp. 210–13. Whether Johnson might have abridged this pamphlet is unknown. "The Art of Deciphering," translated from the Latin of David Arnoldus Conradus, appeared in four installments and was not completed until the September issue (*GM*, 1742, pp. 133–35, 185–86, 241–42, 473–75). It was plausibly attributed to Johnson by Leed in *PBSA* 54 (1960): 106–110. As Leed has noted elsewhere, the March 1742 issue of the magazine is particularly abundant in Johnsonian contributions. Besides the Marlborough essay and the translation of the *Cryptographia*, Leed found possible traces of Johnson's style in the introduction to Richard Glover's speech before the Commons (p. 150), in the translations of two Dutch political papers (pp. 136–39), and in the account of Walpole's fall; see "Johnson and the *GM*," pp. 98–100, but see also note 12 above, and note 59 below. This issue also contains some of Johnson's observations on the wool trade.

34. Burman's life (*GM*, 1742, pp. 206–10) was abridged from the *Oratio Funebris in obitum . . . Petri Burmanni* of Hermannus Oosterdijk-Schacht. It is done in the same manner as the "Life of Boerhaave," which is taken from a similar source. The additions to the "Barretier" (pp. 242–45) were extracted from *La Vie de Mr. Jean Philippe Baratier* by Jean Henri Samuel Formey. The "Essay on Du Halde's *Description of China*," which contains a life of Confucius, appeared in three installments, not reaching completion until September (*GM*, 1742, pp. 320–23, 353–57, 484–86). The final fascicle of the Du Halde had been published in March 1742; Johnson's article was drawing attention to the completed work. The essay on the Du Halde has received detailed analyses by Jacob Leed in the *Bulletin of the New York Public Library* 70 (1966): 189–99; and by Arthur Sherbo in *Papers on English Language and Literature* 2 (1966): 372–80.

35. The essay, which appeared in two distantly separated issues of the magazine (March and November 1743), is discussed below.

36. The projects that drew Johnson away from the *GM*, especially the Harleian catalogue, are discussed in the next chapter.

37. See *GM*, 1742, p. 608.

38. *GM*, 1742, pp. 633–39.

39. These include three youthful exercises—"Friendship; an Ode," "The Young Author," and an imitation of Horace's "Integer Vitae"—as well as an impromptu epigram, "Ad Lauram Parituram," completed from a Latin line proposed by Robert James; see *GM*, 1742, pp. 376–78, and *Poems*, pp. 8, 32, 36–39.

40. *GM*, 1743, p. 550. The verses themselves are a straightforward translation, except for the possible irony in Johnson's overblown rendering of Pope's simple line, "Where nobly-pensive, St. John sat and thought":

> Hic, in se totum longe per opaca futuri
> Temporis Henricum rapuit vis vivida mentis.

In Johnson's version, Bolingbroke, seized by an imaginative fit, is hurried through "shadows" (*opaca*) of the future, with *opaca* suggesting what he really saw: the shadows of the cave itself.

41. In 1742 Johnson pondered writing another drama, "Charles of Sweden," which we may assume was to be in verse, but there is no indication that he ever actually began composition; see *Letters*, I, 23.

42. *GM,* 1742, p. 131.

43. P. 114.

44. Cave, much to our annoyance, may have valued the material on the next page more than the conclusion of Johnson's essay. He had invested in a woodcut depicting the path of a recent comet, which, along with a related letter, occupied that page, the last of an octavo gathering. Three and a half pages had been given over to the essay, and the text would have to be made to fit, for there could be no spill-over without forcing Cave to cancel his illustration; see *GM,* 1742, p. 132.

45. *GM,* 1743, p. 152.

46. P. 588.

47. *Works of Thomas Sydenham, M.D.,* trans. R. G. Latham, M.D., 2 vols. (London: Sydenham Society, 1848–50), I, xi–xii.

48. Birch's account (*General Dictionary,* IX, 458–59) is taken in large part from Anthony à Wood's *Athenae Oxonienses;* he added material in the form of notes. We can be sure that Johnson consulted the *GD,* for he was indebted to certain observations of Sir Hans Sloane, included by Birch in a note, for two points: that Sydenham's suggestion to Blackmore to read *Don Quixote* was probably a joke, and that Cicero was the doctor's favorite author.

49. *GD.*

50. *Treatise on Small Pox* (London, 1723), p. 47, quoted in *GD.* Birch quoted the significant passages from the *Treatise* in the notes to his article on Sydenham; thus Johnson had no need to search out the original.

51. *GM,* 1742, p. 634.

52. Ibid., p. 633.

53. Ibid.

54. Ibid., pp. 633–34.

55. When a young Hans Sloane came to Sydenham highly recommended for his knowledge of anatomy and botany, the great empiric physician supposedly called these studies nonsense, adding, "you must go to the bedside, it is there alone you can learn disease." For this anecdote, as well as a discussion of Sydenham's place among the medical theoreticians of his day, see Kenneth Dewhurst, *Dr. Thomas Sydenham* (Berkeley: U. of California Press, 1966), pp. 47–48, 60–67.

56. See *GM,* 1742, pp. 634, 635 n.; 1743, pp. 528–30. The revised text of the life, originally published in 1749, has been reprinted in Fleeman, ed., *Early Biographical Writings,* pp. 189–95.

57. *GM,* 1742, p. 634.

58. *GM,* 1743, p. 200.

59. Jacob Leed asserted that "the style of the translation from two pamphlets on Dutch politics . . . suggests the possibility that it too may be by Johnson" ("Johnson and the *GM,*" p. 99, n. 3). The text, though, does not seem

Johnsonian to my eye; nor can I find a convincing argument for attributing any of the other translations mentioned above.

60. John Nichols, *Minor Lives*, ed. Edward L. Hart (Cambridge: Harvard U. Press, 1971), p. 348; Cibber's *Lives of the Poets*, 5 vols. (London, 1753), V, 167. These are the two indispensable works for studying Boyse. The biography in the Cibber collection was written by Robert Shiels, one of Johnson's amanuenses on the *Dictionary*, with many anecdotes supplied by Johnson. (The reference to Boyse's groveling may thus be Johnson's.) Hart gathered and edited Nichols's dispersed materials on Boyse, adding some very useful editorial notes. Many of the details of Boyse's life given below are extracted from these two short accounts.

61. Boyse put parts of the *Canterbury Tales* into "modern dress" for three pence per line (Cibber's *Lives*, V, 174), less than a third of the per-line rate Johnson received for *London*. (Excerpts from this modernization of Chaucer appeared in the *GM*, 1740, pp. 404–05.) Dodsley allowed Boyse a paltry two guineas for his verse translation of Voltaire's "ethic epistles" at a time when Boyse's clothes had been pawned (Nichols, *Minor Lives*, p. 348).

62. In 1782, Nichols quoted Johnson as saying that Cave paid Boyse in this manner (see *Minor Lives*, p. 343). In an article in the *GM* shortly after Johnson's death, Nichols generalized that statement, omitting all mention of Boyse and saying that Cave "would contract for lines by the hundred, and expect the long hundred" (*GM*, 1784, p. 891). Boswell incorporated the later account in the *Life* (IV, 409), and it is in this more general way that Johnson's words have achieved widespread acceptance. The original reference specifically to Boyse, printed before Johnson's death, is certainly his authentic testimony. Nichols's reports of Johnson's conversations deserve more careful scrutiny than they often receive; see note 75, below, for the way in which he muddled what Johnson said of Cave.

63. Although most of Boyse's verse is signed "Alcaeus" or "[Y]," some of it appeared in the magazine without either designation.

64. Nichols, *Minor Lives*, p. 345. In the *GM* for May 1740 (p. 251), Cave announced his intention of publishing the second volume of Prévost's *Memoirs of a Man of Quality*. This is the only lengthy translation he is known to have been contemplating over the summer of 1740. Even though it did not appear in print until November 1741, it is a good candidate for Boyse's task. Boyse's statement that translation was "the most profitable business stirring" must be understood in terms of his situation. He was helping a Dr. Douglas (probably John Douglas, a surgeon) make an index, a singularly dull and certainly unprofitable task. And his treatment as a poet by the booksellers made even his poetry of little profit to him; see above, n. 61.

65. See Hart's introduction to Nichols's material on Boyse, *Minor Lives*, p. 341.

66. The only complete life of Hawkesworth is John Abbott's *John Hawkesworth, Eighteenth-Century Man of Letters* (Madison: U. of Wisconsin, 1982). The following account of Hawkesworth is greatly indebted to this work.

67. *GM*, 1741, p. 327; Carlson, p. 253.

68. See Abbott, p. 101.

69. Abbott (p. 215, n. 32) attributes to Hawkesworth a number of short

French translations in the *GM* between 1750 and 1766; Hawkesworth's rendering of Fenelon's *Telemachus* (1768) was highly esteemed in its day.

I also wish to suggest Hawkesworth as the possible translator of the "Description of a House of Ice" (*GM*, 1742, pp. 573–76). The piece is not a direct translation or even an abridgment, but an abridgment-cum-commentary. The translator questions some statements in the original, especially as to how ice candles and ice cannon could be made to blaze and fire without melting or disintegrating. There are stylistic reasons for not attributing the work to Johnson: it has a number of clumsy sentences and it lacks a vigorous introduction, one of the touchstones of Johnson's abridgments. Yet the concluding paragraph seems to me to be an attempt at a Johnsonian reflection:

> When we read in the Fairy Tales, or other Romances of certain Wonders, as transparent Palaces, or such like, we think such Stories quite ridiculous, and beyond Nature. It is always for want of knowing Nature well, that such Writers have Recourse to such miraculous Descriptions. Nature narrowly and studiously observed, presents us with Realities more surprisingly astonishing than the strongest Imagination could ever produce, or the liveliest Fancy describe.

This is certainly not Johnson; he would not have repeated "such" four times in two short sentences, nor would he have called anything "surprisingly astonishing," as if one could possibly be astonished without being surprised. But the attempt to complete the article with a general reflection, the use of such Johnson-like phrases as "Nature narrowly and studiously observed," and the balance of the last two phrases, all seem to me to indicate a mimicking of Johnson's style. For this a young Hawkesworth might be the best candidate.

70. See Hawkesworth's letter to Henry (Abbott, p. 101), and the letter of J. Reading to *TLS*, September 11, 1937, p. 656.

71. Abbott, pp. 21–22; *J. Misc.*, I, 166, 399.

72. Boswell (*Life*, I, 161) suggests that the Preface to the *GM* for 1744 is by Johnson, but Brack (*Shorter Prose*) rightfully considers it doubtful. For a discussion of Johnson's possible authorship of the 1744 debates, see Appendix B.

73. Waingrow, p. 234; for a slightly different version of Hussey's statement, see *Life*, I, 532.

74. *The General Biographical Dictionary*, 32 vols. (London, 1812–17), XIX, 53.

75. These memorandums may have contributed to Nichols's inconsistency in reporting Johnson's statement about Cave's tightfistedness. At the time of Johnson's death, Nichols inserted in the *GM* some of Johnson's recollections of his early years with the magazine, including the statement that Cave was a "penurious paymaster" (*GM*, 1784, p. 891). Nichols questioned this appraisal by glossing it with the first published reference to Cave's having paid Johnson forty-seven guineas for the Sarpi translation; such a payment, he implied, was hardly penurious. Twenty-eight years later in *Literary Anecdotes*, Nichols represented Johnson as calling Cave "a generous paymaster" (V, 23 n.). He repeated the revised version in "Rise and Progress," p. xvi n. Whatever Farmer's evidence was, it may have confirmed in Nichols the belief that Johnson had somehow misrepresented Cave. In an attempt to give Cave his due, Johnson was made to contradict himself. Nichols, it seems, made extensive revisions in

a number of his accounts of Johnson's conversations: see above, note 62; and compare his two versions of Johnson's collecting money to redeem Boyse's clothes: *Minor Lives,* p. 343, and *Life,* IV, 408 n. and 446 n. 2. His earliest versions seem much more likely to reflect Johnson's actual statements than do his later "improvements."

76. Johnson's works filled about fifty-eight pages in the course of six issues. In this and all subsequent calculations, I consider the Supplement as a separate number of the magazine, resulting in thirteen yearly issues.

77. Since many articles end mid-page or mid-column, some rounding off has been necessary. In attempting such a count I have been forced to assume that the great majority of Johnson's miscellaneous articles have been discovered. Of this I am fairly confident, although I have no such confidence about his editorial contributions. But in this count I am limiting myself to fresh compositions. Distinguishing between original works and editorial ones has not always been easy. Whenever the magazine text was substantially Johnson's work, the article was credited to him; if he merely intruded observations into the text of another, the article was not. Thus the articles summarizing and analyzing the various schemes to prevent the exportation of wool (*GM,* February and March, 1742) are counted as his work, while the embargo pamphlet (December 1741) and the two later pamphlets on the wool trade (January 1743), into which he merely inserted remarks, are not. All work in the "Historical Chronicle," including "Foreign Histories," has been omitted from the count as being editorial. Such works as the essay on the Acta Diurna and the translation of *Cryptographia Denudata* are counted; but the life of Sydenham and the description of the Harleian Library are not, for Johnson was paid separately for these before they were inserted in the magazine, and he would then have relinquished all rights to being further compensated for them.

78. Abbott, p. 101.

79. Hawkesworth was not the only one to complain of Cave's stinginess. In a begging letter to Birch, Boyse declared that "Mr. Cave . . . has not used me so kindly as the sense he has expressed of my Services gave me Reason to expect" (BM Add MS 4301, f. 246). In 1747 Boyse was paid a mere half-a-guinea a week by David Henry to compile a history of the recent rebellion (Nichols, *Minor Lives,* pp. 347–48). Henry may have learned the worth of an author from Cave, his brother-in-law.

80. Hawkesworth's letter to Henry: Abbott, p. 101.

81. Straus, *Robert Dodsley,* pp. 82–83.

82. Cave no doubt chose his type size when printing the pamphlet so that the text and prefatory material would precisely fill one sheet; nevertheless, when the Blake was reprinted with the lives of Savage and Drake in 1777, it filled slightly more than one duodecimo sheet. Thus the Blake may be thought equivalent to a single sheet in various formats. Johnson would certainly have been aware of such matters.

83. Goldsmith claimed to have been paid at a similar high rate by Ralph Griffiths to write the *Monthly Review* in 1757. He told Bishop Percy that he had contracted with Griffiths for £100 per year plus board and lodging. But Percy apparently doubted his veracity, saying in his life of Goldsmith only that he received "a handsome salary"; see Katherine C. Balderston, *The History and Sources*

of Percy's Memoir of Goldsmith (Cambridge: Cambridge U. Press, 1926), p. 16; and Percy's *Life of Dr. Oliver Goldsmith,* ed. Richard L. Harp (Salzburg: Institute for English Language and Literature, 1976), p. 60. Goldsmith added that for this salary he was expected to write from 9 A.M. to 2 P.M. daily.

84. If Johnson did indeed receive £100 from Cave for his services while writing the debates, 1743 was a remarkable year for Johnson's earnings. That year Cave paid him fifteen guineas for the *Life of Savage* and at least £13 2s. 6d., probably more, for a "Historical Design." And these profits were supplemented by Johnson's pay from Osborne for work on the Harleian catalogue. These additional undertakings are detailed in the next chapter.

CHAPTER IX

1. James is best remembered for his Fever Powder, which was prescribed extensively throughout the century, most notably for both Oliver Goldsmith and King George III. Although it did the first no good, it seems to have done the second no harm. For a fuller look at James's career, see O M Brack Jr. and Thomas Kaminski, "Johnson, James, and the *Medicinal Dictionary,*" *Modern Philology* 81 (1983–84): 378–400.

2. Allen Hazen (*Prefaces,* p. 69), James Clifford (p. 266), and Arthur Sherbo ("Some Observations on Johnson's Prefaces and Dedications," in *English Writers of the Eighteenth Century,* ed. John H. Middendorf [New York: Columbia, 1971], p. 130) all concur in seeing the proposals as largely if not wholly Johnson's. Nevertheless, the question is not so easily determined; for a dissenting view, see Brack and Kaminski. Sherbo reprints the "proposals" as an appendix to his article (pp. 133–42).

3. *Life,* III, 22.

4. The majority of these contributions were first discovered by Allen Hazen, but he made a number of dubious attributions as well; see Hazen, "Samuel Johnson and Dr. Robert James," *Bulletin of the Institute of the History of Medicine,* 4 (1936): 455–65, and "Johnson's Life of Frederic Ruysch," ibid., 7 (1939): 324–34. Lawrence C. McHenry attributed to Johnson a portion of the life of Oribasius ("Dr. Johnson's Medical Biographies," *Journal of the History of Medicine and Allied Sciences,* 14 [1959]: 298–310), but these passages were merely excerpted from Freind's *History of Physick.* For a complete discussion of the make-up of the *Medicinal Dictionary* and of Johnson's contributions to it, see Brack and Kaminski.

5. *Life,* I, 18 n. and 159 n.

6. *Letters,* I, 23.

7. Voltaire's announcement was noted in "Foreign Books" for July; see *GM,* 1742, p. 391. In the eleven years since its appearance, the *Histoire* had already been through at least twelve editions in French, and the English translation through seven.

8. For Johnson on Voltaire, see *Life*, I, 498; II, 12, 125, 406, and passim. For Seward's remark, see *J. Misc.*, II, 306.

9. For the details of Lord Oxford's construction projects, see *The Notebooks of George Vertue*, VI, contained in the *Publications of The Walpole Society*, 30 (1948–50): 63–64, 117; and F. H. W. Sheppard, *Local Government in St. Marylebone, 1688–1835* (London: Athlone, 1958), p. 103.

10. Oldys is the primary source for estimates of the library's size. In his commentary on the pamphlet "News from France," number 39 in his *Catalogue of Pamphlets in the Harleian Library*, appended to the third volume of the *Harleian Miscellany* (London, 1744–46), he says of the Harleian Library, "setting forty thousand [of its volumes] aside, the remainder alone would make a library sufficient for any Cardinal in Europe." He then asserted that the Harleian Library included an "infinite number of prints, and even pamphlets, which have been computed at little less than four hundred thousand." Thomas Osborne, who offered the library's collection of pamphlets and tracts for sale in 1747, numbered them at over 300,000 (*Daily Advertiser*, February 26, 1747). These figures seem incredible when one considers that the Thomason tracts, the nearly exhaustive collection of pamphlets issued at London between 1640 and 1661, merely total 22,255 items, over 7,000 of which are newspapers (*Catalogue of the Pamphlets . . . Collected by George Thomason*, 2 vols. [London, 1908], p. xxi). Oldys and Osborne probably included broadsides, newspapers, and other ephemera in their estimates. Even then, they may be suspected of exaggerating. An advertisement in the *GM* for October 1742 (p. 551) suggests that the complete holdings of the library, including books, tracts, prints, and drawings, amounted to 300,000 articles.

11. For the disposition of the MSS, see C. E. and Ruth C. Wright, eds., *The Diary of Humfrey Wanley, 1715–1726*, 2 vols. (London: The Bibliographical Society, 1966), I, lxxviii. Vertue was asked to do an inventory of the artwork; see *Notebooks*, VI, 119–20.

12. Thomas Osborne, who was himself accused of charging exorbitant prices in his sale of Harleian books, defends himself in the preface to the third volume of the *Catalogus Bibliothecae Harleianae* (5 vols. [London, 1743–45]) by asserting that if those who grumble at his prices "measure the Price at which they were bought by the last Possessor [i.e., Lord Oxford], they will find it diminished at least Three Parts in Four," pp. [xi–xii].

13. On Oxford's income, Vertue writes, "I have lately heard from pretty good hands that the Earl of Oxfords estate is £22,500 *p* Anñ [and] that his Lady brought him a good £18,000 *p* Anñ" (*Notebooks*, VI, 105). See also Wright, p. xlv; according to the *DNB*, Lord Oxford's debts had reached £100,000.

14. *Notebooks*, VI, 63–64.

15. Ibid., p. 120.

16. Ibid.

17. Thomas Birch informed Philip Yorke of the sale in a letter dated September 16, 1742 (BM Add. MS 35,396), part of which is quoted in Clifford (p. 267). Birch says that Osborne bought the library in partnership with Nathaniel Noel, but no other source corroborates this. Noel, one of Oxford's pri-

mary suppliers of books, did over £11,000 worth of business with the two Earls of Oxford between 1715 and 1728 (Wright, pp. xliv–xlv).

18. Wright, p. lxxviii.

19. *Notebooks,* VI, 63; Oldys is quoted in Sir Samuel Egerton Brydges, *Censura Literaria,* 2nd ed., 10 vols. (London, 1815), X, 331.

20. See Wright, pp. xxi, lxxi. Michael Maittaire dedicated the third volume of his *Annales Typographici* to Lord Oxford; specific references to the Harleian collections appear in the *Annales,* 5 vols. (The Hague, Amsterdam, and London, 1719–1741), at I, 60 (repeated at IV, 274) and at V, 136.

21. See his letter of December 11, 1741, to William Stukeley in *The Family Memoirs of William Stukeley,* 3 vols. (London, 1882), I, 327.

22. The Cottonian Library was made a present to the nation by Sir John Cotton in 1700, but Parliament, which graciously accepted it, was niggardly in its care until the establishment of the British Museum in 1753, at which time Parliament also appropriated £10,000 to purchase the Harleian Manuscripts from Lord Oxford's widow; see Edward Edwards, *The Lives of the Founders of the British Museum* (London, 1870), pp. 134–40, 242–43.

23. The Bodleian's original endowment, only £131 10s. per annum, grew slowly until late in the nineteenth century: a property that brought in rents of £91 10s. in 1609 had increased its yearly value to only £220 by the 1880s. The library's first regular user's fee was not established until 1780, the proceeds of which, amounting only to about £460 per annum, provided the funds for expanding the collection. When the library wished to take advantage of several major book sales in 1789 and 1790, it was forced to borrow over £1550 from various individuals and institutions, including four Oxford colleges. See William Dunn Macray, *Annals of the Bodleian Library,* 2nd ed. (Oxford: Clarendon, 1890), pp. 37, 267, 272–74; and Anthony à Wood, *The History . . . of the University of Oxford,* 2 vols., ed. John Gutch (London, 1792), II, 949–50.

24. According to Thomas Hearne, the librarian at the Bodleian in 1714, the collection then contained 30,169 printed volumes and 5,916 volumes of MSS (Macray, p. 190). Even if it grew rapidly, the Bodleian collection may have been smaller than the Harleian Library at the time of the Earl's death. To merge the two collections would probably have required the construction of a new building. Thus, to purchase and house the Harleian collection at Oxford, the university would have needed a benefaction far greater than the Bodleian ever received before, probably £20,000. Building a library could consume considerably more money than that: Dr. John Radcliffe, who died in 1714, left £40,000 for the establishment of the monumental library that still bears his name.

For the difficulties that Cambridge University experienced in housing the 30,000 volumes King George I presented it in 1715, see Charles Sayle, "Annals of the Cambridge University Library," *The Library,* ser. 3, 6 (1915): 212–17; 220–21. Before the King's generous gift, the entire library was housed in two rooms, and one visitor estimated its size at a mere 6,000 to 8,000 volumes (ibid., p. 211).

25. See the *Daily Advertiser,* April 7, 1743. The second sale is noted in the *DA* as beginning "At T. Osborne's in Gray's Inn" on February 14, 1744.

26. Both catalogues are entitled *Bibliotheca Marckiana* and both were pub-

lished at The Hague. The second catalogue does not appear to repeat many titles from the first sale and may consist of new stock originally held back.

27. Quoted by T. F. Dibdin in *The Director*, no. 7 (March 7, 1807), p. 214 n.

28. *Lives of the Poets*, III, 187. A large part of his trade was in used books, but if a buyer came in search of a title from one of his catalogues, Osborne "would endeavor to force on him some new publication of his own, and, if he refused, would affront him": Hawkins, p. 150.

29. Bk. II, ll. 157–90; *The Dunciad*, ed. James Sutherland, 2nd ed. (London: Methuen, 1953), pp. 303–04.

30. Osborne's letter to Birch is quoted in Clifford, pp. 267–68. Clifford (p. 267) asserts that Michael Maittaire drew up the plan of the catalogue, apparently basing his statement on Hawkins's similar, though more qualified, suggestion: "It is probable that Osborne had consulted Maittaire . . . and that Maittaire might have furnished the heads or classes under which the several books are arranged" (p. 133). But Maittaire, who wrote the Harleian catalogue's Latin dedication to Lord Carteret, states there that he had no other part in the work: "Mihi non vacavit meae opellae quicquam in pensum tam arduum impendere; nisi quod, rogatus, praefandi partes susceperim" (I have not been free to put forth any service in such an arduous task, except, having been asked, I have taken up the part of writing the preface), *Cat. Bib. Harl.*, I, sig. a2ᵛ-[a3]ʳ. Maittaire's bibliographic expertise was not needed; like its title, the organization of the catalogue seems in large part to follow the model of the *Catalogus Bibliothecae Thuanae* (Paris, 1679), the library of Jacques Auguste de Thou, a copy of which was in the Harleian Library (see *Cat. Bib. Harl.*, IV, 837).

31. Osborne had sold catalogues before, but at a much lower price. His *Bibliotheca Bibliothecarum*, a catalogue of 20,000 volumes to be sold at his shop in December 1741, cost a shilling, but even this was refunded to those who purchased books at the sale (*DA*, November 16, 1741).

32. Proposals, facsimile edition (Oxford: Oxford U. Press, 1926). Though dated November 1, 1742, the proposals were not advertised in the *DA* until November 16.

33. The first number appeared a week late, on December 11, 1742; see R. M. Wiles, *Serial Publication*, p. 330.

34. James Yeowell, *Memoir of William Oldys* (London, 1862), pp. xii, xvi, xx. Much of Oldys's work as literary secretary appears to have involved the library, but the MSS rather than the books may have been his chief care.

35. *Records of My Life* (London, 1832), I, 25; cited in Samuel Schoenbaum, *Shakespeare's Lives* (Oxford: Clarendon, 1970), p. 141. (This John Taylor should not be confused with Johnson's friend of the same name.) Oldys never completed his biography of Shakespeare. Schoenbaum (passim) shows Oldys to have been quite a collector of rumor and speculation. For a detailed, though perhaps too reverential, account of Oldys's place in English literary history, see Lawrence Lipking, *The Ordering of the Arts in Eighteenth-Century England* (Princeton: Princeton U. Press, 1970), pp. 66–81.

36. *Daily Advertiser.*

37. At least two works that Johnson knew very well appear in volume II without commentary: #11,425—Knolles's *History of the Turks* (p. 689); and

#11,605—*Voyage Historique d'Abissinie* du Jerome Lobo (p. 706). Many works, we may assume, were never looked at by either Johnson or Oldys, but merely entered by transcribers.

38. These events are chronicled in the Preface to volume III of the catalogue, perhaps revised by Johnson; see Hazen, *Prefaces*, pp. 44–45.

39. Osborne shrewdly produced another publication from the Harleian Library, his two-volume *Collection of Voyages and Travels . . . Compiled from the Curious and Valuable Library of the Late Earl of Oxford* (London, 1745). There is no sign that Johnson aided in the compilation of this work.

40. *Life*, I, 154. George Vertue, in an entry to his notebooks made sometime between October 1745 and June 1746, states that "the Sale of books by Osborne of Ld Oxfords books. &c. sold for £3745" (VI, 138). This sum probably refers to the third and most recent sale of April 1745. Even if the other sales did considerably better, Osborne was at least several years in recouping his investment. As Seymour de Ricci pointed out, "for nearly twenty years [Osborne's] catalogues . . . are full of Harleian books": *English Collectors of Books and Manuscripts* (Cambridge, 1930; rpt. Bloomington: Indiana U. Press, 1960), p. 37.

41. Johnson was at work on a "Historical Design" (discussed below), as well as the *Life of Savage*, late in 1743; yet his letter to Theophilus Levett of December 1, 1743, is subscribed "At Mr. Osborne's Bookseller in Grey's Inn" (*Letters*, I, 25–26). Johnson was obviously balancing several projects at once.

42. For the details, see *Life*, I, 154, 534; and Clifford, pp. 270–72.

43. The Thuanian catalogue has been mentioned above (note 30). The others are the *Bibliotheca Heinsiana* (Leiden, n.d.), the library of Nicolaas Heinsius; and the *Index Bibliothecae* (Rome, 1681) of Francesco Cardinal Barberini.

44. *Cat. Bib. Harl.*, I, 9–15; Wright, p. lxiv. Several of these notes from volume I are reprinted in volume III (pp. 130–31), where they are put in quotation marks to indicate that they are not the cataloguers' own.

45. Johnson and Oldys apparently worked from incomplete sets of these scholars' works and thus pointed out gaps that in fact had already been filled in supplemental volumes. The cataloguers' most significant challenge to accepted scholarship is their discriminating between the 1465 and 1466 editions of Cicero's *De Officiis et Paradoxa* (*Cat. Bib. Harl.*, I, 249–50). For a further discussion of these matters, and for a more detailed analysis of the make-up of the catalogue, the nature and provenance of many notes, and the quality of the scholarship contained in it, see Thomas Kaminski, "Johnson and Oldys as Bibliographers: An Introduction to the Harleian Catalogue," *Philological Quarterly* 60 (1981): 439–53.

46. See especially volumes III, pp. 213–25, and IV, pp. 520–26.

47. Oldys claimed that Robert Harley, the founder of the library, knew the location of every one of his books without the aid of a catalogue—a dubious assertion; see the *Harleian Miscellany*, 8 vols. (London: 1744–46), I, 1. There were several attempts to catalogue the printed books through the 1720s, but these often resulted in specialized or incomplete lists (Wright, pp. xvi–xvii, lxi n., lxxiv). There is no indication that cataloguing kept up with the great expansion of the library during the next decade. Oldys made no similar claim for the second Earl's knowledge of his possessions.

48. Maittaire, who knew as much as any of his contemporaries about the

origins of printing, listed the *Psalmorum Codex* of Fust and Schoeffer (Mainz, 1457) as the first printed book; the great 42-line Bible was generally unknown to have been the first production of Guttenberg and Fust. Such was the state of bibliography.

49. *Letters,* I, 20.

50. See *Letters,* I, 21–22, 24–25. The first of Johnson's three letters (previous note), the only one that refers specifically to a "Historical Design," is undated, but can be placed between August and December, 1743, because of Johnson's references to the biography of Savage then in progress. Although neither of the other letters mentions the project specifically, one closes with Johnson intending to investigate the South Sea scheme, while the other, dated September 29, 1743, is a request for information on "the Lives and Characters of Earl Stanhope, the two Craggs, and the Minister Sunderland" (pp. 24–25), all of whom were involved in the troubles following the bursting of the bubble. The overlapping of the dates and subjects suggests that all three refer to the same project.

51. *Journals of the House of Commons,* v. 24, pp. 262–66. The printed Journals were not to go on public sale, but to be distributed to sitting members and sold to future members of the House.

52. An advertisement for this work appears in the *History and Proceedings of the House of Lords,* 8 vols. (London, 1742–44) VIII [inserted before p. 209], where it is said to be "in great forwardness"; thus it may have been under way at the same time that Johnson was working on the "Historical Design." Ward's bankruptcy brought the project to a halt. When a work of the same title was finally published by Sandby and Thomas Osborne between 1751 and 1761, the Commons Journals were used in its compilation.

53. The *DNB* calls Guthrie's work "the first attempt to base history on parliamentary records." Guthrie does not appear to have consulted the Lords Journals.

54. The House was careful to maintain its privileges, even when it chose not to enforce them. Such was the case of allowing "strangers" in the House; their presence was forbidden by Parliamentary order, yet they were never ejected except at the request of a member; see P. D. G. Thomas, *The House of Commons in the Eighteenth Century* (Oxford: Clarendon, 1971), pp. 138–39.

55. Johnson writes specifically of putting "most of the resolutions &c in the Margin" (*Letters,* I, 20).

56. The primary objection to this theory is the difficulty involved for Johnson and Cave in obtaining access to the Journals, for the printed volumes covering the 1720s were not to appear for many years. Thus Cave's researchers, if not Johnson himself, would have to make transcripts of the MS volumes. Nevertheless, Guthrie and the authors of the proposed *Parliamentary History* faced the same problems but apparently were given access to the MSS.

57. *Letters,* I, 22.

58. *Journals,* 24:266.

59. *Letters,* I, 20. Johnson asks that Cave pay two guineas as each sheet of copy is turned in, adding that "the rest you may pay me when it may be more convenient." Johnson had already received £13 2s. 6d. for this project.

60. The text of the *Life of Savage* filled slightly more than eleven-and-a-half

sheets, for a rate of about £1 7s. per sheet, a rate of pay not far off from the 25s. per sheet paid the compilers of the *General Dictionary* (see above, Chapter 4). Since Johnson's two guineas per sheet appears to be a significant temporary remission of Cave's payments, the total for the historical project may well have been three guineas per sheet or more.

61. Because of Johnson's very different circumstances in 1743 and 1738, this high rate of payment cannot be assumed to have been the rate Johnson received for such early works as the Crousaz and Sarpi translations.

62. *Life of Savage*, ed. Clarence Tracy (Oxford: Clarendon, 1971), p. 134 n.

63. The text of the announcement is printed by Clifford (pp. 273–74), who says that it appeared within two weeks of the first London notice of Savage's death.

64. *GM*, 1743, p. 416.

65. *Life*, I, 165; *Daily Advertiser*. For Roberts's position in the trade, see above, Chapter 4, note 8.

66. "The Making of Johnson's *Life of Savage*, 1744," *The Library*, ser. 5, 22 (1967): 346–50.

67. Boswell prints the *Champion*'s praise and suggests that the paper was written by James Ralph (*Life*, I, 169); Clifford (p. 352, n. 24) gives its date as February 21, 1744. The delay in the life's publication was not without its consequences. The *Savage* was to contain the first printing of Savage's "London and Bristol Delineated," but on December 15, 1743, shortly after Johnson completed his task, Mary Cooper brought out a version of the poem (announced in the *DA*).

68. The anonymous *Life of Mr. Richard Savage* (London, 1727) was attributed by Johnson to "Mr. [Charles] Beckingham and another Gentleman" (*Savage*, Tracy ed., p. 39). The other sources included discussions of Savage's circumstances in the *Poetical Register* and the *Plain Dealer*, as well as an account of his trial for murder; see Tracy's introduction to his edition of *Savage*, p. xv.

69. Pennington, *Memoirs of Mrs. Carter* (London, 1807), pp. 40–41.

70. Tracy, *Savage*, pp. xii–xiii, 70 n. Johnson erred by seven years.

71. Clarence Tracy suggests that Johnson "would have found willing talkers in Aaron Hill, Thomas Birch, James Thomson, and David Mallet, who had known Savage longer than he had" (*Savage*, p. xiii); but the life shows little evidence of their more-detailed knowledge. Johnson may not have consulted any of them, except perhaps Birch.

72. Johnson made use of letters from Savage to some London acquaintances, including Cave. Cave also acquired two of Savage's letters to a Mr. Strong of the General Post Office; these remained in the magazine's files and were printed by John Nichols in the *GM* for 1787, pp. 1039–41. William Saunders, a sometime friend of Savage's in Bristol, provided a letter from Savage printed in the life, as well as other information (*Savage*, Tracy ed., pp. 121–23, 133 n.).

73. In Johnson's relation of the circumstances of Savage's retirement, many phrases are put in italics as if to indicate direct quotations from letters (for examples, see Tracy ed., pp. 110, 113, 116–17, 125). Pope would appear to be the only source for some of this material. Dodsley may have been the go-between, for he appears to have provided some information about Savage's ap-

plications for additional money shortly after his departure from London (p. 155 n.). As J. D. Fleeman has pointed out ("Making of . . . *Savage*," p. 352), all of this material appears in the re-set portion of the first edition.

74. See the editorial note appended to the abridgment of the *Savage* in Cibber's *Lives of the Poets*, V, 32. Nevertheless, the author of the adulatory notice in the *Champion* thought the facts of Savage's life "very fairly related" (*Life*, I, 169).

75. *Letters*, I, 25–27, 37; *Gleanings*, IV, 10.

76. Johnson may have received £100 for his contributions to the *GM* alone. In addition he received over £28 for the *Life of Savage* and the "Historical Design," and an unknown amount from Osborne for the Harleian Catalogue.

77. *Life*, I, 163 n.

78. Hawkins (p. 146) states that "while the catalogue was compiling," Johnson was employed in selecting the pamphlets for the *Miscellany;* but as he makes no mention of Oldys at all with respect to this project, his assertions about its compilation appear suspect.

79. See Gwin J. Kolb, "A Note on the Publication of Johnson's 'Proposals for Printing the *Harleian Miscellany*,' " *Papers of the Bibliographical Society of America* 48 (1954): 196–98.

80. The "Dissertation" is printed in the sixth number of *Phoenix Britannicus*, pp. 553–62. It was severely abridged and extensively rewritten for inclusion in Nichols's *Literary Ancedotes*, IV, 98–111.

81. Hazen, *Prefaces*, p. 59.

82. Note the errors in the following sentences from the Introduction: "These Treatises were generally printed in foreign Countries, and are not, therefore, not [sic] always very correct. There was not then that Opportunity of Printing in *private*, for, the Number of Printers were small" (Hazen p. 57).

83. The thirteenth number of volume II was due on September 15, 1744; it did not appear until September 22 (*DA*).

84. Greene provides a succinct yet thorough discussion of Johnson's contributions to the *Miscellany*, as well as some interesting observations on Oldys's prefaces and notes: see *Notes and Queries*, July 1958, pp. 304–06. All of Johnson's editorial contributions appear in the first four numbers of volume III and are generally restricted to prefaces; Johnson added only one footnote, a gloss for an unusual use of the word "fear" (*Harleian Miscellany*, III, 128).

85. The prefaces themselves were discontinued for the most part after the completion of the third volume. I could perhaps convince myself that the first paragraph of the following preface to "A Packe of Spanish Lyes" is by Johnson, but the second is certainly not:

> This curious Pamphlet, which, our Correspondent informs us, has been sold by Auction at Half a Guinea, is an ancient Specimen of those indirect Means, which an ambitious Court takes to support its drooping Credit with the Publick. How far such Practices are now in Vogue, every Reader knows; and these are now published to oblige that judicious Gentleman Mr. R. Z. who apprehends, by so doing, we shall also gratify all our Subscribers.

> This is the Eleventh in the Catalogue, published with this Collection;
> and contains the Artifices made Use of, by the Spanish Court, to keep
> up the Spirits of the People, at the Time that the King of Spain at-
> tempted, in 1588, to invade England with his invincible Armada, and
> dethrone Queen Elisabeth; because, the Fleet being beaten, dispersed,
> and gone North about, and almost intirely destroyed by Tempest, &c.
> they began to doubt of its Success. See Vol. 1. where you have a true
> and full Account of this Expedition in 1588. (III, 369)

None of the other editorial remarks beyond those identified by Greene seem
to me Johnsonian. Nevertheless, Johnson may have given occasional help to the
project in the waning months of 1744.

86. The 1744 version of the *Life of Barretier* is reproduced in *The Early Biographical Writings of Samuel Johnson,* ed. J. D. Fleeman, pp. 159–88. The proposals for the *Publisher* were reprinted by R. W. Chapman in his article attributing the work to Johnson; see the *London Mercury* 21 (March 1930): 438–40.

87. What might have prompted Cave to back this venture is a mystery. The
sale of 250 copies of a 6d. pamphlet, a respectable sale for a work like this,
would have provided gross revenues of £6 5s. Since Cave would have had to
lay out the cost of paper, the printing charges, Roberts's fee for publishing the
work and Johnson's for revision, he stood to make little money even if all things
went well (which they never did when he published Johnson's works). One cannot help but wonder if Cave was willing to take a small loss so that Johnson
might make a small gain.

88. Roberts was the nominal publisher of the *Miscellaneous Observations,* but
Cave certainly held copyright. The work was announced as published on April
8 in the *DA.* The proposals list the prices of the other editions: Pope's, six
guineas; Theobald's, two; and Hanmer's, three. The proposals are reproduced
in *Johnson on Shakespeare,* ed. Arthur Sherbo, Yale *Works,* vol. 7 (New Haven:
Yale, 1968), inserted between pages 46 and 47.

89. *Letters,* I, 20.

90. See James Osborn, "Birch and the *GD,*" p. 30; and *DA,* January 19 and
22, 1732/[33]. The proposals for the *GD* were reprinted in the *GM,* 1733, pp.
53–54. The first number was published on March 29, 1733 (*DA*). The proposals
state that the first number is in the press.

If Johnson's *Plan of a Dictionary* can be viewed as a type of proposals, it too
follows this same pattern. Although Johnson composed a draft of the plan in
April 1746, before he signed a contract with the booksellers, the *Plan* itself was
not published until August 1747, more than a year after work had begun.

91. P. 112.

92. "Sanguine Expectations: Dr. Johnson's Shakespeare," *Shakespeare Quarterly* 9 (1958): 426–28. Boswell may have suspected the same, for he conjectured
that Johnson spent the remainder of 1745 and part of 1746 on this edition
(*Life,* I, 175–76).

93. See Yale *Works,* vols. 7 and 8, pp. 30, 782.

94. Giles E. Dawson, "The Copyright of Shakespeare's Dramatic Works,"
University of Missouri Studies 21 (1946): 29–32. Dawson prints Tonson's letter to
Cave, dated April 11, 1745, stating his objections to the planned edition. Cave

could not have been ignorant of Tonson's claim, but the appearance of the Oxford edition (1743–44) may have misled him into thinking that Tonson would no longer interfere with other publications.

95. See James Osborn, "Dr. Johnson's 'Intimate Friend,'" *TLS*, October 9, 1953, p. 652. The poem, a translation into Latin of John Byrom's "Colin and Phebe," appeared in the *GM* for February 1745, p. 102, following by two pages "An Invitation to Two Abstemious Friends," discovered by Osborn to have been written by Barrett and addressed to Johnson and Cave.

96. See Appendix B.

97. *GM*, 1745, pp. 135–36. The project was apparently dropped, only to be revived after Cave's death and printed by Richard Cave and David Henry in ten volumes (1763). The body of Johnson's proposals was revised and abridged by another hand for the address to the reader printed in the first volume of this edition.

98. Hawkins (p. 392) initially set Johnson's fee at one guinea per sermon but changed it to two guineas in the second edition of his biography (quoted in *Life*, III, 507). The *Sermon Preached . . . before the Sons of the Clergy* was printed under Hervey Aston's name and has subsequently been reprinted by the Augustan Reprint Society, No. 50 (Los Angeles, 1955), with an introduction by James Clifford. Donald Greene has suggested that Johnson may have also written a charity sermon for his friend John Taylor about the same time (see Clifford's introduction to *Sermon*, p. vii and n. 14).

Boulter's Monument was published in October (see *GM*, 1745, p. 560). Madden noted in a postscript that "some Hundred Lines have been prun'd from it." This would appear to be his own acknowledgment of Johnson's editing; see *Life*, I, 318, 545. The poem runs to 2,034 lines.

99. See W. J. Bate, *Samuel Johnson* (New York: Harcourt Brace, 1977), p. 232; Clifford, p. 285. Boswell gave an earlier date that A. L. Reade has shown to be unreliable: see *Life*, I, 134; *Gleanings*, VI, 115–16.

100. *J. Misc.*, I, 133; *Memoirs of Richard Cumberland* (London, 1806), p. 261; *Life*, III, 195. We have no knowledge of when Hervey gave the latter assistance to Johnson; but he died in 1748, and Johnson was probably not in great need once he began the *Dictionary*. Thus, the relief from arrest must have been given during one of Johnson's periods of distress between 1738 and 1746.

101. *Life*, I, 182; III, 405.

102. Mary Segar, "Dictionary Making in the Early Eighteenth Century," *Review of English Studies* 7 (1931): 210–13. For the lexicographical tradition behind Johnson's undertaking, see James H. Sledd and Gwin J. Kolb, *Dr. Johnson's Dictionary* (Chicago: U. of Chicago Press, 1955), pp. 1–45.

103. The "Short Scheme" is reproduced in volume II of the *R. B. Adam Library*. The contract was dated "18th June 1746" (Hawkins, p. 344 n.). See also *Letters*, I, 29–30.

APPENDIX A

1. *GM*, 1740, p. 251.
2. *Daily Advertiser*.
3. See *GM*, 1741, p. 614.

4. See *GM*, 1742, p. 504.

5. For the terms on which trade publishers sold the works owned by others, see Treadwell, "London Trade Publishers, 1675–1750," pp. 126–27. Wilford had gone bankrupt in 1735, but was back in business two years later; see Belanger, p. 208. Wilford was one of the original proprietors of the *London Magazine,* but his interest in that publication appears to have ended at the time of his bankruptcy. It seems odd that either Cave or Wilford would have sought any working relationship.

6. The passage as excerpted in the *GM* (given above) is apparently taken from Cooper's proposals and contains a number of minor variants from the preface to the 1738 edition of the *Memoirs.*

7. Although the preface to the 1738 edition of the *Memoirs* is by no means a translation of Prévost's original "Avis de l'éditeur," some of its non-Johnsonian elements are taken from that French preface, and some of the Johnsonian passages seem vaguely suggested by Prévost's original.

APPENDIX B

1. Boswell (*Life*, I, 150) confuses the issue by "correcting" Johnson and giving the dates of the actual debates in Parliament (November 19, 1740, through February 23, 1743). Johnson's statement is obviously more accurate, for we may be sure that he generally wrote his accounts not when the debates took place but when copy was needed.

2. It appears from internal evidence that Johnson did two debates, those on navy estimates (*GM*, December 1740) and on registering seamen (January 1741), before taking full responsibility for the debates; see Chapter 6.

3. Hawkins, p. 132.

4. The debate on pay for Hanoverian troops took place on December 10, 1742; that on spiritous liquors, February 22–25, 1743; and that on the Corporation Bill, December 1, 1742, and March 11 and 17, 1743. F. V. Bernard ("Four Debates," pp. 415–16) mistakenly places the Corporation Bill debate in an earlier session of Parliament, an error that weakens his attempt to attribute the debate to Johnson. The debate on pay for Hanoverian troops is probably included in the canon on the unsubstantiated assumption that Johnson wrote the debates in the order of their actual occurrence, rather than in the order of their appearance in the magazine: thus, if he wrote the debate on spiritous liquors, he must have written that on pay for Hanoverian troops, which had occurred first. Until some attempt is made to attribute this debate on stylistic grounds, it must be considered a questionable inclusion.

5. The 1787 and 1825 collections of the debates both include the debate on pay for Hanoverian troops but not that on the Corporation Bill. For an account of the carelessness with which these volumes were compiled, see Hoover, pp. 44–49. These collections have no authority whatsoever.

6. Hawkins, p. 132; Hoover, pp. 144–45. J. G. Nichols emphatically denied, without explanation, that Hawkesworth wrote the debates ("Autobiography," *GM*, March 1857, p. 285).

7. Bernard, "Four Debates," pp. 415–19; Greene, "Some Notes," pp. 77–78.

8. Greene, ibid. Why the debate on the Corporation Bill appeared without the Lilliputian machinery is a mystery, for the subsequent debates immediately resume it. Cave generally dropped the disguise only when he was copying from a printed source, as in the case of the Lords Protests; but I have been unable to find such a source for this debate. Nevertheless, the relatively undisguised text suggests that it was not compiled by Cave's normal means and that Johnson was thus not the author.

9. Hoover, pp. 144–45.

INDEX

Abridgment, legality of, 60, 217–18n.54
Adams, Dr. William, 196
Addison, Joseph, 197
  Cato, 13
Akenside, Mark, 169
Anne, Queen of England, 156, 196
Annual Register, contract for, 75
Argyll, 2nd Duke of, portrayed in
  debates, 141–42
Aston, Henry Hervey. *See* Hervey Aston,
  Henry
Aston, Molly, 22

Baratier, François, 113, 114, 147
Baratier, Johann Philip, 113
Barker, A. D., 212n.25, 220n.29
Barnard, Sir John, 93
  style in Parliamentary debates, 126
Barrett, Stephen, 195
Bayle, Pierre, 37, 74, 189. See also
  General Dictionary
Beauclerk, Topham, 90
Bernard, F. V., 202, 233n.38
  on Johnson's bias in debates, 236n.28,
  237n.41
Bernard, John Peter, 65, 220n.34,
  222n.44
Birch, Thomas, 36–40
  assists Cave, 30, 32
  consulted about Harleian catalogue,
  178
  contrasted with Johnson, 38–39, 114,
  189
  courts Elizabeth Carter, 39, 213n.49
  his diary, 213n.43
  General Dictionary, 37, 65, 74, 158, 193,
  242n.48
  mentioned, 33, 54, 75, 87, 110, 185,
  186, 213n.42, 247n.17

Blackmore, Sir Richard, 159–60, 161
Bodleian Library, 176, 248nn.23, 24
Boerhaave, Herman, 54, 173
Bolingbroke, Henry St. John, 1st
  Viscount, 78, 94, 98, 102, 241–
  42n.40
Booktrade, structure of, 63–65
Boswell, James
  on Cave as Johnson's first employer, 5
  his conjecture on extent of Johnson's
  work on Shakespeare, 254n.92
  "corrects" Johnson on Parliamentary
  debates, 256n.1
  on Johnson's ancestors, 208n.15
  on Johnson's "tolerable livelihood," 85
  melancholy over Johnson's poverty, 86,
  89, 224n.12
  praises Johnson's review of the Duchess
  of Marlborough's memoirs, 155
  mentioned, 7, 10, 11, 33, 34, 38, 47,
  91, 166, 182, 201, 223n.60
Bougeant, Guillaume, *Philosophical
  Amusement upon the Language of Beasts*,
  60
Boyse, Samuel, 33, 162–64, 171
  The Deity, 163, 218n.8
  payment for literary work, 243n.61,
  245n.79
Brack, O M, Jr., 231nn.13, 16
Brett, John, 59, 229n.66
Brooke, Henry, 102
  Gustavus Vasa, 13, 91, 102, 103, 104
Brooke, John, 93
Broome, William, 212n.25
Browne, Moses, 32–33, 40, 88, 212n.28
  offended by Cave, 25–26, 210–11n.4
  wins Cave's poetry prizes, 49–50
Burke, Edmund, 75, 95, 123, 133
Burke, William 229n.67
Burney, Charles, 89

Cambridge University Library, 248*n*.24

Campbell, Rev. Thomas, 195

Caroline, Queen, consort of George II, 8, 68, 69, 86, 87

Carter, Elizabeth, 34–36
courted by Thomas Birch, 39–40
"Fortune," 35–36
source of information on Baratier, 113, 114, 147
subject of epigrams by Johnson, 20, 50–52, 216*n*.26
translates Crousaz's *Examen*, 77
mentioned, 21, 22, 24, 40, 87, 163, 188

Carter, Rev. Nicholas, 34

Carteret, John, Lord, 93, 97, 132, 137
portrayed in Parliamentary debates, 137–38, 139, 237*n*.39

Casimir Sarbiewski, 16–17, 18

Catalogus Bibliothecae Thuanae, 249*n*.30

Cave, Edward, 25–27, and passim. *See also Gentleman's Magazine*
assists in campaign to retain Savage's pension, 88
chaperones Birch and Carter, 39
copyright, violations of and disputes over, 31, 60, 195, 212*n*.22, 217*n*.54
demurs at initial offer of Sarpi translation, 8–9
discontent with Johnson's editorial services, 44–45, 50
early publications, 219*n*.14
entrusts his presses to subordinates, 40
expands staff of *GM*, 161
exploits position with Post Office, 44, 188, 211*n*.13
introduces Johnson to literary acquaintances, 32, 86, 88
jailed for breach of Parliamentary privilege, 29
Johnson's first employer in London, 5
maintains editorial responsibilities, 40, 44
offers poetry prizes, 16, 31–32, 49–50
opens magazine to correspondents, 4
"penurious paymaster" for editors and authors, 74, 163, 166–70, 244*n*.75, 245*n*.79
plagiarizes debates from *London Magazine*, 29–30, 115
position in the booktrade, 65–67
among proprietors of *General Dictionary*, 65–66
provides financial backing for

Johnson's projects, 63, 186–87, 192, 254*nn*.87, 88
publishes Du Halde's *Description of China*, 66–67
seeks improvements in Parliamentary debates from Birch, 37, 213*n*.42
solicits poetry from Johnson, 22, 155
"Sylvanus Urban," pseudonym, 15
uses trade publishers, 78, 187, 192, 199–200, 216*n*.34, 230*n*.9, 254*n*.88

Cavendish Square, 10, 11, 175

Centlivre, Susannah, 11

Chalmers, Alexander, 166–67, 169–70

Chaney, John, 70

Charles XII, King of Sweden, 174

Chesterfield, 4th Earl of, 102, 103, 137
portrayed in debates, 126, 127, 236*n*.34

Churchill, Charles, 215*n*.12

Cibber, Colley, 11

Clay, John, Daventry bookseller, 28

Clifford, James, 208*n*.18, 249*n*.30

Clothing, cost during 18th century, 84–85

Collins, William, 33, 164

Common Sense, 16, 55–58, 108

Congreve, William, 11

Considerations upon the Embargo of the Provision of Victual, 149–50

Contracts for literary work
Annual Register, 75
assumed for Sarpi translation, 72–73, 75–76
General Dictionary, 66, 72, 74, 75
Museum, 169

Copyright, 60, 63, 195
and abridgment, 217–18*n*.54
not enforced for periodicals and pamphlets, 212*n*.22

Corn Bill, debate on, 140, 150

Cornewall, Velters, in debates, 126–27

Cost of living in the 18th century, 84–85, 207*n*.5, 208*n*.13. *See also* Diet of laborers; Johnson, Samuel, personal economy

Cotton, Sir John Hynde, 102

Craftsman, The, 57, 100, 108, 136

Crokatt, James, *The Publisher*, 192

Croker, John Wilson, 21

Crouch, Nathaniel, *The English Hero*, 111

Crousaz, Jean Pierre de, 76, 78–79, 157. *See also* Johnson, Samuel
Commentaire, 63, 77
Examen, 77

Cumberland, Richard, 196
Curll, Edmund, 77, 177

Daily Advertiser, 69, 77, 102
Daily Gazetteer, 58
Debates in Parliament. *See* Parliamentary
  debates; Johnson, Samuel,
  Parliamentary debates
Diet of laborers, 7, 207–8n.12
Dodd, Anne, mercury and "publisher,"
  78, 216n.34, 218n.7, 223, n.52, 230,
  n.9
Dodsley, Robert
  payment of authors, 73–74, 243n.61
  provides information for *Life of Savage*,
    252n.73
  publisher of *The Annual Register*, 75
  publisher of *The Museum*, 169
  purchases copyright of *London*, 19–20
  suggests that Johnson write a
    dictionary, 196
  mentioned, 22, 62, 155, 223n.52
Dodwell, Henry, *Praelectiones Academicae*,
  117
Donne, John, 68
Douglas, James, *Bibliographiae Anatomicae
  Specimen*, 173
Dryden, John, 13
Duck, Stephen, 51
Du Halde, Jean Baptiste, *Description of
  China*, 8, 46–47, 66–67, 70
Duick, John, 49, 215n.24
Du Resnel, Jean François du Bellay, 78,
  79–80, 81

Edial school, 3, 14, 62
  advertised in *GM*, 29
  expenses, 207n.5
  failed investment, 5
Erasmus, Desiderius, 215n.19
Excise, 98, 101
  Johnson's hatred of, 153

Fabricius, Johann Albert, 183
Farmer, Dr. Richard, 166–67, 169–70
Farquhar, George, 11
Fielding, Henry, 12, 163
Fleetwood, Charles
  rejects *Irene*, 11, 12
  promises to produce *Irene*, 107, 238n.1

mentioned, 15, 108, 115, 196, 208n.25
Floyer, Sir John, 30
Folkes, Martin, 178
Fontenelle, Bernard le Bovier de, *Éloge de
  Morin*, 145
Food, cost during the 18th century, 84,
  208n.13, 224n.7. *See also* Cost of
  living in the 18th century; Diet of
  laborers
Ford, Cornelius, 13
Forman, Charles, 77
Formey, Jean Henri Samuel, *Vie de
  Baratier*, 192, 241n.34
Frederick, Prince of Wales, 13, 46–47, 94
Freind, Dr. John, *History of Physick*, 173

Gale, Roger, 176
Gardner, Thomas, 66
Garrick, David, 3, 5, 13, 107, 231n.25
Garrick, Peter, 11
Gay, John, 48, 94
Gee, Joshua, *Impartial Inquiry into the
  Importance of our Woollen Trade*, 153
General Dictionary, 37
  contract, 66, 72, 74, 75, 219n.15
  publication history, 65–66
  source of some of Johnson's early
    biographies, 110, 158
  mentioned, 70, 193, 194
Gentleman's Magazine. See also Cave,
  Edward; Johnson, Samuel
  abridged translations in, 60, 120, 161–
    62
  abridgment of "Weekly Essays," 55, 58
  disputes with other periodicals, 15–16,
    54–55
  distribution to the provinces, 28–29
  "Historical Chronicle," 28
  history and development, 27–32
  Latin poetry in, 16
  Lilliputian disguise for debates, 42
  "Lords Protests" in, 121
  materials gathered for debates, 45, 124
  mathematical problems in, 60, 170
  political neutrality, 27, 123
  predominance over *London Magazine*,
    216–17n.41
  satire absent before Johnson, 43, 55
George I, King of England, 92, 248n.24
George II, King of England, 48, 98, 101,
  105
George III, King of England, 246n.1

Gibbs, James, 175
Giffard, Henry, 12
Gloucester Journal, 29
Golden Rump, The, 103
Goldsmith, Oliver, 38, 245–46n.83,
    246n.1
Gordon, Thomas, 235n.20
Gower, John Leveson-Gower, 1st Earl,
    62–63, 82
Gray, John, bookseller, 238n.1
Greek Anthology, 22
Green, John, 66, 215n.12
Greene, Donald, 103, 135, 136, 146, 191,
    202, 234n.8, 236n.30
Griffiths, Ralph, 245–46n.83
Guthrie, William, 33–34 and passim
  composes Parliamentary debates for the
    GM, 30, 115, 146
  style full of "Scotticisms," 45, 215n.12
  translates Du Halde's *Description of
    China*, 66
  writes a *General History of England*, 185
Guyon, Abbé Claude Marie, *Histoire des
    Amazones*, 120
Gybbon, Philips, in Parliamentary
    debates, 127, 236n.30

Hakluyt, Richard, *Principal Navigations of
    the English Nation*, 111
Handel, George Frederick, 208n.25
Hanmer, Sir Thomas, 94, 193
Hardinge, Nicholas, 186
Hardwicke, 1st Earl of, Lord Chancellor,
    37, 39, 175, 217–18n.54
Harleian Library, 175–77
Harleian Miscellany, 181, 190–92
Harley, Edward. *See* Oxford, Edward
    Harley, 2nd Earl
Harley, Robert. *See* Oxford, Robert
    Harley, 1st Earl
Harte, Walter, 190
Hawkesworth, John, 164–65, 171, 214n.9,
    244n.69
  author of debates in *GM*, 201–2, 203,
    256n.6
  earnings from *GM*, 168–69, 170
Hawkins, Sir John
  anecdotes of Johnson, 5–6, 32, 125
  depiction of Edward Cave, 25–26
  errors or doubtful assertions by, 88–89,
    210–11n.4, 212n.31, 225n.20,
    226n.22, 229n.66, 249n.30, 253n.78

on Johnson's friendship with Savage,
    86, 88–89, 90–91
  on Johnson's Parliamentary debates,
    125, 126, 201, 203, 237n.41
  on printing of the Sarpi translation, 71
  mentioned, 38, 44, 45, 212n.28, 214n.9
Hazen, Allen T., 220n.31
Hearne, Thomas, 248n.24
Hector, Edmund, 3–4, 62
Henley, John "Orator," 187
Henry, David, 168, 245n.79
Hervey, Henry. *See* Hervey Aston, Henry
Hervey, John, Lord Hervey, 137
  in debates, 127–28, 143, 236n.34
Hervey Aston, Henry, 5, 190, 195, 196
Hill, Aaron, 94, 188
Hill, George Birkbeck, 43, 126, 128,
    208n.25, 234n.8
Hoffmann, Friedrich, 173
Hogarth, William, 236n.34
Hoover, Benjamin, 202, 203, 234n.8,
    237n.41
Horace, 18
House of Commons, 41
  Journals, 185
Hussey, Rev. John, 44, 166, 173, 225n.20

Ilive, Jacob, 26
Impressment of seamen, 118
  arguments on, in debates, 132–34,
    136–37

Jacobitism, 105, 174
James I, King of England, 68
James (Stuart), the "Old Pretender," 105,
    174, 202
James, Robert, 158, 172–73, 241n.39
Johnson, Elizabeth (Tetty)
  dislike of London, 11
  her "fortune," 5, 10, 19, 83–84, 106,
    207n.5
  habits and expectations, 85, 190
  sells keepsake cup, 196
  mentioned, 7, 14, 89, 107
Johnson, John, 69–70, 71
Johnson, Samuel: Biography
  contributes essays to Warren's
    Birmingham Journal, 4
  translates Lobo's *Voyage*, 4
  proposes edition of Politian, 4
  writes to Cave from Birmingham, 4

failure of Edial school, 5
travels to London with Garrick, 3, 5
retires to Greenwich to finish *Irene*, 7
proposes Sarpi translation, 8
establishes permanent residency in
  London, 10
fails to get *Irene* produced, 11–14
approaches Cave with "Ad Urbanum,"
  15
offers *London* to Cave, 18
sells *London* to Dodsley, 20
contributes epigrams to *GM*, 21
early friendship with Elizabeth Carter,
  34–36
assumes editorial duties for *GM*, 44
edits Guthrie's debates, 44–45, 108–9
decline in poetic output, 50
defends *GM* in periodical wars, 55–59
editorial work not full-time
  employment, 52
translates Sarpi's *History of the Council of
  Trent*, 68–76
Sarpi translation foiled by rival, 69
translates Crousaz's *Commentary*, 76–78
as translator neither indolent nor
  aimless, 82
friendship with Richard Savage, 85–91
writes *Marmor*, 101
subscribes to Brooke's *Gustavus Vasa*,
  102
writes *A Compleat Vindication*, 102
depression and indolence, 106
applies for position at Appleby School,
  62, 106
fails in application for Appleby
  position, 106
mortgages mother's house in Lichfield,
  107
Fleetwood promises to produce *Irene*,
  107
avoids writing Parliamentary debates,
  115, 118, 121
increases contributions to *GM*, 115–17
agrees to write debates, 122
attempts to sell all rights to *Irene*, 144
total immersion in *GM*, 144–54
gradually disengages himself from *GM*,
  154
contributes to James's *Medicinal
  Dictionary*, 173
contemplates "Charles of Sweden,"
  173–74
compiles Harleian catalogue, 177–82

works on "Historical Design," 184–87
writes *Life of Savage*, 187–88
departure from *GM*, 165–66
contributes to *Harleian Miscellany*, 191–
  92
edits Shakespeare, 192–95
periods of debility or indolence, 192,
  194, 196
seeks to practice law, 195–96
decides to attempt *Dictionary*, 196–97
Johnson, Samuel: Topics
aggressive conversation, 39
biographical practice, 53–54, 110–14,
  158–61, 188–89
colonialism deplored, 43, 112
Crousaz, criticisms of, 79–80
difficulties writing poetry, 155
diffidence, 19, 238*n*.1
earnings for literary work, 20, 71–74,
  84, 166–70, 186–87, 192, 195,
  222*n*.43, 223*n*.2, 246*n*.84
editorial contributions to the *GM*, 44–
  50, 54–59, 108–9, 145–54
epigrams, facility with, 21–22, 51–52
extent of contributions to debates,
  201–3
extent of contributions to *GM*, 59, 63,
  167–68
extent of labor on Sarpi translation,
  74–76
extent of labor on Shakespeare edition,
  193–94
habits of composition, 15, 24, 80–81,
  125–26, 220*n*.23, 256*n*.1
hack work vs. literature, 143
hatred of schoolmastering, 62
not homeless when he knew Savage,
  88–89
"improvement" of speeches in debates,
  119–20, 129
influence on *GM*, 60–61, 120, 161,
  170–71
Jacobitism, 105, 229*n*.67
lack of university degree, 9
mythology in Latin poetry, 18, 51
opposition to Walpole, 59, 92, 97–106
Parliamentary debates, bias in, 132–39
Parliamentary debates, rhetorical art,
  126–31
Parliamentary debates thought genuine,
  dismay at, 235*n*.21
personal economy, 5–7, 10–11, 84–85,
  196, 224*n*.6

on political-economy, 150–53
Pope's *Essay on Man*, attitudes towards, 79–80
poverty, often exaggerated, 83, 85, 89, 196
poverty, sometimes real, 19, 106, 190, 195, 196
pride, 7, 39, 224n.12
rapidity of composition. *See* habits of composition
residences, 5, 10, 11, 89, 226n.22
"Ruling Passion," critique of, 80
on "savage" manners, 43, 112
scholarly ambitions, 9, 63, 69, 76, 81, 174, 178–79, 184, 192–93, 196–97
supposed separation from Tetty, 226n.22
"Sylvanus Urban" as pseudonym, 51, 55
no "Whiggism" in his political pamphlets, 103–4
Johnson, Samuel: Works
"Account of the Life of Peter Burman," 154
"Ad Elisam Popi Horto Lauros Carpentem" and translation, 50–52
"Ad Ricardum Savage," 21–22
"Ad Urbanum," 15, 16–18
"Art of Deciphering," 154
Catalogus Bibliothecae Harleianae, 76, 148, 182–84, 186, 193–94
Crousaz, *Commentary*, translation, 63, 77, 78–81, 199
A Compleat Vindication of the Licensers of the Stage, 59, 91, 102–4, 136
"Debate between the Committee of the House of Commons and O. Cromwell," 118–20, 129–30
"Debates in the Senate of Magna Lilliputia." *See* Parliamentary debates
"Dissertation on the Amazons," 120
economic commentaries in *GM*, 149–53
"Epitaph on Claudy Phillips," 115
"Essay on Du Halde's *Description of China*," 154
"Essay on Epitaphs," 116
essay on the Crousaz-Warburton controversy, 154, 157–58
"Essay on the Origin and Importance of Small Tracts and Fugitive Pieces," 191
"Eubulus" letter, 46–47
"Foreign Books" in *GM*, 146–48, 166

"Foreign History" in *GM*, 145–46, 166
Greek epigram on Elizabeth Carter, 21
Greek epigram on Thomas Birch, 38
History of Tahmas Kuli Khan, edited, 109–10
introduction to Lilliputian debates, 42–43
Irene, 9–10, 14 and passim
Ironic commentary on *Common Sense* in *GM*, 55–56
"Jests of Hierocles," 145
"Life of Barretier," 113–14, 154, 192
"Life of Blake," 108, 110, 122, 169
"Life of Boerhaave," 54, 59, 63, 81, 173
"Life of Burman." *See* "Account of the Life of Peter Burman"
"Life of Dr. Sydenham," 155, 158–61
"Life of Drake," 110–13, 122
"Life of Father Paul Sarpi," 53, 71
"Life of Morin." *See* "A Panegyric on Dr. Morin"
Life of Pope, 76, 80, 176
"Life of Sarpi." *See* "Life of Father Paul Sarpi"
Life of Savage, 87, 186, 188–89, 190
"Life of Sydenham." *See* "Life of Dr. Sydenham"
Lobo, *Voyage to Abyssinia*, translation, 4, 72, 73
London, 20, 98–100, 155 and passim
Marmor Norfolciense, 48, 59, 91, 100–101, 105
Miscellaneous Observations on the Tragedy of Macbeth, 192–93
"On the Acta Diurna of the Old Romans," 117
"Pamphilus" letter on condolence, 47–48
"Pamphilus" letter on Gay's epitaph, 48–49, 59
"A Panegyric on Dr. Morin," 145
Parliamentary debates, 76, 116, 118, 123–43
Plan of a Dictionary, 254n.90
Pope's "Verses on a Grotto," translated into Latin, 155
preface to *Memoirs of a Man of Quality*, 198–200
Preface to Shakespeare, 57
proposals for Anchitell Grey's *Debates*, 195
proposals for "a New Edition of the Plays of Shakespear," 192–93

proposals for James's *Medicinal Dictionary*, 173
proposals "for Printing *Bibliotheca Harleiana*," 155, 178
proposals for Sarpi's *History of the Council of Trent*, 69
proposals for the *Harleian Miscellany*, 190
proposals for *The Publisher*, 192
The Rambler, 22, 39, 48, 129, 156, 165
Rasselas, 129
review of the *Account of the Conduct of the Duchess of Marlborough*, 154, 155–56
sermon for Henry Hervey Aston, 195
"Short Scheme" for the *Dictionary*, 197
"To a Lady who spoke in Defense of Liberty," 22
"To Lady Firebrace at Bury Assizes," 22, 45
Vanity of Human Wishes, 24, 35–36
"Venus in Armour," 22
"Vision of Theodore," 129
Jones, William, 178
Jonson, Ben, 11
Juvenal, 98, 155
Third Satire, 14, 35, 99–100
Tenth Satire, 35–36

Kimber, Edward, 84, 168
Kimber, Isaac, 84
Knolles, Richard, *General History of the Turks*, 13, 249–50n.37
Korshin, Paul, 236n.34, 237n.41
Kouli Khan, 109
Kramnick, Isaac, 96, 226n.33

Langton, Bennet, 90
Latham, R. G., 158
Le Clerc, Daniel, *Histoire de la Médecine*, 173
Le Courayer, Pierre François, 8, 9, 53, 68, 69, 70, 74
Levett, Theophilus, 107
Lillo, George
Fatal Curiosity, 12
London Merchant, 209n.27
Lintot, Bernard, 73–74
account books, 221n.40
Lintot, Henry, 5
Livy, 130, 131
Lockman, John, 65
Loftis, John, 208n.25

London, development in early 18th century, 10
London Magazine
accusations of plagiarism against *GM*, 218–19n.13
competition with *GM*, 15–16
payment of editor, 84
prints original debates before *GM*, 29
"Proceedings of a Political Club," 41–42
mentioned, passim
Lyttelton, George Lyttelton, 1st Baron, 20, 102, 103
portrayed in debates, 136–37, 138

McAdam, Edward L., Jr., 220n.31
Macbean, Alexander, 221n.37
Madden, Samuel, *Boulter's Monument*, 195
Maittaire, Michael, 249n.30, 250–51n.48
Annales Typographici, 183, 184
Mallet, David, 94
Mustapha, 13
Marck, Henry Vander, library of, 177
Martial, 21, 34
Mary II, Queen of England, 156
Maupertuis, Pierre Louis Moreau de, *Book of the Figure of the Earth*, 60
Mead, Dr. Richard, 173, 213n.43
Mendes, Solomon, 87–88, 90, 188
Miller, James, 12
Milton, John, 18, 78
Comus, 12
Miscellanea Curiosa Mathematica, 60
Monarchy Asserted to be the best form of Government, 119, 129
"Moneyed" corporations as source of corruption, 94, 96
Mortimer, Cromwell, 212n.25
Murphy, Arthur, 88–89
Museum, contract for, 169

Nichols, John, 69, 71, 125, 163–64, 166–67, 210n.49
alters Johnson's statements, 243n.62, 244–45n.75
Nichols, John Gough, 210n.49, 256n.6 (App. B)
Noel, Nathaniel, 247–48n.17
Nourse, John, 221nn.35, 37

Oldys, William, 176, 222n.44, 250n.47
co-worker on Harleian catalogue, 179–80, 181, 183

Oldys, William (*continued*)
    compiles *Harleian Miscellany*, 190–92
Opposition, the, 12, 92–95, 96–97, 102,
    104
    portrayed in the debates, 132–33, 135–
    39
Osborn, James, 222n.44
Osborne, Thomas
    character, 176
    buys Harleian Library, 175–76
    hires Johnson to compile Harleian
    catalogue, 177–78
    influences make-up of catalogue, 180–
    81, 183
    publishes *Medicinal Dictionary*, 172
    mentioned, 155, 172–92 passim, 218n.9
Otway, Thomas, 13
Oxford, Dowager Countess of, 175, 176
Oxford, Edward Harley, 2nd Earl, 174–
    75, 176, 179, 182, 183
Oxford, Robert Harley, 1st Earl, 156,
    183, 250n.47
Oxford University, 7, 176. *See also*
    Bodleian Library

Parliamentary debates, history of, 29–30,
    41. *See also* Johnson, Samuel
Parliamentary privilege, 124, 185
Patronage, 9
    engrossed by Walpole, 95, 142
Paul, Lewis, 211n.6
Payment of authors. *See also* Johnson,
    Samuel, earnings for literary work
    magazines, 84, 168–70, 245–46n.83
    miscellaneous, 221n.37, 243n.61,
    245n.79
    translation, 73–74, 221n.40
Pennington, Montagu, 34, 36
Percy, Dr. Thomas, 38, 245–46n.83
Philips, Ambrose, 197
Pitt, William, the elder, 103, 132, 137
    in the debates, 126, 127, 128, 136, 143
Plant, Marjorie, 73
Politian, 4
Political State of Great Britain, 29
Pope, Alexander
    and Crousaz, 78–79, 157
    Dunciad, 97, 177
    edition of Shakespeare, 193
    Essay on Man, 31, 76, 78–81
    Messiah, 9
    model for Johnson, 9, 15

*One Thousand Seven Hundred and Thirty-
    Eight*, 20, 22
    opposition sympathies, 94, 96, 98
    source of information for *Life of
    Savage*, 188–89
    and Thomas Osborne, 177
    mentioned, 18, 19, 24, 51, 69, 73, 163,
    187, 197, 212n.25
Porter, Lucy, 5
Prévost, Antoine Francois, 200
    *Mémoires et avantures d'un homme de
    qualité*, 198
Prevost, Nicholas, 66
Printers, position in booktrade, 63–65,
    66, 219nn.15, 16
Proposals, booksellers' use of, 193
Publishers. *See* Trade publishers, position
    in the trade
Pulteney, William, 93, 95–96, 97, 137
    in debates, 124, 126, 127, 143, 237n.39

Radcliffe, Dr. John, 248n.24
Reade, Aleyn Lyell, 207n.5, 222n.47
Reynolds, Sir Joshua, 88
Rich, John, 12, 208n.25
Richardson, Jonathan, 38
Roberts, James (trade publisher), 187,
    192, 245n.88
    position in the trade, 218n.8
Rowe, Nicholas, 13
Ruhe, Edward, 213n.49

St. John's Gate, 15, 29, 40
Sandys, Samuel, 132, 137
    in the debates, 127, 136, 236n.30
Sarbiewski, Casimir. *See* Casimir
    Sarbiewski
Sarpi, Father Paul, 67–68
    Historia del Concilio Tridentino, its
    importance in the 18th century, 8–9,
    67–68
Savage, Richard. *See also* Johnson, Samuel
    contrasted with Boyse, 162, 163
    not always desperate during friendship
    with Johnson, 87–88
    low ebb of his fortunes, 106
    paid by Cave for poetry, 32
    political discontent, 90–91
    not "Thales" of *London*, 225n.20
    mentioned, 21, 22, 37, 38, 40, 86, 92,
    94, 98, 164, 187, 209n.44
Schultens, Albert, 54

Secker, Thomas, Bishop of Oxford (later Archbishop of Canterbury) , in debates, 127–28
Seward, William, 174
Shakespeare, William, 11, 180
  editions of his works, 192–93
Sherbo, Arthur, 194
Shiels, Robert, 163–64
Sir Francis Drake Revived, 111
Sloane, Sir Hans, 242nn.48, 55
Smith, Adam, 133, 140, 239n.15, 240n.27
Smollett, Tobias, *Roderick Random*, 208n.13
Society for the Encouragement of Learning, 144, 218n.9
Spence, Joseph, 212n.25
Spiritous Liquors Bill, 127, 137
  debate on, 127, 141, 201, 203, 236n.34
Stage Licensing Act, 11–12, 98, 103
Swan, Dr. John, 158
Swift, Jonathan
  hatred of "moneyed" men, 96
  model for Johnson's political pamphlets, 91–92
  place in the opposition, 94
  subscribes to *Gustavus Vasa*, 102
  mentioned, 62, 97, 98
Sydenham, Dr. Thomas, 158–61

Tacitus, 235n.20
Taylor, John (of Ashbourne) , 106, 174, 255n.98
Taylor, John, 180
Theater in London during the 18th century, 11–14
Theobald, Lewis, 193
Thomson, James, 18, 38, 90, 188
  Agamemnon, 12, 13
  assists Savage, 87–88
  place in the opposition, 94
Thornhill, Sir James, 175
Thrale, Henry, 89
Thrale, Hester Lynch, 47, 89, 173
Thucydides, 130, 131
Tonson, Jacob, 195, 196
Tories, place in the opposition, 92–94, 103–4, 226–27n.33
Trade publishers, position in the trade, 64, 223n.52. *See also* Dodd, Anne, mercury and "publisher"; Roberts, James
Trapp, Joseph, 60

Tyrconnel, John Brownlow, Viscount, 188

Universal Spectator, 58

Vanbrugh, Sir John, 11
Vernon, Edward, Admiral, 110, 121
Vertue, George, 176
Voltaire, 174
  Histoire de Charles XII, 174
  "Vanity of Fame," 161
Vossius, Isaac, 176

Wade, George, General, in debates, 126
Wages of laborers in the 18th century, 6–7
Wake, William, Archbishop of Canterbury, 68
Wallmoden, Amalie von, 48
Walmesley, Gilbert, 3, 5, 6, 13, 172
Walpole, Horace, 37
Walpole, Horatio, in debates, 128
Walpole, Sir Robert, 95–97
  allegorized by opposition playwrights, 13–14
  caricature of vice in opposition speeches, 136
  portrayed by Johnson in the debates, 126, 132–35, 143
  mentioned, 15, 87, 92–143 passim, 150, 153
Wanley, Humphrey, 183
Warburton, William, 38, 157
Ward, John, 161
War of Jenkin's Ear, 110, 140
Warren, Thomas, *Birmingham Journal*, 4, 30
Watts, Dr. Isaac, 212n.25
Webber, Samuel, 149, 151, 240n.28
Wesseling, Petrus, 232n.36
Whig, Johnson's understanding of term, ´103–4
Whigs, disaffected, in the opposition, 92–93
Whitehead, Paul, 20
Whitelocke, Sir Bulstrode, *Memorials of English Affairs*, 233n.40
Wilcox, J., bookseller, 6, 109
Wilford, John, 199–200, 218n.13, 256n.5 (App. A)

William III, King of England, 142, 156
Wimsatt, William K., 202, 203
Wood, Anthony à, *Athenae Oxonienses*, 74, 242n.48
Wool trade, 149, 151–53

Wotton, Sir Henry, 68
Wycherley, William, 11
Wyndham, Sir William, 94, 102, 126

Yorke, Philip, 39, 213n.42, 247n.17